COMPUTERS AND POLITICS
High Technology in American Local Governments

COMPUTERS AND POLITICS High Technology in American Local Governments

JAMES N. DANZIGER
WILLIAM H. DUTTON
ROB KLING and
KENNETH L. KRAEMER

COLUMBIA UNIVERSITY PRESS / NEW YORK / 1982

Library of Congress Cataloging in Publication Data
Main entry under title:

Computers and politics.

Bibliography: p.
Includes index.
1. Local government—United States—Data Processing.
I. Danziger, James N.
JS344.E4C65   352'.0004722'0973   81-3251
ISBN 0-231-04888-2   AACR2

Columbia University Press
New York and Guildford, Surrey

Printed on permanent and durable acid-free paper.

To the spice of our lives—
Lesley, Diana, Sherian, Norine.

CONTENTS

PREFACE

This book is a product of the Urban Information Systems (URBIS) Project, carried out from 1973 to 1978 by the URBIS Research Group of the Public Policy Research Organization (PPRO) at the University of California, Irvine. The project was supported by a grant from the National Science Foundation. The purpose of this project was to assess the state of the art in local government computing, to evaluate the impact computers have had on government services and management decision making, and to develop recommendations that local managers and officials could implement in order to make better use of information technology.

The project was conducted in two major phases (see appendix). The first was an extensive survey of computing in more than 700 U.S. cities and counties, which documented the current array of data-processing activities, the extensiveness of computing use, the impacts of computing, and the problems with computing. The data were provided by mayors, city managers, county administrators, county board chairmen, and other chief executive officers in local governments, and by managers of the data-processing installations in these governments.

During the second phase of the research, members of the project did intensive fieldwork in 42 cities specially selected for study. Interviews were conducted with local government personnel, documents and papers were studied, and questionnaires were completed by 50 to 100 personnel about their use, and their evaluations, of computer applications in their governments. One primary objective in this phase was to analyze the impacts of specific policies for the management of computers in local government. Results of those analyses are most fully explicated in this book's companion volume from Columbia University Press, *The Management of Information Systems* (Kraemer, Dutton, and Northrop 1981). A second major objective of the fieldwork in the 42 cities was to determine the political and organizational effects of computer technology in local governments. These concerns are central to *Computers and Politics.*

Clearly, politics and administration are not separate. Consequently, we have dealt with the political aspects of implementation policy in *The Management of Information Systems* just as we have dealt with the management and implementation aspects of the political uses and impacts of computing in this book. Our conceptualizations and discussions in the two books are complementary and each offers a different, if interrelated, set of understandings about the roles of computer technology and the behavior of those who deal with the technology. We hope that each book will provide some answers to current questions about the effectiveness of computing in public organizations.

The intellectual origins of this book about the politics of computing extend far beyond the URBIS Project. When we started the project, most of the literature on computers reflected a rationalistic perspective. Major theorists such as Herbert Simon (1973, 1975, 1977) saw computers as an apolitical technology for improving the rationality of decision making and the efficiency of operations in organizations. It was unclear how useful this literature would be, because it was markedly apolitical and it also tended to be nonempirical, based more on speculation than on evidence.

At the time URBIS was initiated, our main guide to the empirical research on computers in organizations was an inventory of such research by members of our group (Kraemer & King 1977). Whisler's (1970) research on computing in the insurance industry was the primary empirical study available, and provided a grounding for our understanding of the role of automated information systems in complex organizations. Although this work guided our early conceptualizations, it also reflected the kinds of questions that arose in formulating our own research framework. Whisler had studied one private-sector industry with rather "primitive" computers, and had interviewed only one informant per company. Would the effects of computers in insurance companies be similar to their effects in public organizations? Would it be revealed that the major advances in the technology had brought about significant alterations in the nature of the effects? Would the political context of local government be important? In short, we recognized that our approach to the research required sensitivity to the variations in the effects of computer technology among different types of organizations, different levels of technological development, and for different kinds of personnel within an organization.

Our perspective on "the politics of computing" was rather simple in 1974. We generally assumed that computing was likely to shift power toward technical experts and top managers in organizations. This assumption had been influenced by a seminal article by Anthony Downs (1967), by models of organizational behavior (e.g., Allison 1971), and by the literature on the role of experts in organizations (e.g., Ellul 1964; Crozier 1964). As we completed a series of exploratory case studies and then proceeded with the two major phases of the research, it became increasingly clear that the interplay between the technology and the political setting, and hence the politics of computing, could be both complex and variable.

Our understandings were substantially enhanced as we found relevance in other scholars' work and as new research appeared. Three related studies that appeared during our research were especially useful. One was Kenneth Laudon's (1974) series of case studies of computers in state and local governments, that suggested how computers can be shaped to match the institutional agendas of key actors. Another was Eric Hoffmann's (1973, 1977) research on the role of computing in the Soviet Union, that illustrated the degree to which technical expertise can be pressed into the service of dominant political elites. And the third was Langdon Winner's (1977) synthesis of the technology and politics literature, that revealed the connections between our research focus and broader conceptions of technology and society.

The main argument of this book contrasts four alternative perspectives that emerged from many sources. Each provides an approach for understanding the politics of computing in local governments. They are: managerial rationalism, technocratic elitism, organizational pluralism, and reinforcement politics. The refinement of these four perspectives occurred as we analyzed the data collected in the survey of 42 cities. In the ideal world of social science research, one specifies a clear set of competing theoretical frameworks, develops a set of plausible and testable hypotheses, defines them operationally, gathers data to test the hypotheses, conducts formal data analyses, and then writes up the conclusions. This rigorous method has seldom been applied successfully in major research about complex social phenomena. Our study is no exception. In fact, the reinforcement politics perspective emerged in the process of research and data analysis. Data were not collected to allow a "critical test" of this perspective versus the alternatives. Nonetheless, we believe that the complex patterns of control and effects regarding the development and use of computing are best explained by the reinforcement politics perspective. Our research does have the advantage (relative to many studies) of producing a large body of systematic empirical data from survey techniques, consistent and comparable judgmental data from case-coded field appraisals, and suggestive insights from extensive field interviews. These alternative types of data inform the arguments and analyses throughout this book.

Books based on large-scale, multidisciplinary research projects such as URBIS are products of efforts by groups larger than are suggested by the authorship of any individual project publication. Throughout the URBIS project, we have benefited from the critical and unique contributions of many people who should share whatever credit this book merits. We want to acknowledge the contributions of these individuals. Most importantly, we thank two principal collaborators on the URBIS project. Their scholarly contributions to the project and to this book go far beyond our direct citations. Alexander Mood was the key force in shaping the overall research design of the URBIS project. Alana Northrop participated in the design and fieldwork of the second phase, and her critical reviews of our early work helped us formulate the reinforcement politics perspective.

Debora Dunkle, Linda Hackathorn, John Leslie King, Joseph R. Matthews, and David Schetter were invaluable to the URBIS project. Dr. Dunkle's talents in social science data analyses were extremely helpful to our work. Linda Hackathorn ably managed the complex census survey field operations and data-reduction activities. Dr. King has been a critical intellectual resource for the project throughout his involvement in the field research and group discussion. Joseph Matthews' constant attention to the needs of practitioners is responsible for much of the project's value to local government officials. David Schetter has been such a talented research administrator that we have often forgotten the difficulty of administering a multidisciplinary project in the complex bureaucratic environment of university and governmental agencies, procedures, and regulations. In addition, Robert Emrey, Henry Fagin, James Jewett, Fred Tonge, and Enzo Valenzi participated in the initial design of the URBIS project during the summer of 1973.

We also wish to acknowledge the support of others outside the URBIS project. Most important are the many local government personnel whose patient cooperation was essential to the generation of our data bases. Lawrence Williams of the National League of Cities, Mark Keene and Stanley Wolfson of the International City Management Association, John Thomas and Bernard Hillenbrand of the National Association of Counties, and Robert Havlick and James Bohnsack of Public Technology, Incorporated, helped us to gain the support of the specific cities and counties for our research, and helped to disseminate our research findings to their membership. The URBIS National Advisory Committee (along with their affiliations at the time of our project)—Dr. Ruth Davis of the National Bureau of Standards; Dr. Robert Crain of the Rand Corporation; Gerald Fox of Wichita Falls, Texas; Robert Goldman of the Association of Bay Area Governments; Edward Hearle of Booz, Allen and Hamilton; Donald Luria of the U.S. Bureau of Census; Peter McClosky of the Computer and Business Equipment Manufacturers Association; Daniel McGraw of the State of Minnesota; and Dr. Ralph Young of Fairfax County, Virginia— provided critical reviews of our work during the initial design of the project. Our NSF program managers—Dr. Vaughn Blankenship, Dr. Richard Mason, and Dr. Frank Scioli—kept us aware of the need to address both policy issues and intellectual issues in our research. Moreover, they helped us in a very practical way by bringing such experts as Professors E. S. Savas, Merrill Shanks, and Bert Swanson to judge both the substance and the methods of the project at critical junctures.

Penetrating and helpful comments were provided by Professor Kenneth Laudon, who reviewed the entire book. And continuing guidance came from Dr. Vicki Raeburn and Jacqueline Doyle of Columbia University Press.

The Public Policy Research Organization professional staff rendered essential support throughout the project, and deserve special mention for their patience and competence. Doris McBride and Shirley Hoberman kept the project moving and on target. The PPRO secretarial staff, Nancy Brock, Elizabeth Kelly, Sherry Merryman, Helen Sandoz, and Georgine Webster typed and retyped the torrent of manuscripts. And Laurel Battaglia refined and clarified our prose.

The entire book is the joint collaborative effort of the authors. To denote the equal contribution of the authors, the order of authorship is random (and, by chance, alphabetical). Also, to facilitate the preparation of the final versions of each chapter, responsibility for individual chapters was assigned by lottery. Despite the substantial help and advice of many people, the remaining errors and omissions are clearly our responsibility.

CHAPTER ONE

COMPUTERS AND POLITICS

William H. Dutton and James N. Danziger

POSTINDUSTRIAL SOCIETIES have applied high technologies to many
activities during the past decades. This technological development has been
a largely silent revolution—it has been dramatic in scale and scope but has
seldom drawn public notice. Usually the public's attention has focused
sequentially on different technologies whose impacts, costs, or benefits
have been highlighted or dramatized by a major event. For example, mass
transit systems, SSTs, space satellites, and nuclear power plants have been
subject to intense, if brief, public scrutiny as a result of dramatic events such
as the Three Mile Island accident.

One of the most pervasive applications of technology in this silent
revolution has been that of computer technology in organizations.
Computers and electronic data-processing systems are major tools of
modern organizations and components of many other technologies.
Occasionally a dramatic image of the computer has captured the public's
imagination, as did the uncontrolled and threatening computers in the
films *2001: A Space Odyssey, The Demon Seed,* and *Colossus: The
FORBIN Project.* But computer systems usually exist at the periphery of
public attention, because they are seldom perceived to entail the social
benefits or costs of rapid transit systems, SSTs, or nuclear power. Though
computer systems are critical components of rapid transit systems, SSTs,
and nuclear power plants, computing is backstage, out of the public view.
As a consequence, the costs and benefits and the broader impacts of
computer systems are largely perceived as indirect and subtle, if they are
indeed perceived at all. And when people do think of computing, it is
usually as either a minor convenience or as an annoying inconvenience,

depending, for example, on whether the automated bank teller is functioning properly.

However, neither the lack of public scrutiny nor the subtle and indirect nature of computer effects negates the importance of this revolutionary change in the technology of modern organizations. A growing literature posits that computer systems have major consequences for the sociology and politics of organizations, as well as for the broader society. Yet we have little systematic knowledge regarding these consequences.[1] This book explores the impacts of computing on modern organizations by focusing specifically on the politics of computing in certain public organizations— American local governments.

From a political perspective, the nature of a technology's impacts is contingent on the answers to two fundamental questions:

1. *Who controls* the technology?
2. *Whose interests are served* by the technology?

These questions regarding technology correspond to classic issues in the study of politics: Who governs? Whose values are served as a consequence of who governs? Computers and electronic data processing are among the most widespread and general-purpose high technologies implemented by local governments. In this book we shall analyze these empirical questions about control and interests served; but in the concluding chapter, we shall also consider the related normative questions: Who *should* govern computer technology in American local government? Whose interests *should* be served?

Answers to these empirical and normative questions are complex because both the control and the impacts of computer technology in local government are often subtle and variable. However, the general thrust of our findings is clear. First, no single local government interest—managerial, technological, or political—unilaterally controls computer technology. In most local governments, control is fragmented among a pluralistic array of managerial, technical, and political elites. These elites have varying influences on decisions regarding the adoption, design, and implementation of computer technology. Typically, their interests are not monolithic; rather, each group's actions are affected by personal, managerial, professional and technical values and interests. Moreover, although all elites participate directly in decisions regarding the computer package, not all have equal influence on the decision process. Technical elites are often most influential on the particular operational decisions, while some central and departmental managers combine with technical elites to produce more pluralistic outcomes on major developmental decisions.

Second, no single interest in local governments is always served by computer technology—the technology is highly malleable and can serve a variety of interests. In general, it has been shaped by those who directly control it to serve the interests of those who dominate the prevailing structure of influence within the local government. Thus, computing tends to reinforce not only the prevailing structure of control within local governments, but also the prevailing political and organizational biases of those governments. In this sense, computing has been a politically conservative technological innovation.

Our findings conflict with our judgment regarding who *should* control and who *should* be served by computing in public organizations. Since it is a malleable technology, computing need not reinforce the prevailing biases of an organization. We shall argue that control over computing and over computer experts should be decentralized to the users and clients of the technology in order that the technology might serve a broader variety of appropriate public interests.

In this chapter, we provide a background for this book based on the "technology and politics" literature. First we look at the concept of technology, and define our concept of computer technology. We then develop a theoretical framework for analyzing that technology in the context of the local political system. Finally, we discuss the outline of this book in relation to the theoretical framework developed in this chapter.

TECHNOLOGY AND COMPUTER TECHNOLOGY

What is Technology?

Recently there has been increasing interest in technology as a subject of study. Some define it narrowly, in terms of specific tools or machines (Goodman 1970; Mumford 1970). Others use a broader definition in which technology encompasses

> . . . tools in a general sense, including machines, but also including linguistic and intellectual tools and contemporary analytic and

mathematical techniques. That is, we define technology as the organization of knowledge for practical purposes. (Mesthene 1977:158)

Perhaps the broadest definition is given by Jacques Ellul, who defines technology ("la technique") as "the totality of methods rationally arrived at and having absolute efficiency in every field of human activity" (Ellul 1964:xxv). Although this definition might seem overly broad, Langdon Winner (1977:9) notes that Ellul's notion "closely corresponds to the *technology* now used in everyday English."

We shall employ Ellul's general definition of technology and also distinguish three components of a technology. The term *equipment* is used to denote the class of objects normally referred to as technological objects—tools, instruments, machines, appliances, gadgets—that are used to accomplish a wide variety of tasks. The term *technique* defines the body of technical activities—skills, methods, procedures, policies, routines—in which people engage to accomplish tasks (Winner 1977:14–15). In addition, the term *people* is used to highlight the fact that people are critical elements in technological systems, distinct from either the equipment or the technique of the systems.

Within our broad conception of technology, we shall focus on "high" technology. One may place technologies on a continuum ranging from *simple* technologies,—screwdrivers or cookbooks—to *complex* or *high* technologies—computerized missile control systems or rapid transit systems. High technologies are extremely *complicated systems designed by specialists* who usually have formal training, are relatively professionalized, and operate in a team. The full workings of most high technologies are not easily understood by any single person. In sum, we define high technologies as *complex systems of people and equipment guided by technique and designed by specialists.*

Computer Technology as a "Package"

It should be evident from our definition of high technology that our notion of computer technology includes substantially more than the basic machines associated with computing. Computer technology encompasses a complex, interdependent system composed of *people* (e.g., users, computer specialists, managers), *equipment* (e.g., hardware such as computer mainframes and peripherals; software, such as operating systems and application programs; and data), and *techniques* (e.g., procedures, practices, organizational arrangements).

We call this system of people, equipment, and technique within an organization the *computing package.* As we believe computer technology should be thought of as a package, we use "computer technology" and "computer package" interchangeably throughout this book. The "package" metaphor is useful because it encompasses more than conventional concepts of computer technology or a "computer system," and it emphasizes the interdependent components. Moreover, because the arrangements among components can vary from organization to organization, the metaphor suggests that there can be substantial variance in the nature of particular computer packages. For example, an organization might have decentralized or centralized hardware or computer specialists, it might have a computer policy board composed of users, and it might develop many sophisticated computer applications, or only a few simple ones.

An even more inclusive definition of the computing package would include the organizations and networks that comprise the broader "systems-world" of computing and that constitute the societal infrastructure for application of the technology within specific organizations (Kling & Gerson 1978).[2] This systems-world includes computing equipment manufacturers, software vendors, professional associations, communication networks, and governmental agencies, which operate as promoters and regulators of the technology. In order to clarify our analysis of the distinctive features of computer technology within modern, complex organizations, we shall maintain a conceptual distinction between the computer package and the broader systems-world that constitutes the environment within which the package exists.

Since change in one component of the package might produce changes in other components, the computing package is conceptualized as a system of mutually interdependent components within an organization. If those (computer specialists, managers, and users) who design changes in the package do not fully understand the critical linkages among the components, such changes will affect the package in unexpected ways. Moreover, when the computing package interacts with the dynamic systems-world, certain components of the package are likely to change and to produce effects beyond the control of local designers.

TECHNOLOGY AND POLITICS
Dominant Themes in the Technology Literature

Technology has been " . . . a central theme in political thought for the past two hundred years," as Winner (1977:1) notes in his comprehensive study of the technology and politics literature. Within this extensive literature, several dominant themes are relevant to our research. The most general perspective has come from those works that broadly examine the role and significance of technology for society—the writings of Ellul (1964), Ferkiss (1969), and Mumford (1970), for example. Such works provide comprehensive and detailed explorations of technology's impact on the beliefs, values and activities of individuals and groups within society.

A second stream of literature has been characterized by a narrower approach. One primary branch of this literature has been empirical research on the impacts of a particular technology, or technological change, upon a specific social system such as an industrial organization (for example, Mann & Hoffman 1960; Walker 1957; Woodward et al. 1970). Recently, the impact of computer systems on social systems has become an important focus of this work (Gottlieb & Borodin 1973; Kraemer, Dutton, & Northrop 1980a; Laudon 1974; Wessel 1974; Westin & Baker 1972). "Technology assessments" form a second branch of these more specific works. These are policy-oriented analyses that aim to examine the effects of the introduction or alteration of a specific technology, and to develop and evaluate policy and decision alternatives with respect to the technology (Brooks & Bowers 1972; MITRE 1971; Rich 1979). The third branch has focused primarily upon determining the socioeconomic and political factors that facilitate or constrain technological innovations within organizations, treating such innovations as the dependent variable (Bingham 1976; Danziger & Dutton 1977a, 1977b; Perry & Kraemer 1979; Row & Boise, 1974; Yin et al. 1976).

Although diverse and extensive, this literature on technology and politics is unified in its focus on several common issues and related themes. Broadly, this literature can be examined from the perspective of two basic themes:

What factors shape the use of technology?
What impacts does technology have on its environment?

These general issues regarding technological control and impacts are embodied in the conceptual framework schematized in figure 1.1. The figure illustrates the basic relationships between a *technology* and its *environment* and also among elements of the technology itself. Each relationship suggests certain issues regarding technological control and impacts, and these relationships define the theoretical and analytical focuses of this study.

Three fundamental premises underlie this conceptualization. First, the adoption, implementation, and utilization of a given technology are a continuing social and political process in which the technology is constrained—somewhat controlled and shaped—by its environment. This relationship is represented in figure 1.1 as linkage C. As will be seen in figure 1.2, this environment consists of both external (extracommunity and community) forces, and internal (organizational) forces, each set of which might have effects on the nature of the technology. And these environmental "constraints" can operate as forces that either limit or expand the technology.

The second premise is that the existence and use of the technology will have impacts on its environment (linkage I). Some of these effects will be intended by the actors who implement and operate the technology; but unintended effects are also likely to occur. Both can be either beneficial or harmful to the objectives of various actors in the system. Also, they can be recognized or unrecognized, and might or might not result in adaptive responses from the system and its actors.[3]

The third premise underlying figure 1.1 holds that, because a technology is an interdependent system of people, equipment, and technique, changes in one component are likely to produce changes in other components

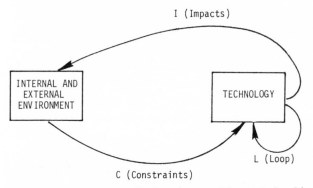

Figure 1.1   Technology, Environment, and Interrelationships

(linkage L). This loop, internal to the technological package itself, adds further complexity to the problem of understanding and controlling the dynamic linkages between the technology, on the one hand, and the environment, on the other. In the next section we shall develop this conceptual framework.

COMPUTERS AND POLITICS

General Approach

Once we move from an abstract concept of technology to an empirical consideration of an observable technology, important issues arise concerning the generalizability of observations. Each particular technology raises many issues peculiar to itself, concerning both its control and its social impact. For example, privacy is not an issue in rapid transit systems, and storage of volatile wastes is not an issue in computing. Different technologies and different organizational settings vary greatly and this has presented a major problem for empirically based research on technology and politics. Are these variations so great that the search for theoretical generalizations across different technologies and organizational settings must be abandoned in favor of single-technology, single-setting theories?

We feel that general theory is most likely to emerge from a body of both multiple-technology, comparable-setting studies, and, particularly, single-technology, comparable-setting studies. That is, we assume that stable and generalizable findings will emerge from studies of similar types of technologies, and that differences in findings across various types of technologies and settings will lead to conditional theories of technology and politics. We believe that single-technology analyses such as this book lay the groundwork for eventual development of general theories on the control and impacts of technology in social systems.

Computers and Politics in Local Government

The conceptual framework for our analysis of the computer package in local government is schematized in figure 1.2. As in our broad "systems" conceptualization of technology and environment (figure 1.1), computer technology is seen as a package that is continually shaped by both its external and internal environments, and that in turn, through the benefits and costs of its information-processing services, itself affects those environments.

At the most general level, we distinguish the *technology* from its *external environment*, from the *organizational system* within which it functions, and from the *outputs* it produces. As defined above, computer technology encompasses the package of people (e.g., data-processing personnel and active users), equipment (e.g., hardware and software), and techniques (e.g., organizational arrangements and procedures) used to provide automated information-processing (computing) services.

Figure 1.2 makes a further distinction, within the *external environment*, between extracommunity and community environments. The *extracommunity environment* of computer technology refers, in part, to relevant political and administrative factors outside the specific local political system, such as the activities of other local governments, and to state or federal policies affecting computing, such as external funding for local computing, privacy legislation, or upward reporting requirements that create demands for local information processing. The extracommunity environment also refers to factors in the outside socioeconomic and technological environment, such as activities of suppliers of computer package components, and the professional communication networks through which the technology is diffused.

The *community environment* refers to the socioeconomic and technological characteristics of the community served by a local government. Relevant community socioeconomic factors might include the size of the community, its social complexity, resource base, and social status. Relevant technological features include the mix of technologies available within the community, as well as general community support for the use of technological innovations.

The *local political system* is the organizational entity upon which this study focuses. It has been formally defined by Easton (1965) as the structures and processes that "authoritatively allocate public values" for its population. Attributes of the local political system of particular relevance to our analysis include such features as organizational structure (e.g., government size), professionalism of government personnel, administrative orientation of the government, and centralization of authority within the governmental system. Also included in this category are certain factors that relate specifically to decisions regarding the computer package, such as the interests and values served by the local government's computer applications, and the question of who controls decisions regarding computing.

As shown in figure 1.2, both the external environment and the local political system can determine the nature and affect the impacts of the

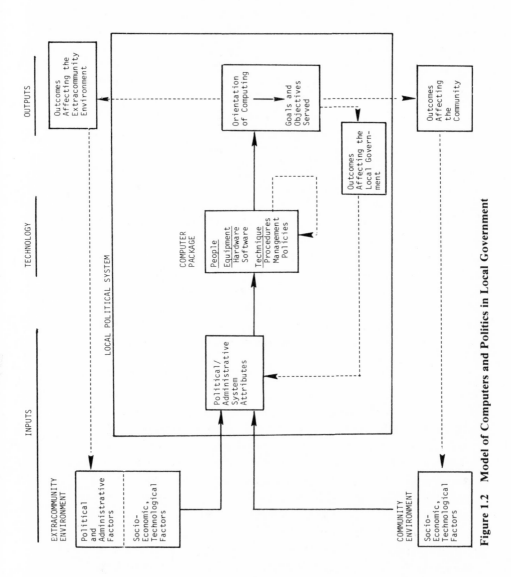

Figure 1.2 Model of Computers and Politics in Local Government

computer package in a local government. The most important features of the external environment are hypothesized to be those attributes of the extracommunity and community environments that shape the technology's "selection environment," and that function as "facilitators." "Selection environment" refers to those environmental factors that define the worth of the technology in its setting;[4] and "facilitators" are those environmental attributes that substantially ease adoption and implementation of the technology (Danziger & Dutton 1977b).

The most important features of the local government (the internal environment of computing) are taken to be certain attributes of the political and administrative system—specifically, the *interests and values* of local government officials and personnel, and the locus of *decisional control* over the computer package.[5] Broadly, five types of interests and values can be distinguished in most local governments: personal, managerial, professional, technical, and public. *Personal* interests and values involve career ambitions, status, and the reelection or advancement of public officials and staff. *Managerial* interests and values are mainly involved in maintaining and enhancing organizational guidance and control—particularly by central and departmental managers. *Professional* interests and values are mainly related to maximizing the autonomy and discretion of professionalized personnel, such as detectives, social workers, and planners. *Technical* values and interests focus on maintenance and enhancement of the technology—in this case, on the computer package and the technical experts. Finally, *public* values and interests are primarily concerned with serving the community as a whole, the clientele of the local government. Any individual, group, or organization is characterized by a mixture of these interests and values. The nature of the use and orientation of computer technology is likely to be contingent on which interests and values are dominant, resulting, in turn, in different interests and values being served by the technology in different local governments.

Decisional control over the computer package may be held by politicians, bureaucrats, professionals, or technocrats, or by coalitions of these groups. For the purposes of this study, the most relevant politicians are elected officials of local governments (primarily mayors and council members) and their staffs. Bureaucrats who might exercise decisional control include top appointed officials (such as city managers and chief administrative officers), central management staff, and departmental administrators; professionals include personnel who have received specialized training and who occupy professionalized roles in the delivery of urban services (e.g., detectives, social workers, planners). Technocrats here include not only specialists in computer programing and systems analysis, but also specialists in the use and analysis of computer-based data. Within any local government, members of each of these groups might exert some influence on computing decisions. And, as with the dominant set of interests and values of a local government, the locus of decisional control is likely to affect the use and orientation of computer technology.

The basic *outputs* of the computer package are termed the "orientation" of computing. This concept refers to the goals and objectives served by specific applications of the technology. Given outputs might produce different benefits and costs as they affect particular actors and groups, and they might involve unintended as well as intended effects.[6] Therefore, we shall analyze in particular detail the variations among governments in the degree to which computing is oriented towards different purposes—for example, towards providing information for managers and policy makers, aiding service delivery functions versus administrative functions, or serving such functional areas as police and finance rather than welfare and parks.

In analyzing figure 1.2 from left to right, we have specified a framework within which to discuss computer technology in local government, with respect to both the forces that seem to *control* the technology, and the *benefits* generated by application of the technology. But the figure also incorporates a focus on the impacts of the technology itself, as an independent variable that might affect its environment. Thus the "feedback loops" that move from right to left indicate that the use of the technology produces various services, benefits, and costs, and that these effects can, in turn, alter the technology's environment, the allocation of values within and outside the government, and decisional control over the technology.

The Politics of Computing

Our concern with the *politics* of computing focuses on the assessment of two phenomena: the relative influence of various groups over decisions relating to the use of computer resources; and the interests served by applications of computer technology. In essence, these are reformulations of the two classic questions posed by Aristotle in his analysis and classification of political systems: Who rules? and Whose interests are served? From the social-scientific literature on local political systems and on organizations, we have adapted four alternative perspectives that attempt to answer these two questions. They are summarized in table 1.1 and are briefly characterized in the next paragraphs.

MANAGERIAL RATIONALISM

Managerial rationalism provides both a normative and a descriptive explication of how decisions are made and which interests are served. According to this approach, an organization constantly aims to increase the extent to which its decision system is guided by criteria of rationality and its actions maximize the interests of the organization as a whole. Such an organization will be controlled firmly by top managers, whose authority is evident on the organization chart. These managers will ensure that decisions are guided by extensive, high-quality information and data, by a comprehensive decision process, and by such techniques as cost-benefit analysis. Although the features of hierarchical control, "synoptic" decision making, and organization-as-a-whole values cannot obtain universally, the managerial-rationalist approach holds that every procedure and action should serve these objectives.

In this approach, computer technology is viewed as a valuable, organization-wide resource that can be strategically employed by those in managerial roles. In a local government characterized by a managerial-rationalist approach, the critical decisions about the adoption, operations, and uses of computer technology will be made by the top managers—chief administrative officers, mayors and councils, and department heads of major staff agencies. And computing will be managed to serve generalized interests of the organization, a set of values characterized in the government sector by the concept of "the public interest." Specifically, computing resources will enhance the quality and quantity of information available to government personnel, and it will increase their capabilities for extensive, sophisticated and analytical decision making and problem solving. The managerial rationalist approach is generally evident in works by Bell (1973), Fuller (1970), Nolan (1973), and Simon (1973).

TECHNOCRATIC ELITISM

The technocratic-elitist approach is premised on the notion that modern organizations are composed of domains of activity within which complex, technical, and highly specialized knowledge prevails. The experts—those with the appropriate "technique," in Ellul's sense—will control the resources within their respective domains. And the interests served by the

Table 1.1 Perspectives on the Politics of Computing

Dimension of Comparison	Alternative Perspectives			
	Managerial Rationalism	Technocratic Elitism	Organizational Pluralism	Reinforcement Politics
Dominant mode of decision making	Rational assessment of costs and benefits to the organization as a whole	Technical assessment of the optimal design and utilization of the technology	Pulling and hauling among coalitions of groups within the organization, given the constraints of hierarchy in subunits.	Political assessment of decisions as they affect each actor's ability to maintain and enhance his position within the organization
Basis of control over decision making	Formal position and authority in organizational hierarchy	Monopoly of technical expertise	Variety of resources, including authority, expertise, time, ability to resist, nature of coalition, etc.	Direct and indirect influence on lower-level operatives, who anticipate the reactions of those controlling the organization and attempt to serve those interests.

Locus of control over decision making	Those at the top of the organizational hierarchy—top managers and elected officials (managers, mayors, council members)	Technical experts (computer experts, management and planning analysts skilled in the use of computer-based systems)	Varies across decisions and especially across decision domains	Those who dominate the prevailing structure of influence within the organization (varies from organization to organization).
Dominant interests served	Organization as a whole	Maintenance and enhancement of the role within the organization of the technology and the technical experts	Groups benefit differentially at different times and with different kinds of decisions and issues	Reinforces the power and influence of those who already have the most resources to influence organizational decisions.

application of those resources will stem from the agenda and values of those experts.

The application of computer technology is a clear example of a domain where sophisticated technical knowledge is necessary for the smooth functioning of the activity and effective use of its products. In the technocratic-elitist view, it is assumed that those who have sophisticated knowledge about computers and about the skillful manipulation of automated information systems will constitute a technical elite, making most of the major decisions for the computer-technology domain and enjoying most of the benefits from application of the technology. Members of this elite will be found primarily in the units providing computing services to the organization, particularly the managers and analysts, and among those with advanced skills in computer software or in data analysis in user departments (e.g., planners, policy analysts). The technical elite is distinguished by its relative monopoly of expertise. It will in fact strive to dominate the decisions regarding computer technology, converting most nontrivial decisions about computer application and use into decisions where technical criteria are paramount. As a result, the interests served by computer technology will be primarily those of the technocrats, in terms of the norms and standards of practice in the computing profession or in the profession of the expert users. In general, computing will serve the needs of the organization and of the users for basic information-processing services; but service of these needs will be incidental and secondary to the attempt of the technocratic elite to control the computing domain, to maintain its autonomy on key decisions, and to expand its domain. Technocratic elitism is discussed in work by Benveniste (1977), Boguslaw (1965), Danziger (1979a, 1979c), Downs (1967), Ellul (1964), Galbraith (1967), and Touraine (1972).

ORGANIZATIONAL PLURALISM

This widely accepted approach holds that numerous actors and groups with some stake in a decision will become active in making that decision, and will receive some benefits from its outcome. In this approach, most commonly associated with Robert Dahl (1961) and the "pluralists," various groups will have sufficient resources to influence decisions on distribution of public goods and services. Not all groups will have equal influence; some will have and use more influence resources than others, some will be constrained by the rules of the game, and, in an organization, some groups will be constrained by the organization's hierarchical arrangement of authority, with its superordinate-subordinate relationships. A central assumption of this approach is that no single group dominates this decision process; rather, there is a variable pattern in participation and influence, with a particular group's will and capacity to participate being a function of that group's resources and agenda.

Although there is considerable disagreement about precisely how one may measure empirically the extent to which a power structure is pluralistic, we shall interpret organizational pluralism to mean that the system is essentially fragmented and nonhierarchical. Thus there will be no unitary control system over an organization-wide resource such as computing. Many people and groups in the local government will be active in decisions regarding computing, since computing resources will be significant to many. Those groups likely to be consistently involved in the decision process, because of their interests in computing and their general influence, are the top managers in appointed and elected positions, the heads of departments and agencies that are major users of computing resources, and the experts in the computing unit itself. Indirect influence and sporadic involvement might be expected from others, such as departments or agencies making limited use of computing resources, citizens affected by the government's computers, and federal and state agencies interested in the local government's computer applications.

The pluralist approach does not assume that the distribution of computing resources will be random. Rather, the allocation of computing resources will depend upon the behavior and competition among groups mobilized in the decision process, and will result from those groups' perceptions of the stakes involved and their willingness and ability to use their power and influence to affect the decision. Although the total amount of computer resources is relatively constant, these resources can be divided among a large number of groups. According to the organizational-pluralist perspective, many groups are likely to enjoy at least some benefits from the use of computer technology. It is not necessarily the case that a particular group's benefits from computer resources will be proportionate to its influence, or to its stake in computing, since decision outcomes are a function of shifting coalitions and a somewhat unpredictable decision process. It is clear, however, that no one group dominates consistently, and that no group is either a consistent "winner" or "loser" among those with some modicum of involvement and influence in the decision process. The organizational-pluralist approach to the politics of technology can be found in Cyert and March (1963), Lambright (1976), Laudon (1974), Lorsch and Morse (1974), Price (1965), and Redford (1969).

REINFORCEMENT POLITICS

The reinforcement politics approach differs from each of the other three approaches in its focus on the *distribution of impacts* from computing resources rather than on the distribution of decision control and the allocation of computing resources. This approach posits that there is a dominant interest or dominant coalition in any given local government. And the central assumption of reinforcement politics is that a resource like computing will primarily serve the interests of this dominant coalition, regardless of who controls computing resources. That is, the decision process regarding computing might be controlled by a rational-managerial elite, a technocratic elite, or a pluralistic array of actors. There is no assumption that any style of decisional control or allocation of computing resources will obtain in most or all local government settings. But in every system of decisional control and allocation, the dominant interests in the organization will fundamentally be served by the uses to which computing is put. Hence computing will *reinforce* the power and influence of those actors and groups who already have the most resources and power in the organization.

In this approach, computer resources are thought of as malleable. They can serve rational-management objectives, they can be employed by the technocratic elite to serve its organizational objectives, they can serve the interests of a dominant coalition of groups, or they can serve the interests of many individual groups. It is assumed that those groups that directly control the uses of computer technology will attempt to guide it to serve the values and interests of those groups dominant in the organization. Thus precise effects of computer technology on the government and its environment will be contingent on the dominant interests and values of that government. The serving of other sets of values and interests will be secondary or incidental. The view that technical experts fundamentally reinforce the established base of institutional power is expressed by Dickson (1974), Marx (1906), Noble (1977), and Straussman (1978). The reinforcement politics approach to the role of computer technology is found in Dutton and Kraemer (1977), Hoffman (1977), Kling (1978c), and Kraemer and Dutton (1979).

OUTLINE OF THIS BOOK

We have outlined the theoretical framework that underlies this book. Later chapters will examine the extent to which there is a differential distribution of benefits from computing; the extent to which the decisional control over computing is pluralistic, or is dominated by an elite; the impact of the environment on the computer package; and so on. These questions will be addressed within the framework of our empirical study of the role of this pervasive high technology in operating political systems.

We begin chapter 2 by describing the computer package as it has evolved in American local governments. We emphasize the fact that computer technology is difficult for anyone to control because it is highly complex, organizationally fragmented, and constantly changing. Yet the pattern of its evolution and current implementation suggests that computing has been implemented in rather predictable ways by local governments. We also indicate that computer technology is important to a wide variety of local government functions. While the distribution of computing resources is much greater in certain departments and agencies, computer impacts are likely to be widespread.

We next focus on issues of control over the computer package. Specifically, we examine the major actors and forces that might determine the adoption, implementation, and use of computing in local government. Chapter 3 considers the computing "milieu"—the environmental and organizational context within which the computer package functions. First, we evaluate an alternative to the thesis that some local actors do control computer technology. Data from 500 local governments are analyzed to see whether variations in the level of computer use among governments are determined by "objective" characteristics of the environment; then a series of case studies of the politics of computing in selected local governments is presented. We conclude that although environmental forces do act as an important constraint, the technology's use is not environmentally determined—it can also be considerably shaped by more unique (that is, nonsystematic) forces in each government's computing milieu. These unique forces often emerge from the influence and control of particular people, whose decisive behavior alters the politics, and outcomes, of local government computing.

Chapter 4 identifies the participants involved in decisions about distribution of computer resources. Are those decisions made by a managerial or technocratic elite, or are they made more pluralistically? The evidence indicates that computing is not wholly controlled by a distinct elite. Although computer professionals are frequent and sometimes dominant participants in many decisions, particularly technical ones, their influence is tempered by the participation of other decision makers. When broader issues of computing use are involved, decisions tend to be made pluralistically, through interactions among top managers, department heads, department staff, and computing staff.

Chapter 5 presents a historical perspective on control over the computer package. We highlight the dynamic nature of control, and how the various key participants have changed over time. We show how certain actors have made strategic use of structural changes such as reorganizations, master plans, and policy boards in order to establish, maintain, and enhance their control over the computing package and, consequently, over broader organizational interests. And we indicate how the growth of computing has contributed to fragmentation of control over the computer package. We conclude that while past political effects have resulted mainly from ownership and control of *computer* resources, future effects might result more from ownership, control, and use of *data* resources.

We then turn to the political consequences of computing as it is now used by local governments. Chapter 6 examines the use of computer-based information in the policy process. This analysis shows that such use is limited and selective. In general, automated information systems tend to be employed where the dominant policy makers are most certain that they can control the access to, the manipulation of, and the use of automated information. It is suggested that a less limited, less selective use of computer-based information would threaten the interests of those who currently control decision-making processes in the local government.

The interests served by computing, particularly the interests served by the current cross-cutting information systems of local government, are further assessed in chapter 7. The analysis reveals that the use of computer-based information for decision making shapes the relative influence of different actors in the local political process. A major conclusion is that the primary political effect of these information systems is to reinforce existing patterns of power and influence within the government.

In chapter 8 on urban services, we demonstrate that the uses of computing tend to reinforce dominant groups by supporting their interests in such goals as revenue generation, centralized fiscal control, bureaucratic growth, and crime fighting, as opposed to such goals as the effectiveness of service delivery, decentralized professional control, bureaucratic efficiency, or public welfare and social services. If computing serves some activities of local government more than others, is this a function of the technology's capabilities, or of political decisions made about the use of the technology? The data suggest the latter. Computer technology serves a variety of interests in local government, but it most clearly serves the interests of central administrators, and the values of social and administrative control.

In the concluding chapter, we present a broad overview of our findings and some of their general implications. We find that computers are used to support certain dominant interests and values of local governments, due to the nature of the decision-making process in those governments. This process is characterized best by reinforcement politics—control over computing decisions tends to follow, and reinforce, the influence of those who dominate the broader structure of influence in the organization. However, the process of reinforcement politics is constrained by important technological and environmental factors that lessen the degree to which any actor or group can effectively control a complex and dynamic high technology.

Our findings are especially notable because most writing on computing (and other high technologies) emphasizes technical-rational aproaches to control, and even to impacts, of the technology. Only a small part of the literature deals with the organizational politics of high technology—most treats any problems as largely correctable by means of better financing, design, and management. In contrast, this book argues that some technological problems are *intrinsic* features of the technology, given the relatively complex and differentiated social system in which it is embedded. Often, these problems are not due to the lack of viable and effective solutions. Rather, they result from differences of opinion and interest regarding the best solution, and regarding the appropriate distribution of control over technological decisions.

We argue, in the concluding sections, that control over computing resources should be more decentralized so that those resources might serve a broader array of interests in the local political process. We explain why more "democratic" control over a government's computer technology is infeasible and problemmatic. But we do offer a set of recommendations for shaping computer technology into a tool that might enhance the rationality, as well as the democratic nature, of local government information systems.

CHAPTER TWO

THE COMPUTER PACKAGE: DYNAMIC COMPLEXITY

Rob Kling and William H. Dutton

COMPUTER USE symbolizes rationality and control. Computer-using organizations are thought to be in control of those data and operations that are automated. Like sympathetic magic, the rationality of computing lends an aura of rationality, control, and efficiency to other parts of their operations (Dutton & Kraemer 1978c; Kling 1978a, 1980). Indeed, if any aspect of an organization's activities is well-managed, one would expect it to be its computing operations. Good management is linked to administrative control; when one questions computing management in an organization, one must question control over computing.

When asked about the management and control of computing in their own organizations, many computer users can point to *someone* they believe is in control of some important part of the computing operation. They can point to the computer-center director or his superiors to explain why some departments get better service than others; they can point to particular programmers and systems analysts to explain why specific applications are designed in a certain way, and how the applications can be altered. They can point to the data-entry and computer-operations staff as people who know in detail the ways in which data are coded and files are manipulated in specific programs. Each of these people is thought to understand and control some important aspect of computing. This complexity is one key reason why it is highly doubtful that any single individual or group entirely comprehends, let alone controls, all of the organization's computing operations and services.

Complexity tends to be an important characteristic of most modern technological and social systems.[1] A complex system is composed of so many parts, interrelated in such an elaborate variety of important ways, that the behavior of the whole system is difficult to analyze. Computer technology in local governments shares this complexity. Large computer programs are often complicated and incomprehensible to technicians who did not design them. (Weizenbaum 1976). Most major computer programs in organizations are written and then modified, perhaps by different programmers, by teams of analysts and programmers over a period of months or even years, so that eventually few people, if any, comprehend programs in their entirety.[2] Compounding this problem is the fact that many organizations depend on several key systems which are composed of hundreds of such programs. And complexity is increased by the rapid development of computer equipment, the greater diffusion of computer applications among the various local government departments and agencies, and the generally dynamic nature of the computer package. This issue is important because it is directly related both to the control and to the impacts of computer technology. The complex nature of the technology is likely to make organizations more dependent on computer experts, thus influencing the structure and power within those organizations.

In this chapter, we explore the characteristics of computing in local government, highlighting various parts of this complex system we call the computing package, and indicating some of the many relationships among these parts. First, it is necessary to describe briefly the rapid development of the technology.

THE DEVELOPMENT OF COMPUTER TECHNOLOGY

A critical factor in the complexity of electronic data processing (EDP) in local governments has been the rapid development of equipment since 1950. Advances in the speed, flexibility, and relative cost of the equipment have been most visible and dramatic. Even before the 1950s, some local governments employed unit record equipment to perform certain basic data-processing tasks. Information was typically stored on punched cards. The early unit record equipment facilitated many of the routine record-keeping, calculating, and printing tasks involving large files, particularly in finance and accounting. By the mid-1950s, a few local governments had begun to utilize the early electronic computers, which could store data and complex programs as well as manipulate data from punched cards or tape. These early computers were limited by both the amount of data they could store, and the number of tasks they could be programed to perform "simultaneously."

The second-generation computers, developed in the late 1950s, dramatically increased the amount of information that could be stored, and the speed with which it could be accessed by the mainframe computer, particularly through the use of magnetic core memories. Second-generation computers were also easier to program, through the use of "high-level" programing languages such as COBOL and FORTRAN that were invented and disseminated in the late 1950s. These computers, although crude in comparison to contemporary digital computers, enabled organizations such as local governments to automate certain clerical and record-keeping activities. As files were usually sequential, and were often stored on magnetic tape, data could be rapidly retrieved or recombined with other elements of a "data base." As we shall see in chapter 5, these were the machines initially adopted by many American local governments.

By the mid-1960s, third-generation machines had been developed, with thousands of transistors and integrated circuits. These computers provided greater technical performance by means of increased reliability, speed, and storage capacity, and they were less expensive than their predecessors. In addition, they incorporated major technical advances that allowed the development of advanced forms of automation without demanding exceptional technical expertise. These computers also used magnetic discs, which could store large amounts of data that could be retrieved non-sequentially ("random access"). Third-generation machines often supported operating systems that facilitated the writing of on-line and real-time applications, without requiring a deep understanding of the hardware architecture and sophisticated engineering. Most operating systems for third-generation machines also allowed "multiprograming"—the "simultaneous" execution of several programs on a given machine. Multi-programed machines with on-line capabilities could simultaneously support several real-time programs that had access to separate data bases, and could also run batch programs to process routine transactions and reports.

These technical innovations enabled many organizations to build new computer applications at costs ranging from ten thousand to several hundred thousand dollars, rather than the millions of dollars that such applications would have cost with second-generation machines. Thus, the third-generation computers made many applications, particularly those requiring on-line access, technically feasible at costs that were well within the budgetary reach of larger cities and counties.

These interactive capabilities also allowed immediate access to and updating of files from terminals in any number of locations in the local government's setting. Moreover, the on-line systems made possible the institution of information networks that greatly facilitated the sharing of data and equipment among government functions and jurisdictions. Rapid access from diverse geographic settings was particularly attractive to local government agencies seeking current information (e.g., budget control), or operating from multiple points (e.g., social service centers), or both (e.g., police field patrols).

During the 1970s, there have been further incremental improvements in computer technologies. The technical flexibility of systems of a given scale continues to improve as features that have been developed for larger and more expensive machines are engineered to fit smaller-scale equipment. Simultaneously, the speed, memory, and communications capability of smaller-scale equipment (e.g., minicomputers) have been increasing rapidly, and the cost of such equipment per unit of computation has been dropping dramatically. Most of these developments can be attributed to advances in integrated-circuit and "chip" technologies, which allow millions of electronic components to be packed into increasingly smaller spaces and to be produced and marketed at ever cheaper prices. Although speeds and capacity cannot continue to increase, and prices continue to drop, indefinitely, these trends should continue well into the 1980s. Clearly, such developments are significant for local-government computing, because they enable smaller governments, and departmental units in larger governments, to consider purchasing their own computing equipment. Software development, on the other hand, has not become less costly. Software development is labor intensive, and though hardware costs have decreased, the portion of the computing budget devoted to labor costs has markedly increased. This increase has offset the decrease in hardware costs.

Computing is often seen as a "hard" technology, and a great deal of emphasis is placed on the information-processing power of computing devices, and on the applications that they support. But the net effect of these shifts in the costs of equipment and people (particularly programing support) is that computing is becoming a more *labor-intensive* technology. People play critical roles at every stage of the development, implementation, and use of the technology. Thus, much of our emphasis in this book is on the people and the related technique aspects of the computer package.

THE COMPUTER PACKAGE

Elements

Ivan Illich (1974) has observed that the adoption of a technology will often require a complex array of commitments that are not immediately obvious to the adopter. In Illich's metaphor, equipment is the central element in a *package*, which also includes the components required for the application of the equipment. The decision to use the automobile, for example, generates the need to develop a system of roads, service centers and service personnel, replacement parts, regulations governing use, and so on.

Similarly, the decision to install a computer draws the local government into a broad set of commitments involving the "computer package." As noted in chapter 1, this package includes equipment, techniques, and people (Kling & Scacchi 1979; 1980; 1981). Minimally, the specific components of the computer package are

1. The CPU (the central processing unit)
2. The data in automated files
3. Data input and output hardware (card readers, tape and disk drives, line printers, cathode ray tube terminals)
4. Skilled computing staff (operators for the hardware, programmers and systems analysts to develop and maintain software)
5. Data input personnel (coders, staff to operate computer terminals or keypunch equipment)
6. Support services (to ensure proper conditions for the hardware, such as temperature control, and both primary and back-up energy sources)
7. Physical and software security systems (to secure the data from unauthorized access)
8. Vendors (to provide equipment and to maintain it)
9. An array of organizational arrangements and policy decisions to manage and control the operation of the computer system (including management personnel, decision structures to establish charging policies, data access rights, priorities for computer use and development, and training programs for users of computing services).

This list of the components in the computer package indicates the extensive commitment of the local government that decides to provide in-house computing services. Even the decision to purchase *all* hardware and software services from an outside service agency eliminates only a part of these responsibilities from the government. (The government's staff still have to decide what to automate and in what sequence. Moreover, they must be able to develop meaningful specifications, review proposed designs, budgets, and deadlines, and finally evaluate the quality of service they receive.)

Moreover, the computer package, like other advanced technologies, is dynamic and expansive. For one thing, it expands with new technical developments that become virtual necessities for continued and efficient use of existing equipment. For example, multiprograming computer systems that permit the processing of multiple jobs concurrently in the same central processing unit (CPU) have been widely adopted to increase the efficiency of machine use. But multiprograming systems require the development of complex supporting software, such as operating systems, which have become necessities for almost every computer installation. Similarly, technical enhancements such as virtual memory and data-base management systems, which are becoming widespread, require the development of additional capabilities.

However, the spread of these increasingly complex and powerful technologies is not driven solely by the demands of those using computers. It is also prompted by the policies of those selling computer systems (Kling & Gerson 1977). For example, in the mid-1970s IBM announced that it was discontinuing technical support for its "OS" operating system, and would support only its "virtual memory" operating systems in its then-popular 370-series machines. Virtual memory is a technical advancement that provides a more flexible way of allowing large programs to utilize cheaper "secondary" memory resources, rather than being limited to the use of expensive "primary" memory. But most computing installations did not have the in-house expertise to maintain old OS operating systems. Thus IBM's shift to virtual memory systems required most OS users to make additional financial investments in virtual-memory operating systems. Many technological improvements are made, and often controlled, by the manufacturers and other suppliers of computer technology. Users often have no choice but to keep up with these new developments, and usually within a period of time determined by the supplier.

At present, the computer package is in a seemingly unending developmental phase. New additions and modifications are continually expanding the total computer package, its use in the operations of local government, its effects on individuals and groups both within and outside the government, and the structures organized to control it.

Complexity

Few people fully understand computer technology. In fact, most computer experts required years of technical training and experience before they could work successfully with it. One need only skim the pages of a computing periodical to appreciate the specialized language of computer experts and the pace of new developments in the technology. Lay people think that most "computer experts" share a common understanding of the general theories involved and of the practical details required to operate specific programs and equipment. In fact, the various kinds of computing work are so specialized and differentiated, that two computer specialists chosen at random are likely to be unfamiliar with the details of each other's work (Kling & Gerson 1978).

However, a person who uses or depends on computer-based services in an organization can develop a working understanding of those segments of the particular computer package he or she deals with every day. The forms to be filled out, "turnaround time," the reports generated, what is required to correct an error, whom to call if something goes wrong—such practical understanding is necessary for one to get on with one's business.

More sophisticated understanding is difficult because of the dynamic nature of the computer package technology (Kling & Scacchi 1979). If the uses of the technology were relatively stable—that is, if operational computer applications would remain untouched for five or ten years—then understanding and working with the package would be easier. But this is not the case. Rather, the computing package frequently undergoes such changes as:

1. The redesign and upgrading of existing applications by those seeking improvements and solutions to current problems.
2. The promotion of new applications.
3. The interdependence of computing operations within the organization. (New, altered, or expanded computing services for other users can have impacts on one's own operations.)
4. The rapid pace of technological development. ("Generations" of equipment last five to ten years and vendors upgrade their equipment

every few years. Automated applications for users must be adapted to these changes occurring in the local computer package.)

5. The complexity and dynamism of the social, technical and organizational arrangements for computing services. (There are periodic changes in such factors as the location of computing facilities and in such organizational policies as the pricing of computer services and the provision of consulting assistance.)

6. The variation in computing technology and applications among organizations and even among different departments and agencies within a single organization. (Thus users must familiarize themselves with new computing environments as they change roles or positions.)

Because of these factors, it is more difficult to get a clear grasp of the elements of the computer package than is the case with most other technologies. We need to know more about the kinds of choices typically facing the users and managers of computer-based services; therefore, the remaining sections of this chapter describe the "state of the practice" in American city and county governments.

Descriptions of the state of the practice are rare, because most researchers of computing in organizations use either gleaming future "technologies" (e.g., desktop color graphic terminals), or examples of idealized, smoothly functioning organizations to communicate their concepts (Danziger 1977). Such portraits are misleading. The computing arrangements that most people deal with are not leading-edge technologies. And very few organizations run smoothly all the time.

In addition, most people who have close contact with computing in organizations have it in only one or two organizations. Because of their limited experience, when they hear promotional accounts of leading-edge technologies, they feel they are behind and must somehow keep up with that mythical leading edge. It is therefore important for people to understand what they have in relation to others. The following examination of the actual technologies current in hundreds of local governments can give a more realistic perspective than either a portrayal of a single exemplary organization or accounts of leading-edge developments.

CURRENT LEVELS OF USE

Proportion of Governments Using Computers

In the early 1960s local governments found it difficult to decide whether or not to adopt a large-scale computer operation. The hardware was expensive and seemed to be changing quickly, there was little expertise available in local government for the development and maintenance of effective software, there was uncertainty about the benefits that would accrue, and there was concern that computer use would seriously disrupt standard operating procedures within the government's agencies.

Over the past fifteen years, however, the range of capabilities of computer technology has expanded, the reliability of the hardware has increased, and the relative cost of acquiring data-processing equipment has declined. As a result, local governments have increased their use of computers (Danziger & Dutton 1977a; Perry & Kraemer 1979).

This increase is clearly reflected in the cumulative percentage of U.S. cities and counties using computers (fig. 2.1). The adoption of computing approaches the classic "S curve" for the diffusion of a technological innovation. After a slow start, use increases rapidly. It is also clear that the largest local governments adopted computers first, and that governments of each decreasing population category have followed the same diffusion curve at lags of about five years. Thus, the "take-off" period for the large local governments began in the late 1950s; for the medium-sized governments it began in the early to mid-1960s; and for the smaller governments it began in the early 1970s.

The larger governments have approached the level of 100 percent adoption over a period of about twenty years. One might expect that social interaction networks and greater experience with computer technology would stimulate a higher rate of adoption among the smaller governments than has occurred, given their later involvement with computers. However, the data do not suggest that smaller governments are adopting computers at a significantly higher rate. Thus the greatest absolute number of initial decisions to adopt computers is likely to occur during the period between the mid-1970s and the late 1980s, as most of the medium-sized and small local governments implement computing.

Even by 1975, however, computing had become widespread. More than 90 percent of the cities with populations greater than 50,000 were using computers in their government operations. A similar proportion of computer users is found among county governments that service populations greater than 100,000. Only among the very smallest city and county governments (those serving less than 10,000 in population) were computers used by less than half of the governments (Kraemer, Dutton, & Matthews 1975; Matthews, Dutton, & Kraemer 1976).

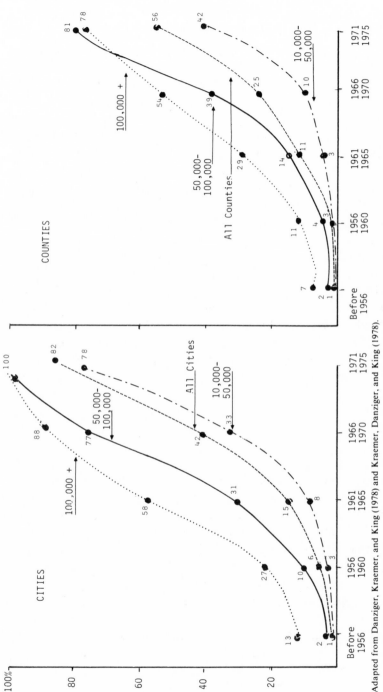

NOTE: This estimate is based upon only those governments that responded and does not include those that were automated but did not answer. Responses are from the 1,063 cities and 400 counties that indicated year of computer adoption. For cities over 50,000 and counties over 100,000, the number of governments using computers is based upon only cities and counties having in-house computers; cities and counties with service bureaus, regional installations or other outside sources were not included. For the smaller cities and counties, all sources of computing were included. Thus the estimates tend to be low for the larger governments and high for the smaller governments.

Figure 2.1   Cumulative Percentage of U.S. Cities and Counties Utilizing Computers

Adapted from Danziger, Kraemer, and King (1978) and Kraemer, Danziger, and King (1978).

Extensiveness of Use

One measure of the extent to which a local government has automated its operations is the total number of applications (from a list of 256 applications) for which computing is utilized (table 2.1). By the mid-1970s the average number of automated applications in the larger city and county governments was about 30, with the largest governments generally having higher average levels on this indicator. The largest city governments (those with more than 500,000 population) use the most automated applications—an average of 65. Generally, county governments are less extensively automated than are comparably sized city governments.

The 30 to 60 computer applications that local governments are able to maintain might seem to be a manageable number. But our field research pointed out several problems that arise from this current level of automation. First, many individual applications are complex systems of computer programs about which very few of the computing staff are knowledgeable. Applications such as budget reporting, utility billing, vehicle maintenance, and criminal history files tend to be large systems of programs developed and modified over long time periods by numerous programmers and analysts. Second, there are very few experts on the full range of computer applications in a given department, much less in the local government as a whole. Most local government officials and personnel have a fragmentary understanding of any given application, of a functional area of applications, or especially of the entire array of applications.[3]

Functional Diversity

As suggested above, the complexity of the technology is increased by the functional diversity of computer applications. That is, not only is computer technology complex, it is also applied to complex information-processing tasks within highly specialized functional areas. As a consequence, few computing experts can independently design, build, and maintain most computer applications without the assistance of experts in each area.

In chapter 8 we examine the functional distribution of local government computer applications, but it is important at this point to stress the great functional diversity of computing. In both city and county governments, it is the finance and police activities that have been most automated. Assessment has been substantially automated in most counties and in those cities that perform this activity. Computer use is also high for certain

Table 2.1 Selected Characteristics of Computing Equipment and Applications

Classification	Governments reporting (N)	Ave. no. CPU's	Ave. total core capacity (bytes)	Median total core capacity	Ave. no. CRT terminals[a]	Ave. no. automated applications currently operational
Total, all cities	647	1.2	155K	94K	9	17
Population group						
500,000 and over	20	4.0	1,986	1,536	72	65
250,000–499,999	28	2.1	531	328	19	41
100,000–249,999	79	1.4	227	144	6	38
50,000–99,999	178	1.1	89	32	2	23
25,000–49,999	174	1.1	54	22	—	6
10,000–24,999	184	1.0	27	16	—	5
Total, all counties	277	1.4	296K	156K	14	23
Population group						
500,000 and over	39	2.6	1,246	640	40	47
250,000–499,999	53	1.5	321	196	15	36
100,000–249,999	98	1.3	133	64	4	24
50,000–99,999	47	1.1	57	24	—	5
25,000–49,999	32	1.0	48	24	—	4
10,000–24,999	12	1.0	36	16	—	4

SOURCE: Adapted from URBIS Group (1977: Table 5).
[a] — = not reported.

administrative record-keeping activities, particularly relating to personnel and purchasing. Among county responsibilities, computer use is common for voter registration and the court system. And where public welfare service has been automated, the number of computer applications is quite high. Among city functions, moderate levels of automation are also evident for utilities services. (Kraemer, Danziger, & King 1978).

But computer applications span a number of other local government functions including public health, planning and zoning, housing, urban renewal, licensing and code enforcement, streets and highways, parks and recreation, public buildings, engineering, the central garage, motor pools, sanitation, water supply, libraries, vital statistics, fire protection, and so on. And some areas are little affected, those that deal (broadly) with planning and maintaining the physical environment and with providing human services being among the least automated (Kraemer, Dutton, & Matthews 1975; Matthews, Dutton, & Kraemer 1976). Again, the cumulative effect of this functional diversity of computer applications in local governments is likely to lessen the comprehensibility of the computer package, even for the computer expert. Teams of functional and technical experts are required to implement any given system, and no single team is likely to be familiar with the full range of applications.

Information-Processing Functions

A basic software question concerns the functions served by current applications—the kinds and range of information-processing tasks performed by computing. To examine this, the following categories of "information-processing tasks" were established: record-keeping, calculating and printing, record-searching, record-restructuring, sophisticated analytics, and process control (Danziger 1977; Kraemer, Dutton, & Matthews 1975). Each of these six types of "information-processing tasks" is distinguished by the primary modality of data-handling that it involves. Hence, in record-searching the critical need is to search a file, given certain parameters, with some regularity, whereas in record-keeping the basic requirement is simply to store and update records, with the need to retrieve specific information occurring only occasionally. On balance, each type of information-processing task in the taxonomy above constitutes a relatively more sophisticated array of automated applications. About three-fourths of all currently automated applications in local governments are used for the more routine record-keeping—nearly 40 percent—and calculating and printing—about 35 percent—information-processing tasks. Only the remaining 25 percent or so serve the more sophisticated tasks—record-searching (8–9%), record-restructuring (7–8%), sophisticated analysis (6–7%), and process control (4%) (Kraemer, Danziger, and King 1978: fig. 1).

Computing operations appear rather simple due to this dominance of the least sophisticated information-processing tasks, but they are more complex than they appear. Local government records and the range of information-processing tasks that have been automated are far from simple and straightforward. These operations are complicated by such factors as legal constraints on privacy, confidentiality, and access and deletion of records (many records must be stored indefinitely); unique state and local reporting requirements; and the entry, updating, and use of the same records by different agencies for different purposes. Such "unsophisticated" record-keeping tasks often pose tremendous technical problems. And the range of automated information-processing tasks introduces some of the same complexities as the diversity of applications. Development of a program that searches personnel records, for example, requires different kinds of technical expertise than those required for development of a program that performs statistical analyses of a community survey or that synchronizes traffic lights. Consequently, computer experts in these different lines of work require very different skills and develop different occupational identifications (Kling & Gerson 1978). Although most computer specialists value technical efficiency, they are a diverse group with different kinds of training, competencies, and experience.

EQUIPMENT

To most people, computer technology is synonymous with the computer itself; and the complexity of the technology is self-evident, since most people do not understand how computers work. Our concept of the computer package entails far more than the computer itself; nevertheless, the role of the computer and its related equipment in the overall complexity of the package must not be minimized. In this section we will identify several important characteristics of computer equipment in local governments, and indicate certain effects that these characteristics are likely to have on the overall complexity of the computer package.

We have seen (table 2.1) that larger governments, serving larger populations, tend to have substantially more equipment. The largest governments are likely to have multiple computer mainframes (CPUs), while those governments with less than 100,000 population typically have only a single mainframe. Similarly, large governments tend to have a substantial number of on-line (CRT) terminals, and greater average and median core capacity than do smaller governments.

Table 2.1 also shows that city governments have higher average levels of computing capacity than do the equivalent-sized county governments. Traditionally, county governments have been less innovative than city governments. But the explanation for this city-county difference is not obvious, since county functions are not necessarily less amenable to computing. Clearly there are many factors influencing the pace of computer innovation in a given local government (Danziger & Dutton 1977; Kling & Gerson 1977). In chapter 3, these factors are dealt with more comprehensively.

Another view of computing equipment focuses upon its flexibility and sophistication, rather than upon capacity alone. In general, more sophisticated equipment can make more efficient use of given computing resources, and thus "do more for less." The typical city or county has a CPU that does batch processing. The cities and counties in our sample do tend to utilize operating systems that allow multiprograming, but most local governments have not yet purchased very sophisticated equipment, and only a minority of local governments have some on-line applications. It is clear that the larger local governments have considerably more sophisticated equipment than the smaller.

Such differences might be explained by the increased needs of larger government units for computing capacity. Since the larger governments are more automated, more sophisticated equipment enables them to better utilize expensive resources such as lineprinters and mainframe processors.[4] Most smaller governments have little on-line computing. But it is important to realize that, as indicated by most of these data presenting group averages, there remain extensive variations. Some small governments use medium-sized machines and have modest interactive capabilities. Conversely, some larger governments have an "undersized" computer package compared to that of their peers. Some reasons for these variations are discussed in chapter 3.

At present, most local governments lack sufficient computing capacity either to provide extensive data-processing services to more than a few operating departments, or to provide interactive data processing, although some of the larger ones do support a quite substantial array of services. Ironically, the fact that most cities have relatively small computing capacities and unsophisticated systems might increase rather than lessen the complexity of the computer package. Most local governments place more demands on their computing equipment than the equipment is able to accommodate; few have backup systems. This can create priority-setting and scheduling problems, delays, and various foul-ups in day-to-day operations. For example, computing equipment, like many mechanical devices, operates most efficiently at somewhat below maximum capacity. If programmers must carefully "pack" every additional instruction or data item into the minimum space possible, their programing time increases almost exponentially. In addition, many large organizations have uneven workloads. Payrolls might come out weekly and utility bills might be prepared quarterly. Without slack computing resources, the peak demand, when both activities coincide, could exceed average use and cause major bottlenecks. Thus our research has suggested that cities with the most advanced computing *equipment*, other things being equal, are far more likely to have successful computing operations (Kraemer, Dutton, & Northrop 1980). However, it is the exception rather than the rule for current city or county governments to have the more advanced applications implemented on advanced computing equipment.

The absence of more advanced development is partially a consequence of the highly visible costs of computing equipment and skilled data-processing personnel compared to the costs of nonautomated information processing. Local governments have never spent a large proportion of local revenues directly on data-processing services. Direct expenditures on data-processing services constitute only about 1.3 percent of the total operating budget in counties, and about 1 percent in cities (table 2.2). The large, but not the largest, governments spend the greatest proportion of their budgets on computers, while the smallest governments allocate the smallest share of their financial resources. While these proportions are not great, they involve substantial amounts of money and tend to be a highly visible item in the annual budgetary process. The average yearly expenditure on computing in a city or county with greater than 250,000 population was more than $1 million in 1975 (Kraemer et al. 1975). However, these figures are likely to underestimate the total expenditures. Many costs of computing do not appear in official computing budgets. Typical budgets often exclude both

Table 2.2 Average Computing Expenditures, 1975

Classification	Governments reporting	Government budget (in thousands)	Budgeted for data processing (in thousands)	Computing as a % of total budget	Computer hardware as a % of total computing budget
Total, all cities	997	$ 21,846	$ 193	.9%	43%
Population group[a]					
500,000 and over	20	334,870	3,596	1.2	39
250,000–499,999	24	107,855	1,108	1.1	37
100,000–249,999	74	50,215	474	1.1	35
50,000–99,999	190	19,625	157	1.0	47
25,000–49,999	266	10,648	66	.6	—
10,000–24,999	423	5,243	28	.5	—
Total, all counties	412	$ 36,587	$ 487	1.2%	44%
Population group					
500,000 and over	48	195,386	2,708	1.8	34
250,000–499,999	51	48,309	811	1.8	45
100,000–249,999	117	22,641	292	1.6	48
50,000–99,999	75	11,517	76	.6	—
25,000–49,999	58	9,205	42	.5	—
10,000–24,999	63	3,868	25	.6	—

SOURCE: Adapted from Danziger, Kraemer, and King (1978: table 4).
[a] These figures are probably underestimates due to incomplete responses from some of the multiple installations in these cities.

the overhead costs of equipment, and the salaries of data input staff and computer specialists in departments using, rather than supplying, computer services. In addition, computing budgets rarely include the time spent by computer users in specifying new systems, reorganizing computer use, and dealing with errors and problems of computing. The actual expenditures on computing are probably two to three times the amounts reported in the table (Kraemer, Dutton, & Northrop 1980).

PEOPLE

A critical component of the computer package in local government is the computing staff. Although the computing operation requires less personnel than many local government operations, as much as 60 percent of its costs are staff-related (table 2.2). Table 2.3 presents basic data about the number and location of computing personnel in local governments. While the absolute number of computing staff increases with increased size of the government, their proportion among all government employees decreases. This may be because of some staff economies of scale, although other explanations are possible. It also seems that there are more computer-related employees in cities than in counties. It may be that counties provide services that require more labor, but counties do report a lower absolute number of computer personnel than cities, given comparable population size.

Table 2.3 shows the distribution of computing personnel. Analysts and programmers account for about 25 to 30 percent in all sizes of governments. Moreover, about one-fifth of all computing personnel are located in user departments in both cities and counties and in all sizes of governments. There are claims that decentralization of technical staff (that is, providing them to user departments) is desirable in large organizations, as it reduces communication problems between the data-processing and the user departments, increases the user's sense of control over and responsiveness from the data-processing department, and does not severely limit the size of the central computing staff (Kling 1977; Kraemer, Danziger, & Dutton 1979). Thus it is somewhat surprising that the decentralization of computing personnel to user departments is no more extensive in the larger than in the smaller governments.[5]

Table 2.3 Computing Personnel in U.S. Cities and Counties

Classification	Computing departments			User departments	
	Total personnel	% analysts and programmers	Personnel as a % of total government employees	Total computing staff	% analysts and programmers[a]
Cities					
Mean, all cities	22.0	24%	1.0%	5.9	36%
Population group					
500,000 and over	112.5	24	.8	30.1	45
250,000–499,999	39.2	30	.9	11.7	25
100,000–249,999	19.6	29	1.0	5.8	32
50,000–99,999	7.6	21	1.1	1.2	25
Counties					
Mean, all counties	37.8	26%	.3	10.2	27%
Population group					
500,000 and over	95.6	27	.3	24.9	19
250,000–499,999	29.6	34	.3	9.5	41
100,000–249,999	14.3	23	.4	3.4	35
Mean, all cities and counties	28.0	25%	.7	7.6	30%

SOURCE: Adapted from URBIS Group (1977: Table 6).
[a]These figures are low estimates due to incomplete responses.

TECHNIQUE

The previous sections focused on the people and equipment composing the computer package. Here we deal with "technique"—that is, the organizational and structural arrangements through which the computer package is maintained and controlled. In particular, we examine the source of provision of computing services, the physical distribution of computer hardware, the organizational distribution of computing staff, and the locus of decisions on technological development. It is important to note that conventional images of computing technique are overly simplified. Most people imagine a single data-processing installation supplying services to an organization, much as a telephone company or an electric utility supplies services to a customer. But most local governments, as well as most organizations, obtain data-processing services from many sources. Computing staff tend to be scattered throughout organizations. And the locus of decisions regarding new development, charging, priorities, and so forth tends to vary.

Source of Computing Services

Local governments can obtain computing capability in several ways: through in-house computer operations, outside service bureaus, private management of a government-owned facility, or sharing of a jointly owned facility with other governments in the region. In 1975, 65 percent of cities over 10,000 in population used in-house computing, 41 percent used service bureaus, 14 percent used public regional installations, and only four cities (all medium-sized) used facilities management by a private firm. Similarly, 59 percent of counties over 10,000 in population used in-house computing, 33 percent used private service bureaus, 11 percent used public regional installations, and only five counties used private management of a government-owned facility (URBIS 1977: Table 2). Many governments use a combination of these arrangements. For example, in most local governments, even those with in-house computing, it is common to find one or more departments occasionally using a private service bureau for some data-processing services, ranging from mere key-punching of data to the purchase of sophisticated computer models for planning or revenue forecasting.

Two sources of computing services dominate, depending on the size of the local government. Larger local governments generally utilize an in-house installation to provide computing services. About 90 percent of the cities with greater than 100,000 population and the counties with greater than 250,000 population are serviced by their own computer installations. In contrast, the small governments (particularly those with less than 50,000 population) have a stronger tendency to procure computing services from outside sources. Among these smaller governments, about as many use in-house as use outside sources for computing. Usually these outside sources are service bureaus, which are private companies that provide a specified level of data processing and software under a contractual agreement. Some smaller local governments also make use of public regional computer installations or other local governments to provide computing services.[6]

Organizational Location of Computer Hardware

In general, the computer services that are provided by the local government tend to be placed in one of two organizational locations. The largest proportion of municipal governments have designated the computing operations as a *subunit of a finance department*. This reflects the historical dominance of finance functions in automated information-processing tasks. Location of the computing unit within the finance department is substantially more common in cities over 50,000 in population (46 percent) than in counties over 100,000 (only about 14 percent). The incidence of the computing unit's location in the finance department decreases in the larger governments. The most prevalent organizational setting in counties is the *independent computing department*. This exists in 44 percent of the counties, but only 19 percent of the cities. A computing operation may also be located *within another operating department* (usually that of police or public works), or within the chief executive's office. About 20 percent of the cities and counties with in-house computer services have one of these latter alternatives—more common in the larger cities and counties.

It is also common for major computer hardware (including mini-computers) to be distributed to various subunits within the local government—this occurs primarily in the larger local governments. Often, this simply reflects the use of federal funding for police computing in larger cities, because such funding often has required the establishment of computing facilities dedicated solely to the police. Also, it may be that departments serving very large populations can make the strongest case that their workload justifies a separate computer. In addition, recent developments in minicomputer technology have made special-purpose computers available and practical for use in various departments, for example, the computer control of chemical mixtures in water treatment plants. Another sort of hardware decentralization is the distribution of CRTs (cathode ray tube terminals) among user agencies. These terminals might serve in data entry and/or data retrieval, or in other real-time data analyses. Again, the larger local governments are more likely to have a significant number of CRTs distributed throughout the government.

Organizational Location of Computing Personnel

While most computing personnel are located within the data-processing unit, a sizable minority are not (table 2.3). The decentralization of computing personnel, especially systems analysts and programmers, to user departments is often advocated. It is suggested that if skilled technical staff are in user departments, the functional needs of users will prevail over the more technical considerations of computing in the development and use of automation. These issues of staff decentralization are more fully considered in chapter 5.

Other Issues

Other important issues that concern the organizational and policy arrangements for the provision of computing will be discussed more fully in later chapters; it is useful to identify several here. A constellation of issues centers around the establishment of priorities among elements of the computer package. These issues include decisions on the acquisition of hardware, the order and pace of applications development, the expansion of computing staff, and the order in which the data-processing needs of all users will be serviced. Other issues include the procedures for charging users for data-processing services (which can be an important determinant of utilization); whether or not there will be formal arrangements for resolving disputes among various departments or agencies about the proprietary rights to use data; and the manner in which the services provided by the computing unit will be evaluated. Clearly, these issues about priorities, charges, data use, and evaluation are fundamental *control* issues. Both the jurisdictional responsibility for and the explicit decisions about these control issues are of substantial importance to the government's top managers, to the departments that use computing services, and to the computing unit itself. Such control issues are a recurrent theme in this book.

COMING CHANGE IN THE COMPUTER PACKAGE

Has the computer package in local government changed dramatically since our 1975 survey? What will the computer package look like in the 1980s? On one hand, there are several pressures toward dramatic change. First, plans of data-processing managers are quite expansionist. Second, the demands for computing services are growing, given new and expanded applications of the technology in such areas as modeling, graphics, word processing, electronic message switching, and "office automation." Third, the rate of new technological development is continuing at an astounding pace, with the development of micro- and minicomputer technology, distributed data processing, and new linkages between computers and other communications technologies such as video discs and two-way cable applications. This pace of change is illustrated by the short life-span of modern computers. For example, two IBM 370/158s that were purchased for nearly $4 million in 1976 had reduced in value so much by July 1979 that they sold at auction for $1.027 million (*Computer World* 1979:1). Such technological developments and user demands underlie the expansionist plans of data-processing managers and create pressures for dramatic changes in the local government's computer package.

On the other hand, there are several pressures toward stability, if not retrenchment. These pressures are mostly financial. Most generally, the urban fiscal crisis of the 1970s has placed important constraints on the expansion of computing. As local-government budgets have been tightened, so have computing budgets. Federal programs that financed much local government computing innovation in the past have been reduced or eliminated. For example, the Law Enforcement Assistance Administration (LEAA) has made major cutbacks in local-government computing support.

In the face of tightening local and federal funding, local governments are finding it increasingly expensive simply to maintain the present quality of their computing staff and operations. Staffing problems are particularly severe because of a widening gap between the salary schedules for computer specialists in the public sector and in the private sector, which is drawing the best talent away from local governments. Fiscal strains, combined with rigid civil service guidelines, are preventing most local governments from narrowing the public-private salary gap in order to maintain the quality of their computing staffs.

In addition, operations problems are severe because of the increasing and often unanticipated high costs of maintenance. As the size of local government computing operations expanded in the 1970s, an increasing proportion of computing budgets was diverted from new development to maintenance, reconceptualization, or up-dating of existing applications to run on new equipment. A rule of thumb among data-processing managers is that a system that requires five analysts to build will require one analyst to maintain. Clearly, this rule entails escalating staff costs for maintenance as more systems are added. The consequence of these escalating costs is illustrated in one large California county where the 1979–1980 computing budget of $6 million devotes only $500,000 to new development.

Because of these countervailing pressures, the computer package has not changed dramatically since 1975. And during the 1980s, the local-government computer package is likely to look very much as it did in 1975. Given current plans for application development and the dynamics of the systems world, there is no doubt that the use and technological sophistication of computing will continue to increase. But the basic nature of the computer package—including its instability—will remain relatively unchanged.

Planned Applications Development

When we surveyed local governments in 1975, there was a widespread expectation that an extraordinary level of development of automated applications would occur in the very near future. Our 1975 survey revealed that cities over 50,000 had an average of nine new automated applications "in development," while counties over 100,000 had an average of eleven applications "in development" (Kraemer, Danziger, & King 1978). Reports indicated that the average government planned to begin development on more than 20 additional applications within the next two years! The most ambitious plans were reported from city governments in the 100,000–250,000 population range, who planned to begin development on (an average of) 28 new computer applications. Interestingly, among county governments it was the comparably sized category that had the highest average figure for planned developments. It would be reasonable to infer from these data that, in many local governments, the number of operational automated applications would have *doubled* between 1975 and 1978—a huge commitment to expansion of their computing operations. However, our observations since 1975 suggest that this expected or desired rate of expansion has not been realized.[7]

An assessment of the stated plans for short-run development of new automated applications reveals that most local governments expected to continue to devote most attention to the automation of internal bureaucratic functions and police functions. The applications most commonly scheduled for development during the late 1970s related to revenue and expenditure forecasting, cash control systems, expenditure monitoring, police service and facility planning, and police manpower allocation systems (Danziger, Kraemer, & King 1978). Continuing focus on automation in the finance and police areas seems likely, since these particular applications are currently automated in few local governments. However, we have noted that in the police area there is some evidence to suggest a lower-than-expected rate of expansion, owing to a decline in federal support for police computing in local government.

Change and Instability

The extent to which new automated applications are planned provides some indication of the dynamism of the computing environment. A more direct measure of the dynamic nature of the computer package is presented in table 2.4. This table reveals various changes in the arrangements of service provision over two years (1973 and 1974), and the changes anticipated during the subsequent year. During only two years, fully 20 percent of the local governments significantly increased the core size of their CPUs. It is even more striking that nearly 40 percent of the governments reported a fundamental change or upgrading of the generation of their CPUs, and that almost 20 percent planned such an upgrading during 1975. Further indicators of major changes are that during the two-year period, more than 30 percent of the governments changed the management of the computing unit, more than 20 percent altered the departmental status of the computing center, and nearly 25 percent changed the physical location of the computing installation.

We must conclude from the data in table 2.4 that the recent rate of major changes in local government computing is astounding. Between one-third and two-thirds of the governments were involved, during only three years, in each of a series of substantial changes in provision of computing services. Each of these alterations in the computer package has the potential to create major instabilities for the organization. The computing staff must adjust to the altered arrangements, and changes in machine generation or management can disrupt both the internal standard operating procedures

Table 2.4 Change in EDP Arrangements in U.S. Cities and Counties

Classification	CPU size	Development priorities	Generation of machine	EDP management	Physical location	Department status	Mainframe vendor	Installation relations	Number CPUs
				Change in: (% of governments)					
Cities									
Change over last two years	57	42	40	31	21	22	17	12	10
Changed planned over next year	—	24	17	6	14	11	8	7	8
Counties									
Change over last two years	64	64	38	31	26	23	15	13	8
Change planned over next year	—	25	18	4	23	13	4	11	7

SOURCE: Adapted from URBIS Group (1977: table 3).
NOTE: — = not reported.

of the computing unit, and its provision of data-processing services to user departments.

The concept of the "technological loop" characterizes the interdependence of computer package components. Thus most of these decisions by a local government to alter one aspect of its computer package have further implications (Kling & Scacchi 1980). Some alterations, such as shifting from one mainframe to another "upward compatible" mainframe, may, under the best conditions, require only staff time to reprogram some of the older applications and operating-system interface. But other alterations could consume wider resources. For example, the decision to convert to a new operating system requires increased language skills among technical staff, as well as sufficient time for staff to undertake all the conversions while maintaining existing system performance. The implementation of a data-base management system, or the expansion of on-line capabilities, substantially increases the amount of core that must be available. Some demands, such as that for additional staff time, may be temporary. Others, such as those for increased primary or secondary storage, are more likely to be permanent.

Alterations that add new resources, on the other hand, often appear to create equilibrium. That is, if more core, increased disc space, or additional input/output channels are added, then it should be possible for current computer users to be accommodated with less stress. This is often, but not always, the case (Kling & Scacchi 1980). When there is substantial unmet demand (a condition on which the case for new resources may be based in the first place), new uses or users might disturb the allocation process as they seek to exploit the additional available computing.

Hence, most important attempts for "more" or "better" or even "different" components in the computer package will be unbalancing for other components. In such a dynamic milieu, a local government need not be committed to leading-edge technology to experience substantial and nearly constant change. In fact, a local government would be unlikely to accomplish a steady-state computer package without a firm policy of constraining its rate of innovation (Kling & Scacchi 1980).

SUMMARY

The computer package is composed of equipment, people, and technique. It is best understood as a fluid, interactive, and open system that is less an organized system than a dynamic one, having developed incrementally as new technological and organizational demands have been addressed (Kling & Scacchi 1980).

This discussion indicates the complexity of coping with, let alone managing and controlling, computing activity in public agencies. Because of this dynamic complexity, few people in local government really understand the package or its major elements. In our field research, we often found that although experienced users might understand traditional computer technology and its application to their own areas, they could not understand the practical applications of recent advances in the equipment (e.g., data-base management) for themselves, for others, or for the organization of the computing package in their own agencies.

A major concern in this book is to explore the extent to which *any* local government actors control the computer package. Effective control of the technology rests, to some considerable extent, upon the ability to understand it. If no one fully comprehends the computing package, then effective control is doubtful and instability is likely. Yet the computing package has developed in relatively similar ways in many local governments. These patterns of development and use do not seem either chaotic or random and they suggest that some kinds of control mechanisms operate within the local government.

Generally, our observations suggest that the computing package is highly complex and hence might be difficult to control, due to such factors as:

1. The incomprehensibility of many older, larger computer programs
2. The rapid development of computer equipment
3. The specialized language and skills of computer experts
4. The extensiveness of computer use (most local governments have 30 to 60 automated applications entailing hundreds of programs)
5. The functional diversity of automated applications
6. The nature of local government records
7. The range of information-processing tasks that have been automated
8. The great demands placed on computing equipment with relatively little capacity and sophistication
9. Staffing problems due to the limited supply of experts and inadequate public-sector salary schedules
10. The diversity of sources and arrangements for purchasing and regulating computing services
11. The great dynamism and instability which characterizes the computing package as a whole.

As this chapter has revealed, this dynamic complexity seems to place severe constraints on the degree to which even computer experts can rationally control the computer package. Moreover, it is likely to make nonexperts— politicians, bureaucrats, professionals, and lay citizens—very dependent on experts whom they expect to understand and control the technology in ways that will serve their interests.

The issue of whether computer technology is controlled or controllable by *anyone* in the local government setting is related to, but different from, the issue of who, in fact, controls it. A broad array of issues about the computer package hinge on patterns of control: the acquisition of additional or different hardware; the location of hardware; the locus of management responsibility for the quality and responsiveness of computer service provision; the mode of obtaining computer services; the size and departmental location of computing staff; the determination of priorities for development of new automated applications; priority setting for day-to-day operations; proprietary rights concerning data; policies for pricing computer services.

There are various people who have rather predictable interests in computing and who might exert some control over these various aspects of the local government computer package. These include the chief executive and his staff, the chief administrative officer, the elected legislative body, the department head in charge of the data-processing unit, the computer installation manager, the skilled computing staff, governmental agencies that use computer services, and perhaps a policy board of representatives from user departments. In the chapters that follow, the influence and control over the computer package of all of these people or groups will be assessed.

CHAPTER THREE

THE COMPUTING MILIEU

James N. Danziger and Rob Kling

IT IS CLEAR from the data in Chapter 2 that there is substantial variability in the computer package among American local governments—variability in the speed of adoption, in levels of resources, and in number of automated information systems. How can we account for this?

We find at least three general explanations for this variability, two of which are generally based on an examination of the "milieu" in which the computer package exists—its environmental and organizational contexts.[1] One of these explanations holds that the nature of the computer package in most governments is largely shaped by the effects of a few basic characteristics of its social, economic, and political-administrative contexts, and that analysis can specify how these characteristics systematically influence the package. A second explanation shares the emphasis on the computing milieu, but holds that a given government's computer package is shaped by unique, local conditions and decisions that vary unsystematically from government to government. Finally, the third, "null" explanation holds that variability cannot be explained by references to the milieu. In this chapter we shall try to see if we can explain the between-government variations in the level of computer use through examination of variations in local governments' computing milieus. We shall analyze both comparative data about computer milieus in many local governments, and detailed data from selected case studies.

VARIABILITY IN COMPUTER USE: SYSTEMATIC EXPLANATIONS[2]

Conceptual Approach

There is extensive research that indicates that variations in such matters as public policy outputs and structural arrangements (taken as dependent variables) are systematically influenced by characteristics of the government and its environment (taken as independent variables).[3] This method of analysis, which has been termed the "demographic approach" (Wilson 1968:3), is based on a more or less explicit causal model grounded in systems theory. The level of (the value of) the independent variable is said to "cause" or to "produce" the level of the dependent variable. This research has been criticized as atheoretical, since it rarely provides an adequate explanation for the statistical relationships identified (see Danziger 1978:81–123). That is, such research typically offers an ad hoc explanation or no explanation at all for apparently related phenomena (for example, how a higher proportion of Catholics in a population "causes" higher welfare payments per capita). Nonetheless, the approach has produced many positive findings, in that many systematic associations have been identified between a given dependent variable and some of the independent variables.

We shall employ, as indicators of the computer package, characteristics that correspond to the ones typically used in research on technological innovations. These measure the speed of adoption of the technology, the extensiveness of its use, and the level of resource commitment to it. In particular, we shall examine four operational indicators of the level of computer use: 1) the speed with which the government initially adopted computer technology; 2) the extensiveness of current use of computing, measured in terms of the total number of currently operational automated applications; 3) the government's commitment to computing, reflected in the financial resources allocated to the computer package (measured by both the proportion of total expenditure allocated to support computing, and the expenditure on computing per capita); and 4) a summary measure of computer utilization, combining values for the three variables specified above with a measure of the extent to which a given government has developed automated applications in each of four different kinds of information-processing tasks that can be performed by the computer.[4]

Figure 1.2 indicated the conceptual elements with which to identify critical sets of milieu variables that might affect the computer package. Each generic category to the left of the computer package in figure 1.2 consists of phenomena that might constrain (that is, might importantly shape) the nature and level of computer use. These sets correspond to those evident in existing research on the determinants of technological innovations in general and of computer use in particular. They measure aspects of the extracommunity environment, the community environment, and the political-administrative system. Let us specify the hypothesized relationships between computer use and these explanatory variables.[5]

EXTRACOMMUNITY ENVIRONMENT

As most analyses of computing in organizations emphasize the critical importance of local forces (Simon 1977; Stewart 1971; Whisler 1970), one might not expect that extracommunity factors would operate as a dominant constraint on computer use. But research on technological innovation suggests several extracommunity factors that might facilitate the adoption and use of computer technology. One is the presence of *external funding support*. Federal agencies and some state agencies have been extremely active in the provision to local governments of grants for funding computer technology (chapters 4 and 5 will describe the dynamics of these activities in detail). We hypothesize that external funding support for computing might increase computer use. A second aspect of the extracommunity environment that might operate as a facilitating factor is the *regional network* of the government. Research has determined that some regions are considerably more innovative than others (see Yin et al. 1976:155). Since innovative governments who are spatially proximate and who communicate with each other may provide a support network and, through shared knowledge, reduce the risks and uncertainty attached to innovative activities, we hypothesize that there will be differential levels of computer use across regions.

COMMUNITY ENVIRONMENT

Certain characteristics of the community environment may rather directly shape the nature of a local government's computer package. Some may reflect the likely need or demand for the capabilities computer technology can provide. Others may facilitate the implementation or use of the technology. One obvious characteristic is the size of the *population* served by the government. A government serving a larger population will tend to have more extensive records, a larger number of transactions involving information, and a greater number of employees. Generally, a larger population should lead to greater scope and complexity of the government's information-processing environment, and this in turn should increase the need for futher application of computer technology. Similarly, we hypothesize that those governments with greater *population growth* will tend to utilize computing more fully as an efficient means to meet increased information-processing workloads by capital- rather than labor-intensive innovations. Finally, we also hypothesize that the governments with greater *local financial resources* will be best equipped to undertake the adoption and expansion of so expensive a technology as a major computer package.

POLITICAL-ADMINISTRATIVE SYSTEM

Among the attributes of the local government system itself, we hypothesize that two sets of determinants regarding computer utilization may be critical. These are the general value orientation of the government, and the nature of control over decisions regarding the computer package. The analysis of American local government generally has contrasted two ideal-typical *value orientations*—"political" versus "reform."[6] The political orientation assumes that resources are scarce relative to demands, and that there are basic value conflicts among groups. Hence, the government is structured to resolve these conflicts and to distribute scarce public goods and services. In contrast, the reform orientation holds that shared values are prevalent and that conflict can and should be minimized. Hence, the reformers attempt to restructure local government so that partisan politics are eliminated, and so that public goods and services can be provided in a professionalized, businesslike manner ("there is no Republican or Democratic way to pave a street").

The substantial use of computer technology in local government operations is most compatible with this professional, reform orientation. Thus we hypothesize that our measures of computer utilization will be positively associated with reform-oriented governments, which we identify by the presence of certain structural attributes (e.g., at-large elections, nonpartisan elections, a professional chief executive) and behavioral practices (e.g., the existence of measurable program objectives) in each local government.

The second set of critical determinants within governments has to do with the *distribution of control* and authority over decisions regarding the computer package. We assume that the use of computer technology will be more extensive where those whose agendas are served by the technology also have substantial decisional control over its development and use. As we expect that computer use will be associated with a professional-management orientation, we also expect that use will be greater where administrators, rather than elected officials, have more authority over computing decisions, and where control is centralized.[7] We also hypothesize that use of an innovative technique tends to be stimulated when authority over decisions is held by those users who enjoy the benefits of the technology. Thus we hypothesize that the level of computer utilization will be higher where administrative officials or the users of computer services have greater control over computing decisions, where elected officials have less control over these decisions, and where control is centralized.

Table 3.1 summarizes the relationships that have been hypothesized between the observed levels of computing use in local governments and the milieu forces that might shape that use. The analysis relies upon methods for measuring the linear association between variables—Pearson product-moment correlation coefficients and path analysis. Since the data are cross-sectional, it is necessary to infer the nature of the dynamic effects among the variables over time.[8]

Findings

The empirical relationships of computer-utilization levels to the various explanatory variables are displayed in table 3.2. The units of analysis are the 304 city governments and 190 county governments surveyed in the first phase of our research (in 1975). The table presents the statistical associations between each dependent and independent variable. Thus the data reveal the extent to which intergovernmental variation on the dependent variable is systematically associated with variation on any particular explanatory variable.[9]

SPEED OF ADOPTION

Among the explanatory variables, the set most consistently related to more rapid adoption of computer technology in both cities and counties is that of political-administrative system attributes reflecting a reform orientation to government (table 3.2). It is uncertain whether the attributes reflecting the current distribution of decisional control regarding the

Table 3.1 Hypothesized Relationships Between Computer Use and Explanatory Variables

Explanatory Variable	Measure	Hypothesized Relationships with Greater Computer Use
Extracommunity environment		
Region	Western and southern versus northeastern and north central states	+
External funding for computing	External funding received for computing during 1973–75	+
Community environment		
Population size	Population 1970 ($\log_{10}$)	+
Population growth rate	Population 1970/population 1960	+
Personal income per capita	1970	+
Political-administrative system attributes		
Value orientation		
Professional management practices	Use of measurable program objectives	+
Reform structures	Index of presence of CAO, at-large elections, and nonpartisan elections	+
Professional chief executive	Existence of CAO or manager	+
Control of computer package decisions		
Control by administrators	Data-processing manager's appraisal of level of involvement by role-types in critical computer package decisions	+
Control by users		+
Control by elected officials		−
Pluralism of control		−

Table 3.2 Actual Relationships Between Computer Use and Explanatory Variables—City/County

	Speed of Computer Adoption	Extensiveness of Computer Use	Financial Commitment to Computing		
			Percent Budget to Computing	Computing Expenditure Per Capita	Index of Computer Utilization
Extracommunity environment					
Region	.17** / .27***	.13* / .34***	.19** / .23**	.18*** / .33***	.25*** / .46***
External funding for computing	.01 / -.03	.27*** / .22**	.15** / .18*	.24*** / .16*	.26*** / .20**
Community environment					
Population size (log₁₀)	.31*** / .28***	.53*** / .49***	.08 / .07	.26*** / .09	.46*** / .38***
Population growth rate	-.06 / .04	.01 / .23***	-.14* / -.04	.06 / .25***	-.10* / .29***
Personal income per capita	.07 / .14	.04 / .32***	.02 / -.12	.09 / .17*	.07 / .27***
Political-administrative system attributes					
Value orientation					
Professional management practices	.24*** / .13	.27*** / .21***	.13* / .03	.16* / .20**	.25*** / .09
Reform structures	.18** / .25**	.07 / .13	.15** / -.11	.05 / .16	.16** / .18**
Professional chief executive	.18** / .21**	.12* / .23***	.17** / -.14*	.11* / .16	.17** / .27***
Control of computer package decisions					
Control by administrators	-.01 / .12	-.03 / .20**	.14* / .06	.13 / .22**	.01 / .26***
Control by users	.00 / .04	.31*** / .13*	.09 / .21**	.18** / .14*	.26*** / .18*
Control by elected officials	-.15* / -.11	-.09 / -.22**	-.13* / .08	-.06 / -.14*	-.25*** / -.17*
Pluralism of control	.03 / .08	.07 / .04	.07 / .04	.09 / .06	.12* / .07

NOTES: Pearson product moment correlations for $N = 304$ cities and 190 counties
Significance levels: *** $<.001$
  ** $<.01$
  * $<.05$

computer package reflect much about control at the time when the adoption decision was made; but none of these measures is notably associated with the speed of adoption. It is clear from the table that those governments with larger populations and, by inference, more extensive information-processing needs, tend to adopt the computer package earlier. Other aspects of the community environment are not significantly associated with the speed of computer adoption. Finally, there is a tendency for governments in the western and southern regions to have adopted the technology earlier than those in the northeast and north central regions.

EXTENSIVENESS OF COMPUTER USE

The variations among governments in the number of currently operational automated applications is substantially related to the explanatory variables. There is a particularly strong, positive association between the size of the population served and the extensiveness of computer use. However, in a clear city-county contrast, the other variables of community environment (population growth rate and the measure reflecting local financial resources available) are significantly associated with computer-use extensiveness in county governments, but are virtually unrelated to it in city governments. There is no apparent explanation for this contrast. The two indicators of the extracommunity environment are also linked with the extensiveness of computer use, with regional location being especially important in counties, and external funding support being important in both cities and counties. In counties, more automated applications tend to exist where administrators and users, rather than elected officials, control decisions regarding the computer package. In city governments, the only striking relationship regarding control is that greater user control of computer decisions is associated with more extensive computer use. Finally, the extensiveness of computer use in both cities and counties is substantially correlated with a reform orientation in the government, and especially with the existence of professional management practices and a professional chief executive.

FINANCIAL COMMITMENT TO COMPUTING

Although the differences are not dramatic, there is sufficient variation in the correlations between the independent variables and the two alternative measures of financial commitment to the computer package to indicate that these measures tap somewhat different aspects of this commitment. A larger percentage of the budget is allocated to computing, and there is higher expenditure per capita on computing, in those cities and counties that receive external funding support for computing, that are in the western or southern regions, that utilize professional management practices, and that are characterized by greater user control over computing decisions. The other correlations are quite varied. Among the strongest associations are those between a higher level of expenditure per capita on computing and larger population in cities, greater population growth rate in counties, and administrators' control over computing decisions in counties. There are several correlations that are clearly contrary to the hypothesized pattern, two of which are statistically significant: a larger share of the budget tends to be allocated to computing in those cities with lower growth rates and in those counties with no professional chief executive. Broadly, the data in the table appear to reflect some systematic effects on financial commitment to the computer package from certain aspects of the extracommunity environment, community environment, and political-administrative system. But the findings are too mixed to support broad generalizations that incorporate both dependent variables and any type of explanatory variable.

INDEX OF COMPUTER UTILIZATION

The computer utilization index combines the values on the four dependent variables in table 3.2 with a fifth indicator measuring the general sophistication of the government's computer applications. The index is meant to provide a summary measure that captures the overall commitment of a government, over time, to the computer package. This computer utilization index has the most consistently significant associations with the explanatory variables of any dependent variable in the table. For county governments, the computer utilization index is associated in the hypothesized direction with every explanatory variable in the analysis, and every correlation is statistically significant except those with professional management practices and pluralism in computer decisions. The relationships are especially strong with the region variable, and with all three indicators of the community environment. Among city governments, most explanatory variables are associated significantly and in the hypothesized direction with the utilization index, although there is significant negative correlation with population growth rate. Population size, region, external funding for computing, and the extent of control over computing decisions held by users and not by elected officials are the variables most notably related to the index of computer utilization for cities. Thus in both cities and counties, all three general categories of independent variables have considerable explanatory power with respect to intergovernmental variation in computer utilization, broadly measured.

SUMMARY

Several generalizations emerge from a broad assessment of the data in table 3.2. In the first place, none of the three types of independent variables, whether extracommunity environment, community environment, or political-administrative system, seems to provide a powerful and compelling explanation of variation in computer use. Second, no single explanatory variable seems to act as an extraordinarily powerful constraint on the level of computer use. The need for computer technology given a large population and its information-processing environment is one of two explanatory variables that has consistent and substantial positive associations with all indicators of computer use. The second such explanatory variable is region—governments in the western and southern states have more quickly and fully committed themselves to the computer package than have governments in the northeast and north central states. At a somewhat more moderate level, the extent of computer use seems to increase with both a strong value orientation toward professional management practices and greater user control over computer decisions.

A third generalization is that nearly every association, whether statistically significant or not, is in the direction hypothesized in table 3.1.[10] At the least, the variables do not contradict the patterns of relationships posited above. Finally, a fourth generalization is that the patterns of association *do* vary noticeably in magnitude between cities and counties. However, these variations are not dramatic or unambiguous enough to suggest the specific forces in cities and counties that might explain the different patterns in the two types of governments.

Multivariate Analysis

The bivariate analyses in the preceding sections are a useful means to determine the level of statistical association between the dependent variables measuring computer utilization and each individual explanatory variable. However, this method is not sensitive to possible interactive effects among the explanatory variables, and it is not capable of specifying a set of explanatory variables that might account for a larger amount of variation than any single variable. The use of multivariate statistical techniques is one means to determine the relative importance of each explanatory variable while accounting for the impact of others, and to estimate the best linear combination of the explanatory variables.[11]

Table 3.3 reports regression analyses that estimate the relative importance of various independent variables in accounting for the between-government variations on the computer utilization index in table 3.2. The criterion for inclusion in the table is that a variable's regression coefficient is at least twice its standard error. Overall, about 38 percent of the variation among cities and about 45 percent of the variation among counties in the computer utilization index can be explained (in the sense of the R^2 statistic) by a combination of key independent variables. Only three of the eight variables in the table are common to both city and county analyses, supporting the decision to analyze the two types of governments separately. However, there are evident similarities in the structure of independent variables included in each analysis, and each of the three types of conceptual explanatory variables is represented by at least one variable in the regression analysis.

Table 3.3 Multiple Correlations Between Independent Variables and Computer Utilization Index

Independent Variables[a]	Direction	Multiple R	Multiple R^2	Increase in R^2
Cities				
Total population (log_{10})	+	0.46	0.21	0.21
Elected official control	−	0.52	0.27	0.06
Pluralism of computer decisions	+	0.57	0.32	0.05
Southern & western U.S.[b]	+	0.59	0.35	0.03
Professional management practices	+	0.61	0.37	0.02
Presence of outside funding	+	0.62	0.38	0.01
Counties				
Southern & western U.S.[b]	+	0.46	0.21	0.21
Total population (log_{10})	+	0.60	0.36	0.15
Departmental user control	+	0.64	0.41	0.05
Presence of outside funding	+	0.66	0.43	0.02
Professional chief executive	+	0.67	0.45	0.02

SOURCE: Adapted from Danziger and Dutton (1977b; table 1).
[a]Variables were entered with independent regression coefficients at least twice their standard error.
[b]Coded as: south or west = 1; northeast or north central = 0.

The interdependent effects of the variables in table 3.3 can be further clarified by the exploratory use of path analysis in figures 3.1 and 3.2.[12] For comparative purposes, all eight variables from table 3.3 are included in the analysis, and the variables are organized in terms of the three general conceptual categories. While there is some variation in the path models for cities and counties, both analyses present a quite consistent model of the structural pattern of milieu forces producing higher or lower levels of computer utilization. First, the government's level of need for computing services is represented in each path model by the community environment variable of population size. Second, both indicators of the extracommunity environment (outside funding support for computing, and region) have positive, direct relationships with the level of computer utilization in both cities and counties. Third, each model supports the view that the level of computer use is influenced by the value orientation of the government (evidenced in counties by the existence of a professional chief executive, and in cities by both the use of professional management practices and, indirectly, the existence of a professional chief executive). Finally, computer utilization tends to increase in those governments where greater control of computing decisions is held by departmental administrators (as represented by user-department control over computing decisions, and pluralism of computer decisions), and tends to decrease with greater control of these decisions by elected officials.

The multivariate analyses provide support for the prior findings that computer use is constrained by particular characteristics in the computing milieu. Each path model for the computer utilization index includes the community environment measure of size, both aspects of the extra-community environment, and indicators of both the value orientation of the government and the distribution of decisional control over the computer package. The data indicate that the combination of these milieu variables "explains" (in a statistical sense) less than half of the inter-governmental variation on the computer utilization index in cities or counties. However, one might also conclude that a small set of milieu variables does explain a substantial amount of the variation. Thus these data are reasonable support for the view that the *level of utilization of the computer package* is *systematically constrained by characteristics of the computing milieu and is not merely the result of random or idiosyncratic local factors.*

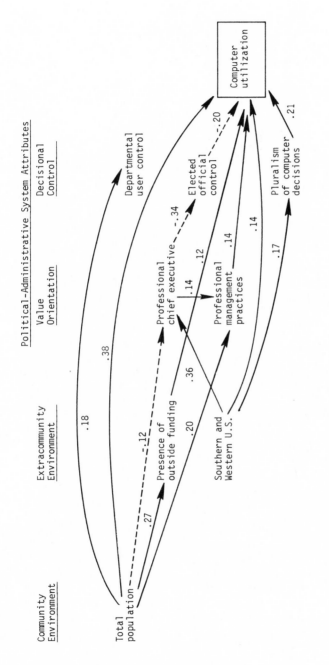

Community
Environment

Extracommunity
Environment

Political-Administrative System Attributes

Value
Orientation

Decisional
Control

SOURCE: Adapted from Danziger and Dutton (1977b: fig. 1)

NOTE: Path coefficients displayed are standardized regression coefficients. Each arrow or path indicates a direct effect. All the direct path coefficients are significant by the standard convention of being twice their standard error. Broken lines indicate negative coefficients.

Figure 3.1 Path Diagram of Computer Utilization Index and Selected Independent Variables in Cities

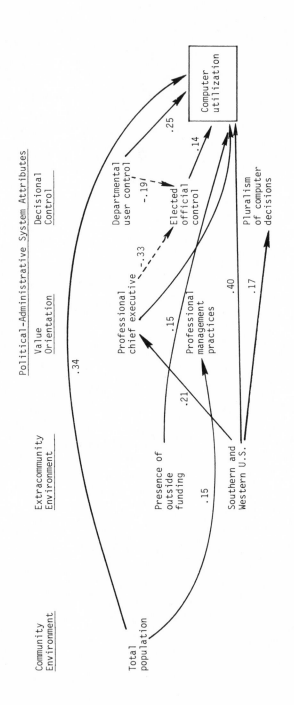

SOURCE: Adapted from Danziger and Dutton (1977b: figure 2)

NOTE: Path coefficients displayed are standardized regression coefficients. Each arrow or path indicates a direct effect. All the direct path coefficients are significant by the standard convention of being twice their standard error. Broken lines indicate negative coefficients.

Figure 3.2 Path Diagram of Computer Utilization Index and Selected Independent Variables in Counties

Political–Administrative System Attributes

Community Environment

Extracommunity Environment

Value Orientation

Decisional Control

Total population

Presence of outside funding

Southern and Western U.S.

Professional chief executive

Professional management practices

Departmental user control

Elected official control

Pluralism of computer decisions

Computer utilization

.34

.15

.21

.15

-.33

-.19

.25

.14

.40

.17

VARIABILITY IN COMPUTER USE:
CONFIGURATIVE EXPLANATIONS

Statistical analyses of comparative data for many units of analysis provide one useful means to generalize about those characteristics of the computing milieu that seem to have a systematic effect upon the level of computing in local governments. Although our statistical analysis in the preceding section indicates that we can account for nearly half of the between-government variation in computer use, that still leaves more than half unexplained. It may be that important milieu characteristics were excluded from that analysis or were inadequately measured. But it is also possible that in many cases the variation in computer use is best accounted for by unique, local factors and/or by an unusual mix of the critical variables specified above. Consequently, this section aims to provide further insight into the dynamics underlying the level of computer utilization by employing an analytic approach that is more sensitive to the particular configuration of critical forces in a given government.

Despite the causal language in the previous section, it should be clear that the analytic models do not imply rigid determinism. Computer systems do not appear magically in cities and counties. Rather, they are initiated by advocates powerful enough to mobilize resources and organizational support. Factors such as a large population or external funding support do not automatically cause an increase in computer technology. Rather, officials serving a larger population generally tend to see a greater need for the technology in order to cope with extensive information-processing that such a population generates. And external funding for computing provides officials with opportunities to use moneys that are outside the normal bureaucratic struggle for the government's limited financial resources. Thus "objective" measures of milieu factors do not translate directly into levels of computer utilization, because the felt need for computing or the willingness to innovate can vary among different public officials and different organizational contexts, and because the milieu factors can interact in nonlinear ways.

An examination of "deviant" cases can provide certain insights. In some governments, the level of computing is quite different from what would be expected from the regression equations specified in the previous analysis. In this section, we present six case studies, each of which was in the extreme 15 percent of the distribution of cities or counties based on a ratio of the estimated score (from the regression equation) to the actual score of the government on the overall index of computer utilization. Two of the governments (Brockton, Massachusetts and Quincy, Massachusetts) are extremely low on this ratio—that is, they score much lower on the computer utilization index than would be predicted on the basis of their values on the key milieu variables. Four governments have extremely high levels of computer use relative to the estimated level (New Orleans, Louisiana; Lane County, Oregon; Grand Rapids, Michigan; and Kansas City, Missouri). These six case studies might enrich our understanding, for both the deviant and the more "normal" instances, of how a particular configuration of actors and characteristics can create a computing milieu that powerfully affects the nature of the computer package.[13]

The Sterile Computing Milieu: Brockton, Massachusetts

Brockton is a small industrial city south of Boston, with an ailing economy and partisan, ward-based politics. Both the city council and city administration were characterized by factionalism and fragmentation, with the government organized into 17 independent departments and about ten semiautonomous boards. In 1975, the city used a limited amount of computing for financial functions and virtually none elsewhere. Brockton is an instance where most of the critical features in the computing milieu tended to be in the directions likely to depress the level of computer use, and these factors were exacerbated by the politicized environment and by local officials' unrealistic expectations about the computer package.

Because of Brockton's relatively small size (population 89,000), the need for complex information-processing capabilities was not great. The city did not actively pursue outside financial support for computing, and few local governments in the region were undertaking extensive use of computer technology. These extracommunity and community characteristics were not likely to stimulate computer utilization; and attributes of the political-administrative system and the related failure of local officials to understand the subtleties of the computer package seem to have had even greater limiting effects.

A professional orientation to government operations has been identified as one key stimulus for computing use. The absence of such an orientation in Brockton was most evident in the police department, which, along with the finance department, is typically a cornerstone of municipal computing development. In the late 1960s, the police department was in total disarray, the city council having added to the problem by appointing seven different police chiefs in seven years. In 1975, an outside consultant presented a devastating report on local police operations, criticizing nearly every aspect of police activities and organization. Thus in a period when LEAA was generously funding police computing innovations, the Brockton local police force was characterized by little professionalism and much disorder. After the consultant's report, the city for the first time recruited a police chief from the outside. Despite his professionalism and long interest in applications of computing to police work, he faced a deeply divided police force resistant to reform. Computing was given low priority in the new police chief's attempt to implement some of the 294 actions recommended by the consultant because, the chief realized, it would provoke staff resistance at a point when basic structural reforms in the department were of greatest importance.

In 1973, a mayor was elected who was committed to "good management" and professional operations in government. One of his early initiatives was to push for a computing operation within the city. But the absence of professionalism in the council and departments gave rise to a series of obstacles. The cost-conscious council was unwilling to provide much financial support for the computer package, so the job of data-processing department manager did not pay well, and consequently the city was unable to recruit a well-qualified person to assume it. Another obstacle was a decision characteristic of a partisan, patronage-based government—that the new data-processing department would be staffed only by people who were already employed in city departments, and who would then receive on-the-job training as programmers and systems analysts. In addition, most departments were unwilling to cooperate with the data-generating and data-handling needs of the data-processing unit, and the departments were not forced to comply with such needs by the city's top officials.

In view of these obstacles, the possibility of adequate data-processing services was low. Nonetheless, the politicians insisted that the use of computer technology should produce quick and significant cost reductions and other efficiencies. When it did not, the data-processing manager and the computer technology "lost credibility" in city hall. Councilmen complained that computing "leaves a bad taste in our mouths" and observed that they had "heard lots of promises but saw no reductions in staff." From the politicians' viewpoints, the city was spending $100,000 per year on computing and receiving few benefits from money that could have been providing public goods and services to their citizen-supporters. There was no leading official in the city who understood or would act on the premise that to build a satisfactory computing operation, it is just as important to invest in skilled technical staff, require departmental cooperation with the computing installation, and allow time for automated systems to be routinized as it is to purchase computer equipment.

In sum, the confluence of historical and current forces has produced an environment that is not yet conducive to the development of a viable computer package. Thus Brockton is an example of a sterile milieu for the growth of computing—a partisan political-administrative environment with little extracommunity or community support for computing, where professionalism is not a dominant presence, where factionalism precludes strong leadership, and where those concerned have little understanding of the complexity and needs involved in nurturing an effective computer package.

The Rise and Fall of Computing: Quincy, Massachusetts

Quincy is a suburban-industrial city of 88,000 on the fringes of the Boston metropolitan area. Like Brockton, it is a city of highly partisan, ethnic politics, and this politics is grounded in patronage and competition among factions. Quincy operates generally through machine politics, and the use of professional management techniques such as computing has never been particularly attractive to any political leadership group. Most department heads are appointed by the leading politicians and share the partisan perspective. Thus it seems Quincy would be another sterile computing milieu.

In fact, however, Quincy did have highly sophisticated computing at one time. The Law Enforcement Administration Agency (LEAA) provided a very large grant to Quincy and several adjoining cities for implementation of a sophisticated computer system whose function was to determine an "optimal" allocation of police patrol personnel. This system, called Hypercube, was developed by Professor Richard Larson of MIT. Apparently, LEAA felt that several small Massachusetts communities close to MIT would be most appropriate sites in which to implement and test the system, despite the limited interest or experience with computing in cities like Quincy. Under the LEAA grant, Quincy and the adjoining cities developed an extensive automated data base regarding crime activities and police efforts. A highly skilled civilian staff was primarily responsible for operating the Hypercube system.

While there was some general enthusiasm in the city for the visibility that this experiment in sophisticated computing provided to Quincy, there was limited enthusiasm among the police; in fact, there was considerable resistance within the police to the kinds of results (that is, reallocations of police patrol) that the Hypercube model suggested. The mayor and the police chief each had a particular view of how best to allocate police officers, but the Hypercube model suggested a third allocation pattern, different from either. It is significant that the strongest opposition to the model came from the mayor rather than from the police chief. Ultimately, given the political nature of the city, it was the mayor's preferences that decided the allocation of patrol officers. And, because neither the mayor nor police chief found that the Hypercube model effectively aided them in their bureaucratic struggle to achieve their own preferences, it was discredited by these significant actors.

A sophisticated computer and skilled staff had been imported and were serving the city. The question now facing Quincy was whether or not to expand automated information systems within the police department. Two factors were central to the resolution of this question. One, noted above, was that the Hypercube model had no strong support from any influential group inside the city. Only the technical experts working on the model were enthusiastic about its use. Not only the mayor and the police chief, but also other ranking police officers and the patrol officers were skeptical or even hostile to the use of such a model and, by implication, to the use of computers.

The second important factor was the nature of the LEAA grant for the system. As are many other federally provided grants, the LEAA grant was meant to support the development and implementation of the automated system, but not to fund it forever. After the initial grant period, LEAA discontinued funding to Quincy and the other cities. Quincy and the participating cities were obliged either to continue funding the automated system, or to end it. Most of the participating cities felt that the costs of maintaining the automated system substantially outweighed the benefits. The few supporters of the system fought a rear-guard action; but these supporters had limited political influence within the cities. The cities decided that they were not willing to pay their share for maintaining the automated system. Finally, the system was "unplugged" and taken away.

Thus ended police computing in Quincy. There has been no further pressure for an automated information system in the police department, and there is not sufficient support from politicians or top administrators in

Quincy to develop computing in other areas. The finance director would like to acquire relatively simple accounting machines; but this interest has been mild and has not produced a policy-initiative leading to the adoption of automated systems.

The milieu in Quincy was not responsive to the use of a sophisticated management technique such as computing, and the experience of importing computing, in the form of a sophisticated system for the police, was an unsatisfactory one for the most powerful political groups affected by the automated system. Because of these factors, little support developed for implementing even the more basic and straightforward uses of automated information systems in the city. While it is quite probable that Quincy will ultimately develop its computer package, that development is likely to be slow and to be considerably more limited in extent than is evident in other cities similar to Quincy.

Importing Computing: New Orleans

A common response to perceived inadequacies in computing services is to upgrade the hardware and/or staff of the computer package. New Orleans is a large city-parish (population 593,000) which provides an extensive range of public goods and services and thus has a clear need for a large-scale computing operation. New Orleans presents an interesting example of a sequential response to inadequacies in the computer package.

In the early 1970s, the fundamental problem with New Orleans' computer package was the absence of skilled computer staff. The area had a limited pool of talented computer specialists, and city salaries were not competitive with those in the private sector. Thus, hiring was done at a rather low level and it was difficult for the government to retain those who did build their technical skills and competence. The city data-processing staff became a training ground for personnel, who then departed for better jobs in the private sector. Given these staffing problems, the city had great difficulty in providing more than the most rudimentary computing services. Agencies with more sophisticated or analytical computing needs usually went outside the city (e.g., to the local universities).

As dissatisfaction with data-processing services grew, management began to blame the shortcomings in computer services on the nature of the computing hardware rather than on the quality of personnel. Equipment was upgraded—it was assumed that better hardware would somehow enhance the quality of data-processing services, independent of the quality of staff. Moreover, it was assumed that some staff might take jobs and stay longer if more sophisticated equipment was available for their use. Thus New Orleans initiated a phase of continuous hardware development, with increases in core size, acquisition of new mainframes and peripherals, and the adoption of more sophisticated programing schemes.

Not surprisingly, the policy of importing advanced hardware and software exacerbated the problems caused by inadequate technical staff. As the discrepancy between the sophistication of the equipment and the competency of the staff grew, data-processing services deteriorated further. The next response was to replace the data-processing manager; but the new manager was neither highly skilled technically nor knowledgeable in the managerial aspects of the computer package. Thus, this change of management did not resolve any problems.

By the mid-1970s, the top leadership in New Orleans recognized the problems caused by inadequate data-processing staff. They tried a new strategy—the importation of skilled staff. The general approach to such importation of the computer package is often termed "facilities management" (FM)—the hiring of an outside expert group to provide some or all aspects of the computer package. Maximally, the FM firm provides virtually all data processing, using its own hardware and software and its own staff.

New Orleans opted for a special version of FM that is termed "systems development." A private firm was contracted to develop and implement the major computing systems that had been specified in negotiations between the firm and the city's leadership. The contractors were to use the city's hardware, and all systems that were developed were to be owned by the city. The sophisticated staff necessary to develop and implement these systems would be brought in by the FM group. In theory, these computer specialists were to work with existing local staff in order to provide the locals with some training in the use and maintenance of the systems that were developed. The contract held that when the agreed-upon systems were completed, the FM group would depart.

As a consequence of these decisions—first to upgrade the computer equipment and then to import skilled technical staff to develop sophisticated automated systems—New Orleans is now considerably above its "expected" level of computing development. However, the pattern of development in New Orleans is indicative of certain underlying problems that arise when an organization attempts to import computing. In the first place, the early period of overdevelopment of equipment led to a considerable mismatch between that equipment and the people needed to operate it. Secondly, during the period of systems development under FM, there has been substantial instability in the interface between computing services and user departments. While there now seems to be considerable support for the activities of the FM organization, the transition period has been lengthy. As a consequence, a decade of importing computing in New Orleans has not yet produced the level of benefits from computing services that might be expected, given the sophistication of hardware and software and extensiveness of applications.[14]

Data-Processing Manager as Entrepreneur: Lane County, Oregon

Until the late 1960s, there was nothing exceptional about computing in Lane County, Oregon. Then an extraordinary period of growth began in both the extensiveness and the sophistication of computing services there. The county began to provide computing services to the city of Eugene and to four other cities in the county. In essence, Lane County became a modified version of a regional computing facility. It even gained national recognition as one of the leaders in the use of computing to serve government.

Although such phenomena usually have multiple causes, the dramatic development of computing in Lane County is primarily due to the emergence and efforts of a data-processing manager with vision, managerial skills, and political skills. While this individual did not have extensive technical skills regarding computer equipment (hardware and software), he was quite sophisticated as a management administrator and he did have a sound understanding of the "technique" aspects of the computer package.

The manager initiated an aggressive, if gradual, program to draw virtually all government agencies into positive, cooperative relationships with the data-processing installation. Programmers were assigned directly to user departments, and worked under the joint supervision of the data-processing unit and the user department. Such decentralized programmers were meant to combine the perspective and the operational style of the user department with their own technical insights in the design of automated applications. Thus, they were able to design and modify automated applications that served the user's needs more fully and also conformed to the needs of the data-processing installation.

The data-processing manager used many techniques to retain highly skilled technical staff in the government. He reclassified technical staff into civil service categories which, although they did not correspond to the job descriptions (e.g., "mechanical engineer"), did provide salary levels comparable to those the staff could command in the private sector. He acquired sophisticated hardware and encouraged the development of intriguing new applications in order to sustain the interest of skilled technical staff. Finally, he generated a very high level of enthusiasm and team spirit—data-processing staff received considerable intrinsic pleasure from their involvement with the computer installation. All of these strategies enabled the manager to retain a dedicated, highly competent, and sophisticated technical staff, despite the salary constraints and bureaucratic tendencies common to local government.

Although the decentralization of computing staff to user agencies was the centerpiece of the strategy to involve users in the data-processing operation, the manager also employed other techniques. He promoted an active computer policy board, composed of representatives from many user agencies, which generated continued enthusiasm and interest in the uses and development of computer services. In allocating computer resources, the manager tried to protect small users as well as to serve large users effectively. And effective promotion and provision of computing services to the five cities in the area led to their increased support for the county's data-processing operation. The manager also gave the top executives of every government materials illustrating the accomplishments and benefits their government enjoyed from computing. Because of this strategy, almost all agencies in the government supported his program and his requests for further resources. This increase in activity enabled further expansion, as well as the efficient use of those resources in providing relatively similar services to the various governments.

While none of these techniques or strategies is extraordinary, and while many government data-processing units have attempted one or more of them, it was the special capabilities of the data-processing manager to blend these techniques with skill and subtlety that enabled the county's computing operation to be both successful and expansive. By his nurturing of the skilled staff, provision of high-quality service to many users, and continual communication of the many benefits from the data-processing operation to top elected and appointed officials, this manager provides a model of the entrepreneurial style of extending computer use.

The Innovative Manager and External Funding:
Grand Rapids, Michigan

Computing developments in Grand Rapids illustrate both the role of the "innovation-oriented" manager and the impact of federal funding. Grand Rapids, the home city of former President Gerald Ford, had a population of 172,000 in 1976 and had been slowly declining in population since the late 1960s. Although only twice the size of Brockton, Massachussetts, Grand Rapids has adopted very large and complex computer packages dealing with police, court administration, financial reporting, and payroll personnel. These extensive systems are in addition to many of the more conventional computer applications that the city operates. This extensiveness is even more remarkable because it was only in 1965 that the city first obtained a computer.

This growth is attributable first of all to the city manager, who attempted to build his peer-professional reputation by being an innovator. Some of his innovations were practical, such as program budgeting, and some more symbolic, such as Calder artwork in, on, and around city hall. His first foray into computing innovation occurred in 1969 when, after difficulties in hiring and retaining skilled staff, he contracted computing operations to a private facilities-management firm—the first such FM arrangement in any American local government. This was immediately followed by another innovation—the creation of an office of Systems and Fiscal Management headed by a former aerospace manager lured from the West Coast. This office was put in charge not only of managing all computing and information system efforts by the city, but also of implementing new program budgeting, fiscal forecasting, and cost-accounting procedures.

Computers were to be a part of these new procedures, but were viewed primarily as a tool for aiding their implementation. Moreover, despite this push for innovation, municipal automation was further limited in its scope and sophistication because of difficulties in implementing these grandiose plans. In 1973, however, this situation changed. After home-town boy Ford entered the White House, the city manager and other municipal staff began seeking federal support for municipal automation and for the city's other innovations. The new director of Systems and Fiscal Management played a major role as agent for the city manager and was very successful in procuring federal support for local computer systems. By 1976, the city maintained five computers to support operations in finance, police, courts, water, tax assessment, voter registration, water supply, and urban planning.

The development of SPARMIS (Standard Police Allocation Resource Management Information System) illustrates the particular role of federal funding in Grand Rapids. Moreover, it illustrates the problems created by extensive simultaneous innovations, because the facilities management innovation ultimately became a major factor constraining the success of the city's other computing development efforts. The city manager and systems manager suggested to Michigan state officials that they seek LEAA funds to develop SPARMIS, using Grand Rapids as the development site. They argued that a single information system could be developed in Grand Rapids, and then either transferred directly to other cities or at least used as a prototype by other cities in the state. The city was awarded funds by LEAA in 1973 and a private firm was awarded a contract for developing SPARMIS. By November 1975, the system was "finished," and it operated for several months before it became inoperable. The development firm sent several programmers back to Grand Rapids at its own expense to "fix" SPARMIS and correct inconsistencies within the program.

However, the facilities management company that ran the city's computers argued that their contract did not commit them to maintaining such "new systems." Consequently, the FM organization did very little to keep SPARMIS free of problems. The accuracy of data in SPARMIS, and the system's performance, deteriorated, and police personnel at all levels became extremely unhappy with the system, because they could not trust its reports. This situation also characterized the other systems developed at the same time as SPARMIS.

Grand Rapids was able to garner considerable external funds through the efforts of an innovation-oriented city manager and his staff, and through the accident of Ford's accession to the presidency. These factors enabled the city to adopt far more extensive and sophisticated computing systems than it seemed to need or might otherwise have been able to afford. But problems can emerge with extensive and simultaneous innovations. And, as the example of SPARMIS illustrates, quite different resources and commitments are required for adoption than for routinization and operation of automated systems (see Yin et al. 1979). The disjunction between the development of costly computing innovations and the attempt to contain the costs of the computing package (by means of the FM innovation) limited the city's effective use of the package.

The Synergistic Computing Milieu: Kansas City, Missouri

With a population of 507,000, Kansas City has an extremely large and complex information-processing environment; the need for basic computing services is obvious. And in fact, the city is characterized by very extensive computer utilization. Administrative activities in the city are managed by a highly professional city manager and staff of four assistant managers, each of whom supervises a different broad area (e.g., finance, human services). Within this structure of authority, major departments are allowed considerable autonomy, due in part to the management style of the top leadership, and in part to the size and historical power of major departments. Department heads and middle-level managers also tend to be professionals and to be the type of officials who are receptive to innovation.

We have noted several times that the most extensive users of municipal computing tend to be those in the finance and the public-safety functions. In Kansas City, this pattern reached an extreme form. The finance department and the police each operated its own independent and very large computer installation, with sophisticated equipment and technical staff. In addition, the municipally operated airport and the water works agency each had a small, independent computing operation. Both the police and the finance computing centers were developed under the strong leadership of a department manager whose objective was to expand the use of computer technology to the limits of its current capabilities.

One of the most striking outcomes of these analyses is that the two quite different approaches produce extremely similar explanations of variation in the level of computer utilization. The statistical analyses suggest that certain factors are systematically associated with the level of computer use. Multivariate analysis has identified more precisely a set of characteristics in the computing milieu that seems to account for variation in the index of computing utilization, which measures the speed of adoption, the extensiveness and sophistication of automated applications, and the resources committed to the computer package. Higher scores on this computing utilization index are associated with a larger population (and thus a larger information-processing environment); more innovative regions; external funding support for computing; evidence of the professional, reform orientation to government; and greater user and administrator control and less elected-official control over decisions regarding the computer package.

Thus important elements of the extracommunity environment, the community environment, and the political-administrative system do tend to have major and systematic effects on the level of computer use.

The six case studies of particular local governments with quite high or low levels of computer utilization reinforce the findings in the statistical analyses. The cases reveal that some or all of the structural constraints identified tend to be of significance, even in the "deviant" cases. However, these cases also illuminate two important observations about the computing milieu.

First, the impact of the characteristics of the computing milieu is not merely additive. The clearest case of nonadditive effects is Kansas City, where all the elements seem to operate in a synergistic manner and produce an especially high level of computer use. Moreover, the presence or absence of any one important element is not always critical in its effect on the level of computer use. In an obvious example, it should be evident that a government outside the most innovative regions can, like Grand Rapids, have an extensive computer package nonetheless. Similarly, while large size seems a critical factor not all large governments make extensive use of computing. And governments serving moderate- or even small-sized populations can implement quite extensive computing, as in Grand Rapids and Lane County. While external funding is often an important facilitating factor, providing slack resources for computing innovation, other milieu characteristics may, as in Quincy, counter its effect by producing a milieu that is not conducive to the growth and routinization of computing. And major external funding is not a necessary condition for extensive computing, as indicated by Lane County.

The police chief in Kansas City during the 1960s was Clarence Kelley, who was later appointed director of the F.B.I. An active, professional manager, Kelley guided the development of a nationally renowned police computing operation in his department. He used a combination of local funds, federal subsidies, and support from the city's computer vendor to develop extensive automated systems for visible police functions. Not only was the chief effective in capturing a significant share of local budgetary resources by arguing the critical needs of the police in Kansas City, but he also aggressively applied for (and often received) external funding for particular computing innovations, particularly from LEAA. Moreover, the department negotiated an agreement with the computer vendor, IBM, to use Kansas City as the site to develop a special package, LEMRAS, as a prototype system for determining the allocation of police manpower across precincts and shifts. Kansas City police took advantage of their dominant position in the region to justify the development of computing systems (for example, ALERT, an on-line wants and warrants system) for police throughout northwestern Missouri. And they utilized the relatively independent position of police operations from local council control in Missouri to support their desire to maintain an independent computing center.

The finance director in Kansas City during the period was a professionally oriented manager who considered himself a data-processing specialist. He vigorously supported the development of operations-oriented computer systems, promoted the expansion of computer use throughout city operations, and fought to maintain the computer installation under the finance department. He was particularly aware of the need for the computer installation to provide efficient and attractive automated systems to all city departments, and to placate those users who experienced problems with computer services. And he encouraged further use and development of computing by not charging departments for computer use. As a consequence, the data-processing division was the largest subunit in the finance department, provided the finance director with an area of rapid growth in his organizational domain, brought him national professional visibility, and assured him a base of technical expertise and information for effective monitoring of municipal operations.

Thus Kansas City is a local government where all of the critical milieu factors tend to occur in the directions found to stimulate greater computer utilization. It has a large population and a professionally oriented administration in which the department heads of the two normal big users are both strongly committed to the expansion of computing. Moreover, it is a milieu in which pluralistic computing activity has been allowed and is dominated by the two largest user departments, and in which external funding support and the regional centrality of the city have been exploited. We term Kansas City the "synergistic" milieu because effective, computing-oriented department heads and most other critical factors seem to interact positively with each other, producing with their cumulative force a level of computer utilization substantially higher than might have been expected.

CONCLUDING OBSERVATIONS

It is generally agreed among researchers that analysis is improved by employing "multiple operationism"—a variety of different types of data and alternative methodologies (Webb et al. 1966), and we have followed this approach in this chapter, and in this book as a whole. We have used both systematic statistical analyses linking empirical measures of the computer package with characteristics of its environment, and also configurative case studies of the computing milieu in individual instances where the level of computing is especially high or low.

Second, there are other, unique factors that have great importance in particular governments. The will and capacity of certain actors to achieve their goals, one of which is to promote the use of computer technology, is a critical factor in several of the cases, including Kansas City, Lane County, and Grand Rapids. That such commitment may not be enough to produce an effective computer package is clear from studies of Brockton and New Orleans. Another factor that is not considered in the statistical analyses is the role of the personnel in the computer installation, particularly its manager. The data-processing manager in Lane County is the clearest example of the powerful impact that the computer specialists can have, either through skillful entrepreneurial activities or through highly effective provision of data-processing services. Conversely, incompetent data processing, as in New Orleans prior to the use of an outside service agency, or inadequately controlled provision, as in Brockton's unsatisfactory experience with a service agency, can severely limit the development of the computer package. The intervention of external actors can also have considerable influence, as in the provision of prototype police systems in Kansas City by the computer vendor and in Quincy by an academic institution. Similarly, the unique circumstances that propelled Gerald Ford to the vice-presidency and then the presidency led Grand Rapids to seek extensive federal funding support for computing.

Both approaches support the conclusion that certain characteristics do produce computing milieus that are substantially different and that are more or less conducive to the adoption and growth of the computer package. To some extent, these milieu characteristics might be understood to act deterministically, in the sense that the actual level of the characteristic does operate as a constraint that shapes the extent of computer utilization. But it seems most appropriate to understand these characteristics as contingent factors, both in the sense that they interact with other milieu factors in complex ways and also in the sense that their impacts can be importantly altered by other factors that do not have a systematic effect in most governments. It is the interplay of these latter configurative forces, within the key constraints that operate more systematically across most computing milieus, that constitutes the essence of what we call "the politics of computing." This politics is evident in the domains of both computer-resource politics and information politics. Chapter 4 begins the exploration of these domains, with a detailed analysis of the identity and activities of the participants in decisions regarding the resources in the computer package.

CHAPTER FOUR

THE PARTICIPANTS IN COMPUTING DECISIONS

Kenneth L. Kraemer and
James N. Danziger

WE HAVE NOTED the dynamic, changing nature of the computer package. In virtually every local government, there is a constant flow of decisions regarding such issues as whether to acquire new computer equipment, whether to automate particular government functions and tasks, and whether to centralize or decentralize the computing function within the government. Who makes these decisions?

Once it has been decided to adopt the technology, there are three key decisions involved with computing. The first is concerned with the organization of the computing unit within the government. Where is it located? In what department? Is it under centralized or decentralized control? The second is concerned with the management of relations between the computing units and the user departments with respect to computing development and day-to-day use. What applications, and with what priorities, will be selected for development? Which departments will enjoy priority in computer operations? What charges should be made for computer services? Should users be involved in the design of applications and in setting operational policies? The third decision involves the evaluation of computing services and the benefits from computer use. What are the methods of evaluation? Who participates in evaluation? Whose benefits and costs are considered? Who acts on the results of evaluation studies?

The case studies in chapter 3 provided revealing examples of how various participants can significantly influence the nature of the computer package in a particular local government. Such examples support the view of those organizational theorists (Child 1972; Weick 1969) who maintain that certain participants, as a matter of strategy or policy, will attempt to shape the nature of critical aspects of their environments by their decisions and actions. In this chapter, we begin with a discussion of the principal participants involved in decisions on computing. Each participant's primary interests regarding the computer package are specified, and the participant's agenda is linked to one (or more) of our general perspectives about computer technology. We then assess data concerning the level and nature of participation of the actors in computing decisions. A major concern here is in determining whether one set of participants controls computing decisions, or whether decision making is more pluralistic. Although primary attention must be paid to evidence of *direct* influence and control, we shall also be aware of instances where certain actors seem to have powerful *indirect* influence.[1]

PRINCIPAL PARTICIPANTS

Decisions regarding control and use of local government computing involve a diverse set of participants who vary widely in their scope of interest and in their involvement with the computer package. Almost every participant has some interest that can be classified as personal and professional, and most also have some technical and/or managerial interests. Therefore, our analysis will focus on dominant interests, in order to make distinctions among participants more clear.

Table 4.1 (following Sayre & Kaufman, 1960:67–89) classifies the participants according to variation in their scope of concern (broad or narrow), and their level of involvement (high or low), in local government decision making regarding the computer package. The major participants distinguished are regulators, suppliers, providers, users, consumers, and supporters. We assume that a particular participant's interests and stakes in local government computing will provide a partial explanation of that role's scope of concern and level of involvement. We also assume that a participant's institutional position and influence vis-à-vis computing decisions will affect involvement.

Table 4.1   Classification of Participants

Level of Involvement	Scope of Concern	
	Narrow	Broad
High	A. Regulators and Suppliers: Frequent involvement in a narrow range of "big" decisions, e.g., reorganization or equipment purchase.	B. Providers and "Big Users": Frequent involvement in a broad variety of decisions and actions, e.g., priority setting, choice of applications, evaluation of services, charging policy.
	Includes chief executives, central administrators, local legislative body (council, board) computer policy boards, manufacturers, consultants, software firms, service bureaus.	Includes the *computer elite* (data processing manager, senior systems analysts and programmers, computer experts in user departments), the *information elite* (planners, policy analysts, management or budget analysts), and the top administrators in operating departments which use computing extensively.
Low	C. "Small Users" and Consumers: Occasional involvement normally regarding a specific issue, e.g., design of applications.	D. Supporters: Wide interest but little involvement in local decisions.
	Includes professionals in user departments with limited use of computers.	Includes lower-level systems analysts and programmers, computer operators, data entry clerks, federal and state agencies, regional agencies, professional and quasi-professional organizations.

Regulators and Suppliers

Regulators include those within the local government who, owing to their positions of formal authority, can have direct involvement in computing decisions and can exert substantial influence to maintain their interests. This group includes chief executives, top central administrators, and local legislators (e.g., city councils and county supervisors). Regulators are frequently involved in computing decisions, but they tend to focus on a narrow range of concerns—usually the "big decisions," such as reorganization of the computing unit or major equipment purchases.

Chief executives, whether elected or appointed, tend to see computers as a management tool, serving the goals of organizational efficiency and central control, and they generally support the wide application of the technology within the government (Dutton & Kraemer 1978b). Top central administrators in such organization-wide functions as finance and personnel serve the chief executive. Consequently, they tend to share the view that computers should facilitate managerial efficiency, particularly through the use of automated applications to monitor and control the operations of line departments and staff. Of course their own interest in getting a greater share of computer resources is indirectly served by this view, since finance and personnel functions are major instruments of managerial control.

The line department heads who serve on computing policy boards are also users of data-processing services; thus they are as concerned with getting a greater share of those computing resources for their unit as with regulating the computing unit. Similarly, elected officials are both regulators and users; however, in most local governments, politicians have not yet made much use of computers to serve their professional and personal goals, such as obtaining information about their constituents. As regulators, politicians are concerned with cost efficiencies both in the expansion of the computer package and in its application to various information-processing tasks.

These people have various interests and motives regarding computing, and particular individuals have their own unique patterns of interest. But it is generally the case that managerial concerns are most important to chief executives and central administrators, professional interests to line department heads, and personal and professional interests to elected officials.

Suppliers are private-sector participants, including the manufacturers, software firms, service bureaus, and facilities-management firms that provide computer equipment and services (Kling & Gerson 1977). Suppliers, like regulators, are centrally involved in major computing decisions and the level of their involvement on these issues is very high. They are primarily interested in promoting specific equipment or services, and in expanding the application of computers. Although their role is usually indirect, the private vendors can have substantial influence on computing decisions because they are often the first source of information about computing for those governments that are considering the adoption of computer equipment or applications. And they are a source, and frequently the only source, of information about new equipment, software, applications, and services. The private vendors profit quite literally from growth and development of computing; hence their participation is based on their entrepreneurial goals and is aimed not only at providing specific equipment and services, but also at encouraging continued expansion and upgrading of existing resources.

Providers and Big Users

Both the providers of computing services and the "big users" of these services (table 4.1B) have frequent involvement in computing decisions, covering a broad array of strategic and operational decisions, such as selecting computer applications for development, setting priorities for development of applications and for computer operations, centralizing or decentralizing computer services, evaluating computer services, and establishing pricing policies for computer services. Providers and big users may even dominate the decision process.

Providers can be distinguished as providing either computing services or information services. The providers of computing services, or the "computer elite," are the top computer specialists, both within the computing unit and elsewhere in the government. This group includes the managers, senior systems analysts, and programmers in the computer unit, and skilled computer experts in the user departments. Activities related to the computer package are fundamental to the careers of those in the computer elite. As a consequence, members share certain perspectives. They are highly concerned and involved with all decisions about the computer package. Expansion of computing is seen as essential to their salaries, promotions, and job security. And they see the development of effective and sophisticated automated applications, and of technically advanced hardware, as critical to their professional status and recognition. Thus their professional and technical interests tend to merge, and both these and their personal interests are served by increasing the centrality of computing to the organization, and by increasing their own influence and control over the computer package.

However, the computer elite is not a homogeneous group. Computer experts in the user departments share with the central computer staff an interest in the sophistication and the expansion of computing, but the two groups differ in other interests. Departmental computer experts are interested in computing development that will enhance their own professional goals, which are more closely identified with departmental interests than with the central computer unit's interests. Computing development and technical computing concerns are most important to central computer staff, but the substantive aspects of each automated application are most important to departmental computer staff. And the greater the dispersion of computer experts to various departments within the government, the greater will be the likelihood that some of their interests will conflict from department to department and with the central computer unit. Thus, when the computer elite is dispersed, it is much less homogeneous than is suggested by the technocratic elite perspective. It is fragmented into different constituencies. Despite this, it is clear that the computer elite can be a major force in computer decision making, because of both its role as primary provider of data-processing services, and its relative monopoly of technical expertise (Danziger 1979a).

The providers of information services, the "information elite," include planners, policy analysts, and management and budget analysts. To an even greater extent than the computer elite, the information elite is composed of discrete sets of participants who, although sharing basic technical skills and values, are dispersed among different organizational units and have operational agendas aligned with the goals of those units. They typically serve as staff to the regulators and the central administrative departments, and many operate as policy groups within the government. Decisions about centralized data systems and sophisticated analytical applications are critical to their careers and to their control over information. They will advocate centralized data systems that cross departmental boundaries because "they view such systems at least in part as means of gaining control over the information channels vital to all operating departments—and thereby capturing some of the latter's power" (Downs 1967:208). They will also advocate development of sophisticated analytical applications (statistical analysis, modeling and simulation, graphic display and mapping) because they view the reduction of their analytical uncertainty as the technical key to the legitimacy and influence of their policy advice.

If those in the information elites can combine technical sophistication with knowledge about policy issues, they will influence their superiors and the actions of operating units (Downs 1967; Lowi 1972). They also will advance professionally, and gain peer recognition and some measure of independence within their domain. As they depend on the nature of government data systems and the computing capabilities that support those systems, they will use their expertise to influence many of the decisions regarding the computer package. They fully understand that seemingly technical decisions about computer configuration, systems software, and data-management software shape their ability to control information as much as do decisions about new applications, development priorities, and the centralization of data systems.

Big users are those departments that use most computing; more specifically, they are those individuals (usually top- or middle-level managers) who authorize each department's use of data-processing services and products. The data in chapters 2 and 8 indicate that the finance, police, utilities, personnel, budget and management, and courts departments tend to use computing most extensively. These users want effective, trouble-free automated applications that enhance the professionalism and performance of their departments. Such improvements are likely to lead to cost and staffing efficiencies, better information to guide and monitor operations, or provision of new services. Big user departments are highly dependent on computing, and in most cases, want to expand their automated applications. This increases their stakes in decisions and their interest in gaining greater expertise in, and control over, the provision of computing services. Most big users see computing as a scarce resource that is subject to the kinds of competitive allocation processes that are best characterized as organizational pluralism. For all these reasons, big users are actively interested in all issues regarding the operations and development of the computer package.

"Small Users" and Consumers

"Small users" and consumers (table 4.1C) are only occasionally involved in local government computing decisions. These decisions usually relate to a specific issue such as the design of a computer application, the specification of a computer analysis, or the format of a computer-generated report. While the intensity of their interest in a computing service may be quite high, these groups are concerned about limited and well-defined issues, and their attention to such issues is sporadic rather than sustained.

Small users are those departments and agencies that consume few computing resources because they make limited, or only occasional, use of computing services. In most local governments, the small users include those agencies responsible for such functions as libraries, streets, parks, and social services (see chapter 8). While certain departments can be identified as likely to be either big or small users, it is important to note that this designation indicates a generalized level of use across most governments. Whether a particular department is a big or small user in a specific local government is dependent upon a number of factors. For example, within a given government, the functions of some departments are more amenable to automation, the leadership in some departments is more committed to the use of computer technology, and some departments are more effective in the competition for computer resources.

The small user is usually concerned with decisions involving specific automated applications for the agency, and lacks the technical expertise and/or political influence to have a major role in the full range of computing decisions. However, the current trend is for the staffs in many small user departments to view computers, and particularly the information they can provide, as a means to improve the professionalism of their operations and maintain their autonomy from central managers and politicians. Hence, there is growing interest among small users in decisions about the allocation of computer resources. In general, both big and small users have the same basic agenda—each wants the providers of computing to be responsive to its needs, the allocation systems to provide it with sufficient computing services, and the products of the service to be information and data-processing capabilities that support its professional and departmental goals.

Consumers are the recipients of computing services. This category is quite diverse, encompassing the personnel in many agencies of both the local government in question and other governments, as well as those citizens who are served by automated applications. Government personnel are usually interested in getting more effective information processing from an automated application—better-quality or more extensive information, error reduction, operational convenience, improvement of the work environment. The experience of citizens with the government's automated information systems is limited, as most current applications do not involve the provision of services directly to the citizens (see chapter 8). Because citizens' concerns as consumers of computing services are quite narrow and focused, their involvement with decisions is intermittent, and most lack the interest and/or the influence to play a major role in those decisions.

However, it is possible for a particular consumer to have considerable indirect impact, as, for example, when another government agency places specific standards or formats on data that the local government is expected to provide. In general, the interests of governmental consumers about decisions concerning the computer package are primarily professional and secondarily personal and managerial, while for citizen-consumers the interests are mainly personal.

Supporters

Supporters include two broad categories. One group, within the local government, consists of those personnel who perform the basic tasks necessary for the operation of computer technology. This group is composed of "lower-level" computing staff, such as less-skilled programmers and operators, data entry clerks, and those personnel in operating departments who generate data for computerized systems. The second group of supporters is external to the local government and includes federal, state, and regional agencies, and professional and quasi-professional organizations that facilitate local government computing by means of financial or technical assistance or other means of encouragement. As indicated in table 4.1D, both types of supporters have a broad interest in local government computing but little direct involvement in local decision processes. However, both groups can have quite significant indirect influence on those decisions.

Lower-level computing staff have a subtle influence on major decisions and the operation of the computer package. In particular, the computer elite must consider the constraints upon the package resulting from the skill levels and the behavior of lower-level computing staff. These staff do tend to share the technical-professional interests of the computer elite in the expansion, sophistication, and autonomy of the computing operation; but if their capabilities are inadequate, it is unlikely that the overall quality of computing services will be high, and there probably will be many problems due to poorly designed automated systems and unreliable computer center operations. And if the computing staff is insensitive or uncooperative in their relations with departmental users and consumers, there will be comparable shortcomings (Danziger 1979a; 1979c). Similarly, if there is either active or passive resistance from those in operating departments who must provide data for automated systems, systems are likely to be unsatisfactory. Thus those who counsel organizations about the "proper" management of their computing operations insist that those who make critical decisions about the computer package must be sensitive to the points where lack of skills or lack of cooperation from lower-level staff can reduce the value of the technology (Bostrom & Heinen 1977; Hedberg & Mumford 1977; Lucas 1975).

It is generally true that most local governments have introduced computer technology on their own initiative and have developed their own patterns of use. But chapters 3 and 5 indicate that substantial impetus also has been provided by factors in the external environment, particularly by various federal, state, and regional agencies. The federal agencies that have been most influential are the departments of Commerce, Justice, Transportation, Housing and Urban Development, and Health, Education and Welfare (Kraemer & King 1978a,b; Kraemer & Perry 1979).

One of the most important influences has been the provision of grants-in-aid from government agencies for the development of a particular computing capability in the local government. Clearly, these grants are "carrots" that are meant to induce the local government to undertake a computerized system that is of value to the external agency. For example, the Law Enforcement Assistance Administration provided substantial funding to upgrade local police computing capabilities (as in the Quincy, Massachusetts case in chapter 3) and to tie local police into information networks such as the National Crime Information Center (Colton 1978; Laudon 1974; Marchand & Bogan 1979). Occasionally, state and federal agencies have provided a developed automated system for transfer into the local computer package (Kraemer 1977).

In addition to "carrots," small "sticks" also have been used by agencies at various levels of the federal system, to prod the local government to upgrade its computing package. Typically, reporting requirements that have been imposed on the local government to satisfy a mandated or grant-aided program are most appropriately handled by developing an automated information system. For example, federal and state bureaucracies require such detailed reports on the distribution of social welfare services that many local agencies are computerizing at least the basic records on welfare recipients.

Professional associations play an indirect role in local government computing decisions. The major urban management associations, such as the International City Management Association, the National League of Cities, and the National Association of Counties, promote the use of computers and other technologies as tools of modern management, and they provide information about computers to their members. And specialized groups, such as Public Technology Incorporated, the Urban and Regional Information Systems Association, and the Municipal Finance Officers Association, provide orientation and training courses for local officials, exchange information about specific computer applications, produce magazines and newsletters, and offer technical assistance to individual governments. All of these activities create a climate of greater acceptance and lower risk on those occasions when a local government must make decisions about the use and expansion of its computer package (Bingham 1978b; Dutton & Kraemer 1979b).

Explanation for Participants' Involvement

Each of the four basic approaches outlined in chapter 1 suggests an explanation for the activities and influence of various participants in computing decisions. From the perspective of *managerial rationalism*, the government's top managers, who correspond generally to the regulators in table 4.1, are concerned with effective and rational control of the growth, use, and impacts of computer technology. Given the complexity and inherent instability in the computer package, the regulators will attempt to plan the development of the technology in their government, and to allocate computer resources wisely among alternative users in order to serve organization-wide objectives. Thus, this approach predicts active and dominant involvement by the regulators in all major computing decisions regarding the adoption of new computer applications, the setting of development priorities, and the performance of the providers of computing services.

The view of *technocratic elitism* posits that bureaucratic units that have a relative monopoly of expertise will exert substantial influence and control over their own domains (Downs 1967; Durkheim 1947; Lowi 1972b). Given the highly technical nature of the computer package, it is reasonable to assume that the computer elite could dominate decisions relating to the development and application of computers in the local government. There are studies that indicate that technical language, issues, and criteria are central and often critical in key computing decisions (Danziger 1979a; Laudon 1974; Mann & Williams 1960; Pettigrew 1975; Pettigrew & Mumford 1975). Several studies also indicate that decisional control could be dominated by another set of technically sophisticated actors—those expert *users* of automated information that we have termed an "information elite" (Downs 1967; Hoffmann 1973; Lowi 1972b). These could be big users, small users, or consumers of computer services, in terms of table 4.1. They may be planners, policy analysts, or others with sufficient expertise regarding the use of computing software and information to influence computing decisions independently, or to share in those decisions with the computer elite.

According to the *organizational pluralist* perspective, no groups enjoy dominant and continuing control over decisions regarding the computer package. Rather, there are many factions with substantial stakes, and each uses its own resources to steer computing decisions toward its own agendas. Thus regulators will use their authority to guide computing toward their objectives, the information elite will invoke their knowledge about computing, the computer elite will manipulate their direct control over computing services, and users in functions of critical importance to the policy (e.g., police, finance) will assert their political influence to gain more computing resources. From this perspective, computing services are allocated in terms of a process of competition and bargaining not unlike that employed to distribute budgetary resources. Everyone gets a relatively "fair share" of computing services, and no participant is able to dominate the decision process.

Finally, the *reinforcement politics* perspective predicts that some participants or set of participants will powerfully control the decision process regarding the computer package. It does not specify, a priori, which participant(s) will be powerful; rather it hypothesizes that some participants will control the process and that others will have very little influence. And those in control will make decisions that primarily serve the interests of those who control the broader organization. Reasonable candidates for this kind of dominance are the regulators, the computer elite, the big users, or the information elite.

INFLUENCE ON CRITICAL DECISIONS

The involvement of external participants, particularly private suppliers and governmental agencies that offer funding, can be quite important on decisions regarding the local government's computer package. But their involvement generally occurs on a *sporadic* basis, focuses on a *specific* automated system, and operates *indirectly* on the government's decision processes. While these external participants occasionally set general constraints or provide opportunities, it is those within the local government who have continuous involvement and direct influence, and we shall concentrate on these internal participants in the following analysis. The data used for the analysis include the appraisals of both data-processing managers and chief executives in the 713 city and county governments, and also of many users of data-processing services in the 42 city governments.

Operational Decisions

The day-to-day operations of the computer package depend on many narrow-gauge decisions, such as the appropriate programing language, the proper design of a form for collecting and coding data, the order in which already automated tasks will be processed by the computer, the format of output for an automated application, or the adequacy of a particular computer service. These decisions have an important technical component, and one might predict that the most powerful influence on many of these decisions would be brought to bear by the members of the computer elite.

However, a strong case can be made in favor of other participants having significant influence. These technical decisions powerfully affect the nature of the computer package and its utility for others who are users and consumers of that package. Scholars examining the impacts of high technologies on organizations have been increasingly interested in the "socio-technical interface"—the nexus between the technical experts and the users of the technology (Bostrom & Heinen 1977; Hedberg & Mumford 1975). An important question in our study is whether technical considerations are elevated above the functional and operational needs of the users. Does the computer elite make any attempt to bridge this gap? Is the information elite active and influential enough to mitigate the potential problem? And do department users have enough control to ensure that their needs are met by computing services?

Table 4.2 may illuminate our assessment of influence and control. The data indicate the general level of involvement of user departments in various activities related to computer services, as reported by the data-processing managers of each computer installation. There is substantial variation in the participation of users, both from installation to installation

Table 4.2 **Data-Processing Managers' Perceptions of Participation of User Departments**

Activities	Users Participate (%):				
	Never	Seldom	Often	Always	(N)
A. Review designs for a new application	6	19	36	38	(473)
B. Provide informal feedback on problems with the data-processing unit	5	15	49	31	(474)
C. Work as a member of technical group in designing an application	15	29	40	16	(474)
D. Formally evaluate applications used	16	44	29	23	(470)
E. Sign off, accepting an application	26	27	24	23	(464)
F. Provide test data for an application	19	35	31	15	(473)
G. Participate in assigning priority to data-processing projects	39	28	19	14	(473)
H. Sit on a policy board overseeing the computer unit	59	16	10	16	(471)
I. Initiate major changes of computer applications (such as changing the flow of information, the input or output)	13	46	35	6	(473)
J. Perform systematic analysis of benefits and costs anticipated from a proposed computer application	23	48	21	8	(473)
K. Perform systematic analysis of benefits and costs derived from implemented computer applications	34	48	14	4	(473)
L. Complete questionnaires or evaluation forms on satisfaction with data-processing services	60	30	8	1	(468)
M. Do the programing necessary for an application	77	13	4	6	(474)

NOTE: The question asked was, "What is the frequency with which users of your data-processing unit do each of the following?"

and from activity to activity. The table indicates that in most installations, departmental users (usually top- or middle-managers) are very active in four activities: (A) reviewing designs for new applications; (B) providing informal feedback on problems with the data-processing unit; (C) participating in design teams; and (D) formally evaluating the applications they use. In at least two-fifths of the installations, the users always or often participate in (E) signing off to accept an application; and (F) providing test data. Thus users do assert control in certain critical areas related to their own applications.

Departmental users are least active in certain of the most technical activities shown in the table: (M) programming applications; and (J) and (K) performing systematic cost-benefit analyses of applications. Fully 90 percent of users report that they (L) seldom or never perform any systematic evaluation of their satisfaction with the performance of the data-processing unit. And it is revealing that (G) users are seldom involved with decisions about priorities among projects, (H) rarely sit on computer policy boards,[2] or (I) do not often initiate major changes in automated applications. These latter activities are not fundamentally technical and are domains that seem important if departmental users are to assert control, or at least influence, over the behavior and services of the data-processing unit.

We have seen that departmental users influence activities directly related to their own automated applications. Tables 4.3 and 4.4 provide evidence that the data-processing unit has considerable control over the more technical aspects of the computer package. As might be expected, the government's data-processing unit is almost always the major source of application design and programing. Of the 476 installations reporting on the proportion of programs that were written in-house, 30 percent said "all" were, 50 percent said "most" were, 7 percent said "about half," 7 percent said "few," and 7 percent said "none." In one-third of the installations, some user departments are active in application design, although they are less involved in programing (table 4.3). Also, about one-third of the

Table 4.3   Sources of Computer Application Design and Programing

	Installations (%)	
Sources	Source has Designed Applications[a]	Source has Programed Applications[b]
A. This data-processing unit	96%	95%
B. Outside consulting firm	38	30
C. User departments	36	19
D. Hardware vendor	32	29
E. Other local governments	30	26
F. Commercial software vendor or firm	21	20
G. Private service bureau	6	7

NOTE: N = 470 data-processing installations.
[a]Question: "Please indicate whether or not each of the possible sources listed below has designed computer applications at your installation in the last two years."
[b]Question: "Please indicate whether or not each of the possible sources listed below has programed computer applications at your installation in the last two years."

installations have used outside suppliers (private consulting firms, hardware vendors, or other governments) to provide application design or programing for at least one application during a two-year period (table 4.3). And table 4.4 indicates that the data-processing unit has substantial or absolute control over forms design in fully 91 percent of the data-processing installations.

A somewhat different perspective on the activities of various users is provided by table 4.5. This table indicates that 40 percent of the users in the 42 cities have participated at some time as members of a group designing a computer application. If the large sample of detectives and police is excluded, the proportion of those personnel who have participated in this activity increases to fully 60 percent. When we view these responses at the city level, rather the individual level, we see that there is substantial variation among cities in the overall level of user involvement in design. However, such individuals as the heads of finance agencies and department heads seem to participate in design across most governments. Table 4.5 also provides some support for the influence of an information elite, because budget analysts and planners also participate in design in most governments. In general, then, the surprisingly high levels of participation reported by users in table 4.5 must be viewed as evidence opposing the notion that the data-processing unit operates in total insulation from user groups.

The users of computer services do report substantial involvement with computer personnel in operational decisions, but the nature and quality of these interactions—that is, the user-technician interface—is of fundamental importance. For example, it is not clear whether the responses in

Table 4.4 Data-Processing Control Over Design of Forms

Degree of Control[a]	Installations (%)
No control	1%
Little control	8
Substantial control	77
Complete control	14
Total	100%

NOTE: N = 480 data-processing installations.

[a]Question: "How much control does the data-processing unit have over the design of forms used by departments to collect information for automated operations?"

Table 4.5 Involvement of Municipal Personnel in Design

Selected Officials and Groups	% Indicating:		
	No involvement in design	Some involvement in design	(N)
Elected Officials and Staff			
Mayor	91%	9%	(11)
Mayor's staff	45	55	(20)
Council	74	26	(51)
Council staff	67	33	(6)
Central Administrators and Staff			
Chief appointed official	42	58	(19)
Appointed official's staff	43	57	(53)
Head of balance-reporting unit	6	94	(33)
Head of budget-monitoring unit	18	82	(28)
Budget analysts	30	79	(66)
Accountants	28	72	(74)
Departments			
Department heads	29	71	(310)
Department administrative assistants	39	61	(105)
Division heads	30	70	(69)
Department accountants	54	46	(69)
Planning			
Planning director	42	68	(21)
Planning staff	31	69	(16)
Data base custodians and analysts	11	89	(63)
Traffic Ticket Processing			
Directors	20	80	(30)
Supervisors	40	60	(40)
Clerks	84	16	(101)
Police			
Data-processing specialists	17	83	(6)
Manpower allocation supervisors	46	54	(37)
Manpower allocation analysts	24	76	(45)
Records-division clerks	72	28	(47)
Detective supervisors	66	34	(74)
Detectives	92	8	(394)
Patrol officers	94	6	(423)
Total	60%	40%	(2176)

NOTE: Each respondent in the 40-city survey was asked: "Have you worked as a member of a group designing a computer application for your department?"

table 4.5 reflect meaningful participation in a continuing design phase, or whether they reflect brief, symbolic participation promoted by the computer staff in order to co-opt users into their design efforts and thereby satisfy user demands for greater involvement. Other questions, to those users who reported *direct* contact with the personnel of the computing unit in their cities, suggest that the quality of interactions is often unsatisfactory. More than one-third (37%) of the users indicate that use of technical language by the computer staff is confusing. And 36 percent observe that the computer staff are more interested in the computer's capabilities than in solving user department problems. Moreover, 37 percent of the users agree that the computer staff are more interested in working on new automated applications than in making improvements in existing ones. While less than a majority of the users agree with any of these observations, a majority (53 percent) do agree with one or another of them. And most importantly, agreement with any of these statements, particularly either of the latter two, is quite explicit criticism of the behavior of computer personnel, and seems a clear indicator of shortcomings in the relationship between technical experts and the users of computer services (Danziger 1979a; 1979c). When these shortcomings are brought up (and our fieldwork suggests that they are increasingly voiced), pressure is increased on the computer staff for real attention to users' interests.

Cumulatively, the many small decisions about data requirements and sources, procedures for the processing of data, the format of data outputs, and the like, can determine which groups are served by an automated application or system, and how effectively the information-processing needs of different groups are served. The data in this section indicate that the skilled staff of the computer unit substantially influence decisions regarding these more technical aspects of computer services; but the data also reveal that users can and do participate in the many operational decisions related to the computer package.

This qualified conclusion is not unexpected. The computer elite do sometimes parlay their central position and technical knowledge and skills into dominance over the users of their services. Indeed, even the decisions that have significant nontechnical components are sometimes reformulated by the computer staff into issues appearing to be primarily technical, thus making users feel incompetent. But there is substantial participation by users in various operational decisions and activities related to the users' domains of interests. And the evidence broadly demonstrates that while the computer elite might seek to control operational decision domains by using expertise, users also seek to influence these decisions. Where the involvement of users is considerable and effective, their interests are likely to be internalized by the technical elite. However, where user involvement is limited or merely symbolic, the computer elite are likely to control operational decisions by using expertise "to maintain either the fiction of uncertainty or to steer the organization into areas where uncertainty will be in [their] hands" (Perrow 1972:67).

Planning and Management Decisions

While those with expert knowledge might sometimes prevail over the relatively technical issues regarding the provision of computer services, several of the explanatory approaches predict that the regulators and/or the big users will have a powerful role in the more critical decisions regarding computer development and utilization. There are broad policy issues involved when decisions are made regarding such concerns as the acquisition of a new computer mainframe, the organizational location of the data-processing installation, the priorities for developing new automated systems, and the evaluation of computer services.

The manager of the data-processing installation has a quite comprehensive view of the role various participants play in management decisions regarding the computer package, and table 4.6 reports their assessments of the relative influence of key actors who might participate in six major decisions involving planning/management of the technology. In analyzing these responses, it should be noted that on four of the decisions the managers were asked to specify all actors who had some statutory responsibility or major involvement (A, B, C, and E), and on two of the decisions they were asked to specify only the one most influential role (D and F). Neither type of question lends itself to precise distinctions, but the overall pattern of responses does provide considerable insight into the relative influence of different participants.

The data indicate that the major regulators—chief executive officials and the legislature—are most active in those areas where general decisions about resource allocation or administrative organization are involved (A, B, C). This may reflect their concern for broad management issues, or it may merely record their *pro forma* action in areas where they have

Table 4.6 Data-Processing Managers' Perceptions of Control Over Decisions

Decision	Managers Indicating (%):							
	Chief executive official	Data processing	Dept. head over data processing	User dept.	Local legislature	Inter-dept. board	Inter-governmental board	Other
A. "Must approve budget requests for new computer mainframes and systems."[a]	33%	78%	NA	73%	15%	32%	NA	NA
B. "Must approve requests for new peripheral equipment in user departments."[a]	57	65	48%	41	52	10	7	9
C. "Must approve major reorganizations such as changing the departmental status or location of EDP, or consolidating several independent EDP units."[a]	69	44	46	6	53	9	9	7
D. "Is primarily responsible for evaluating services provided by this (data processing) installation."[b]	12	30	23	21	3	7	4	2
E. "Provides a major input into whether or not a new set of EDP applications will be adopted."[a]	33	78	NA	73	15	32	NA	NA
F. "Has authority for setting priorities for the development of new applications."[b]	18	25	26	3	3	15	5	5

NOTES: $N = 475$. NA = Not ascertained.

[a]Respondents indicated all categories which apply; therefore, the percentages across will add to more than 100%.

[b]Respondents were asked to indicate the one best answer.

statutory responsibility. Our field research supports the latter view. It is particularly evident that the elected council rarely takes an active and important role. And while some managers, CAOs, or other chief executives do attempt to play a significant role in decisions, they tend to focus most of their attention on questions about major equipment acquisitions. The limited influence attributed by data-processing managers to top executives in the key areas of applications development and priorities and of service evaluation (D, E, F) is indicative of the perfunctory attention that many top managers give to the less concrete and tangible, but possibly more critical, development decisions regarding the actual application of the computer package. And in nearly all cases the local legislature is substantially less influential in these other decisions than are the chief executives. The data-processing managers also report that intergovernmental boards, typically composed of regulators from several local governments that share computing resources, are seldom a significant force in decisions regarding the local computer package. Thus the data suggest that in most governments the regulators neither regulate nor manage the computer package in any major sense.

However, there is an important theoretical argument suggesting a different interpretation. Bachrach and Baratz (1963) note that when decision processes by subordinates are functioning satisfactorily, higher-level policy makers frequently choose not to intervene. These apparent "nondecisions" are nonetheless significant. Nondecisions by the regulators could result from general satisfaction with the quality of data-processing services provided by the computer unit. There is some support for this interpretation in the fact that fully 55 percent of the chief executives and council in the 42 cities rate their data-processing services as good or excellent. Moreover, our field research indicates that the regulators' influence operates, as often as not, through a few critical decisions, such as removal of the data-processing manager, relocation of the data-processing unit, or replacement of the in-house computer staff by a private firm that manages the government's computer facilities. Such decisions, which usually result from severe dissatisfaction with data-processing services, make the latent decision power of the regulators manifest and serve notice to the providers about the regulator's expectations. Such periodic decisions can be powerful indirect influences on the behaviors and activities of the computer elite.

In contrast to regulators' indirect influence, the users of computer services, particularly the big users, exercise direct impact on critical decisions about the adoption of automated applications. Studies of technological innovation identify local government departments as frequent sources of initiative for innovations (Danziger & Dutton 1977b; Feller & Menzel 1976; Perry & Kraemer 1979; Yin et al. 1976). Moreover, user departments must at least consent to innovations that affect their operations, even if the initiative stems from elsewhere. And the successful routinization of an automated information system can require, more than many other technological innovations, acquiescence and even enthusiastic commitment from department users, since they could sabotage its effective use. The user departments also are attributed approval rights on the acquisition of peripheral computer equipment in about two-fifths of the governments, and primary responsibility for evaluating computer services in about one-fifth of the governments. And user departments, through their participation on policy boards, probably influence the crucial area of setting development priorities. The role of user departments is quite limited in most of the areas where regulators are active (e.g., budget requests and reorganization of computer installations). Thus, individual user departments are attributed great influence on major decisions in those areas where their stake is most direct and immediate—specifically, in adoption of new automated applications, approval of new peripheral equipment, and, possibly, setting priorities on new applications.

It is quite clear from table 4.6 that data-processing managers attribute the most pervasive influence on critical control decisions to the providers of data-processing services. The data-processing installation or its department head (usually the computer installation managers, but sometimes the finance department head, when the installation is located in that department) is most often a source of major input on decisions regarding the adoption of automated applications, has authority for setting priorities on the development of new applications in the majority of governments, and has primary responsibility for evaluating the installation's computing services in the majority of cases. Moreover, the providers are attributed nearly the same level of involvement and influence as are the regulators on issues regarding requests for peripheral equipment and budget requests. Only on decisions about reorganization of computing installations are the providers notably less significant than the regulators.

It is often advocated that an interdepartmental board of regulators, users, and providers make the critical control decisions regarding the computer package. Such a board, it is contended, will combine the perspectives of the most important management elements with those of the users, and take into account the technical advice of the computer elite. Table 4.6 reveals the data-processing managers' assessments of the impact of such boards on key decisions. Only in the area of applications development and priorities are the policy boards attributed significant influence. They have major influence on the adoption of automated applications in about one-third of the governments, and primary authority for setting application priorities in only 15 percent of the governments.

It seems useful to explore in more detail the role of the computer policy board to illuminate various issues about the control of the computer package. As noted above, such a board could serve as a representative structure through which policy could be determined regarding the development and operations of computer services. In fact, it could serve the agendas of *any* of the within-government participants discussed in this chapter. As a management and planning unit, it seems particularly well-suited to address the needs of the regulators. It could ensure that the computer package is directed to serve organizational objectives, that there is a rationalized allocation of computer resources, and that the computer elite is held accountable for its performance. The users of computing services might view the policy board as a forum within which their demands for resources would be met, in accordance with their legitimate needs and their political influence. And the computer elite might see it as a means to buffer the demands from the multiple and often competing user groups, to co-opt both regulators and users into a structure supporting the maintenance and development of computing, and to reduce the uncertainty regarding the stability of computer development plans over an extended period.

Only 40 percent of the local governments indicate that they even have a policy board, or an interdepartmental committee that recommends policies relating to computers and data processing (table 4.7). And of those that do have such boards, only 60 percent meet on a regular basis. Thus less than one-fourth of the governments have clearly constituted computer policy boards. This percentage rises to approximately one-half, 69 percent of which meet on a regular basis, among the local governments that have automated an above-average number of functions.[3] Thus, about one-third (34%) of the governments that might be expected to utilize policy boards have institutionalized them.

Those who tend to be best served by existing computing services—departments that are big users and the chief executive's office, and, not surprisingly, the data-processing unit itself—are represented on most policy boards. Departments that are small users or nonusers of computer services, the local legislative body, the citizens, are represented on few such boards (table 4.8). And the primary functions of computer policy boards are to recommend priorities on new developments and to represent top officials on questions of computer procurement, new developments, and user satisfaction with data processing (table 4.9). Consideration of issues regarding access to data or confidentiality of information are reported in less than one-third of the boards. About the same proportion of the boards is active in recommending operational priorities for computer use, and very few provide "technical guidance" to the data-processing manager.

Table 4.7   Use of Data-Processing Boards

Question[a]	No	Yes	(N)
"Is there now a board or committee which recommends policies relating to computers and data processing for your government?"			
All local governments	60%	40%	(562)
Local governments with more extensive and higher automation[b]	51	49	(178)

	No, only "on call"	Yes, on a regular basis	Both regular meetings and "on call"	(N)
"Does this (policy) board meet on a regular basis?"				
All local governments	40%	36%	33%	(223)
Local governments with more extensive and higher automation[b]	31	36	33	(88)

[a]Asked of chief executives.
[b]See note 3 for definitions.

Table 4.8   Officials Represented on Policy Boards

	Membership (%)	
Official	Yes	No
A. Chief executive's office	79%	21%
B. Data-processing department(s)	72	28
C. Departments which are major users of data-processing services	70	30
D. Legislative body, council	38	62
E. Departments which are minor users of data-processing services	22	78
F. Departments not now using data-processing services	18	82
G. Citizens	14	86

NOTE: Only executives of cities and counties with policy boards were asked: "For each group or unit below, indicate whether or not they are represented on this policy board" (N = 233 governments).

It is difficult to demonstrate on the basis of these data that computer policy boards are the tool of any particular participant or interest. At most, only one-third of the local governments most active in computing even have institutionalized policy boards, and their character may vary from government to government. Where they do exist, the boards' focus is

Table 4.9   Functions of Policy Boards and Committees

Functions	Yes	No
A. Recommend priorities for new developments	66%	14%
B. Represent top officials on questions of computer procurement, new developments, and user satisfaction with data processing	75	25
C. Recommend priorities for day-to-day operations	34	66
D. Act on requests for access to data	32	68
E. Develop guidelines for protecting confidentiality and public	30	70
F. Technical guidance to data-processing manager	19	81

NOTE: The following question was asked of chief executives only in cities and counties with a policy board: "What are the functions of this policy board?" (N = 233 governments).

usually upon issues of applications development, equipment procurement, and user satisfaction with data processing. The most powerful regulators and users (including the chief executive's office as user) are represented along with the computer elite, but the computer elite frequently plays a singularly important role in shaping the issues addressed by the policy board, and in providing the information relevant to assessing these issues.

Although the computer elite might set the framework for discussion and decision, representation on the board also ensures that the concerns of big users will be considered. Indeed, as long as the powerful users of computing services are well served, the computer policy board is not likely to be receptive to major alterations in the organization or the relative distribution of computer services. Most tend to be biased toward expansion of computer services, primarily to the big users. They are concerned with appropriate resource allocation, but do not usually ask critical questions about slowing the growth rate of the computer operation; indeed, they usually advocate continuous expansion. Although the computer elite can manipulate the board's agenda and information considerably, it cannot determine the decisions reached on most boards. The board members represent powerful units within the government, and they set the constraints (that is, what functions and areas will be developed, in what priority) for the expansion of computing. The members do grant the data-processing manager considerable discretion, enabling the computer elite to plan for equipment, staff, and other needs regarding the computer package; they provide some short-run certainty about the computer elite's organizational environment; and they grant the computer elite relative autonomy over certain aspects of internal operations.

ASSESSING OVERALL CONTROL

Our analysis of control over the computing package by policy boards corresponds to our broader conclusions in this chapter. We have identified the potential and actual participants in decisions regarding the resources in the local government computing package, and have specified levels of involvement and influence. Let us now see which, if any, of the four explanatory perspectives seems to characterize the configuration of influence over the computing package most accurately.

It seems that we can dismiss the managerial rationalism approach. There is very little evidence that top managers with organization-wide concerns (termed "regulators" in this chapter) dominate the decision processes. Their involvement in the more operational and technical decisions is similar to that of many users of computing services, and their direct involvement in the broad, critical decisions that are their fundamental domain is less than would be expected according to managerial rationalism. They are clearly less active and influential than the computer elite in such crucial areas as priority setting for new applications, and they are less responsible than users for evaluating the performance of the data-processing unit. Top managers seem to focus their attention on major equipment decisions. While these decisions do affect the computer package, they seem to be less critical to its overall impact on government operations than are the decisions about applications development and technique—areas where there is little evidence of managerial rationalism.

Yet managerial influence cannot be dismissed altogether. Top managers' behavior might reflect a decision not to interfere with computing activities, leaving these domains to subordinates (e.g., the user departments and computer staff), as long as computing services are satisfactory. These managers can and do intervene when there is severe dissatisfaction with data processing and when they do, they exercise their latent power and serve notice about their expectations. These occasional decisions probably have a powerful influence on the behavior and activities of the computer elite and on the other participants in computing decisions.

There seems considerable support for the dominance of a technocratic elite. The technical complexity of the computer package, the relative monopoly on expertise of the computer personnel, and the stakes of these personnel in controlling their domain all would lead to this dominance—in fact their influence may be overriding on the most technical issues and on those that they can successfully pose as ones driven by technical criteria. Many users also report a quite technocratic bent among the computer elite, and an asymetric control relationship may exist in the user-technician interface.

However, there does not appear to be a unified technocratic elite; rather there are several elites with independent domains and fragmented constituencies. The information elite operate in an information-use domain, at the service of the government's top managers as well as their own bureaucratic interests. When members of the computer elite are dispersed to the user departments, they participate in operational decision processes but must take the service of those departments into account. Only the computer elite in the central data-processing unit tend to act from a unified technocratic perspective.

There is considerable evidence that the control of the data-processing unit is tempered and limited by other participants. There is a surprisingly high level of user involvement, even in such relatively technical areas as the design of automated applications. Such widespread participation by department staff and top management representatives inevitably draws the computer staff into negotiations and bargaining. More importantly, while the computer elite may have the major role in setting the agenda and the framework for consideration of the "big" decisions about computer development and operations, the regulators and the major users of computing services also have sufficient power to counteract that influence. Particularly in those governments where there is an active computer policy board, but also in many other governments where regulators and major users are less formally organized in their dealings with the computer elite, the common pattern is for these other participants to set broad constraints on the computer package in such areas as development priorities, delivery of computer services, and organization of the computer units within the government. These constraints result from interactions among those participants with high stakes in computing and those participants with significant general influence within the governmental system (e.g., top managers and their staff). In addition to the computer staff, the most influential participants are primarily regulators and big users; but on certain decisions, even external supporters and suppliers can exert substantial indirect influence. Thus, while the computer staff may be very potent, other participants have significant roles in determining the critical decisions about computing, and the notion of absolute technocratic elitism is not supported.

These observations offer strong support for the perspective of organizational pluralism. It is clear the regulators, users, and technocratic elites are all actively involved with computer package decisions, particularly the broadest ones. Thus the pluralist perspective is clearly supported, in that no one group uniformly dominates all decision processes. There is considerable evidence that although *several* relatively independent elites appear to dominate different decision processes, they are not fully autonomous. First, it is generally the case that operational decisions are strongly influenced by the computer staff. Similarly, that elite can often transform the nature of the decision process on many issues by defining those issues primarily as technical, or by biasing necessary information strongly in favor of its own preferred solution. Moreover, the computer staff can deflect the decisions toward their preferences during the implementation process. However, even operational decision making is shared by the computer staff with department users who have their own computer experts, and sometimes with policy boards composed of powerful users and the information elite. These groups do not always acquiesce in the computer staff's preferences.

Second, it is generally the case that big users tend to be particularly active in decisions about the computer package, to develop "special relationships" with the computer elite, and to be overrepresented on such decision bodies as computer policy boards. The considerable segmentation of power in many local governments, especially the larger ones, is a related factor that enables major departments to use their power and autonomy to effect advantageous (and even quite independent) direction to their computer package. Thus in many governments, the big users tend to enjoy increasing benefits and influence. Even where top managers have become more influential over computing decisions, it is as much because of their increased involvement as big users as because of concern about organization-wide management of the technology. But the interests of big users can be successfully challenged by the small users. Top managers sometimes intervene on behalf of small users when organization-wide interests seem to be subordinated to big-user interests. And the computer elite's interest in constant expansion sometimes coincides with these actions against the big users. This system of organizational pluralism means that in any particular decision the interests of the big users might not dominate.

It is unclear from our analysis whether the reinforcement politics perspective provides a valid general characterization of the nature of control over computing. While the regulators, particularly top managers but also elected officials, could dominate all computing decision processes, they participate in only a few. Instead, they often rely upon their representatives (staff aids, department head over data processing, or the computing unit manager whom they have appointed) as participants, and they appear to be content to let most decisions evolve from the pluralistic interplay of many interests—big users, small users, department heads, staff, and technocratic elites. It seems, however, that direct participation is not the key to influence or control by the regulators. Their influence is indirect but it might be powerful. It stems primarily from occasional decisions that indicate dissatisfaction with data-processing services, and secondarily from the expectations created by these interventions. Consequently, those who do participate in computing decisions may act in the interests of those in power, thereby ensuring that their interests are served without direct participation. If this were the case, the reinforcement politics perspective would be clearly supported. In short, while the pattern of participation regarding the computer package in most governments appears pluralistic, it remains for later chapters to analyze whether the *impacts* of this pattern also support a pluralistic interpretation or, instead, reveal that reinforcement politics is the operative driving force in computer decisions.

CHAPTER FIVE

THE BUREAUCRATIC POLITICS OF COMPUTING

William H. Dutton and Kenneth L. Kraemer

BY IDENTIFYING the major participants in computing decisions, we have begun to characterize the bureaucratic politics surrounding the control of computing in local government. We here extend that characterization by tracing the historical evolution of control over computer technology in local government.[1] Such a historical account reveals the dynamic nature of the politics of computing, and shows how the relative influence of different actors has changed rather dramatically since the time computing was first introduced.

A historical account also highlights the important roles that structural arrangements have played in reinforcing the influence of dominant organizational elites. Participants in the politics of computing have used structural changes such as departmental reorganization, master planning, and contracting as strategies for maintaining and enhancing their control over the computing package and, thereby, their broader organizational interests. And just as the relative influence of different participants has changed, so have structural arrangements. As new participants gain control of the organization, new structures are developed to ensure that the technology serves their interests. Such a strategic perspective (Karpik 1978) on organizational structures contrasts with the more common rational perspectives on structural arrangements that emphasize organizational efficiency, in contrast to organizational control, as a goal of decision makers. Finally, a historical account provides an explanation of the findings outlined in the previous chapter, by discussing how and why a pluralistic array of participants has become involved in the politics of computing. That is, we attempt to illuminate the motives, stakes, and strategies of the various participants in the politics of computing.

To provide such an account, we must rely far more on our general understanding and knowledge of local government computing than on systematic empirical evidence. And in the interests of clarity and brevity, we discuss the historical evolution of computing as it has tended to occur in most of the larger local governments.[2] As we have seen, there are extensive variations among local governments. Keeping this in mind, it is useful to portray the central tendencies that have characterized the historical evolution of computing.

HISTORICAL STAGES IN THE EVOLUTION OF COMPUTING

There have been four distinct stages that have characterized the evolution of the bureaucratic politics of computing in the larger American local governments:[3] 1) introduction and conquest; 2) experimentation and expansion; 3) competition and regulation; and 4) reassessment and consolidation (table 5.1). The following discussion matches these four stages, and their characteristics, to the political relationships that have surrounded computing.

Table 5.1   Computing Development Stages

Computing Development Stages	Description
Introduction and conquest	Initial adoption of computing in larger governments; mainly limited to finance use and controlled by finance
Experimentation and expansion	Early development of computing; few applications extant; resources plentiful; expansion outside finance to utilize resources and to justify more
Competition and regulation	Middle stage of development; applications in many departments; high demand; limited resources to satisfy demand; regulation needed to sort out demands
Reassessment and consolidation	Mature stage of development; executive control of computing; reexamination of application development patterns; emphasis on government-wide priorities

Introduction and Conquest: The Mid-Late 1950s

In the large cities and counties during the 1950s, the chief policy concern was deciding whether to adopt the technology, and if so, how to set up a framework within which computing would operate in the government. How would the computer be used? Would computing be applied broadly in the government? Would it be organized as a support service? Who would control it? Who would manage it? How would it be financed? Who would have access? In the uncertainty that characterized the early days of computerization, most of these issues were reduced to a question of where to locate computing. Other critical issues, such as use and control, were considered secondary, to be decided by whatever department was given responsibility for computing. As it turned out, the question of location was central to the policy question: *whom would computing serve?*

Many departments in the city were already being served by their own electrical accounting machines (EAM), the small, inexpensive, limited-purpose forerunners of the computer (e.g., sorters, collators, and tabulators). These had been decentralized throughout the government in departments with large-volume data-processing operations, such as utility billing, tax billing, general accounting, voter registration, traffic ticket processing, and statistical processing. Since the computer was a general-purpose tool, it could be used for all of these tasks and more. But the computer was expensive and required expensive technicians to operate it. The high costs of early computers dictated that there be only one centralized computer installation in the government, and that it replace the previously decentralized EAM installations in order to be cost-effective.

Because of the expense and the centralizing effect of the computer, decision making about acquisition of the computer and about the location of the computing unit in the government fell to the chief executive. The major impetus for the move to computing, however, usually came from finance department heads, because they were the largest users of EAM equipment and they saw computers as far more flexible than EAM technology for finance operations. These people, aided by equipment vendors, provided the chief executives with their earliest vision of the computer-a glorified accounting machine with its primary potential use for routine printing and calculating tasks, and its primary contribution for replacing the "army of clerks" in city and county hall. Since computing would have to serve other departments, it would be a support service in the government—like finance. These perceptions, supported by the computer's immediate use for utility billing, tax billing, payroll operations, and accounting, led most executives to choose the finance department as the site of the computer.[4]

As might be expected from this decision, first priority for development and use of the technology was given to the finance department. Billing, accounting, and budgeting applications were considered easiest to computerize, were expected to have the greatest payoff, and were most desired by the finance director. Since computing was a support service, it was financed from the general fund as an administrative overhead expense, and provided free to user departments. EAM equipment in the departments was eliminated as soon as the data-processing functions it performed were transferred over to the computer. And the other departmental budgets were decreased to reflect the loss of EAM units while the finance department budget was increased to reflect the gain of the computing unit. By and large, these and other administrative matters about computing were decided by the finance director with the knowledge and consent of the executive's office.

Thus, the very introduction of computing into the government brought shifts in resources from some operating departments to finance, and made those departments dependent upon finance for their data processing, whereas previously they had been independent. Yet, at this stage, it was inconceivable to most departments that there might be broader political consequences from computing. The computer was just a tool, limited to performing or assisting fairly rudimentary tasks in the government. In serving finance first, the computer was merely being used to meet the most obvious need, and to gain the fullest advantage from the equipment. Besides, in serving finance, the computer also was serving all departments. Or was it?

The advent of computing coincided with a push for financial reforms in local government (see Schick 1966), including the executive budget, performance budgeting, the uniform chart of accounts, cost accounting, and most importantly, the establishment of centralized support services (finance, purchasing, personnel, and administration). Computing directly supported both the budgeting/accounting reforms and the move toward centralization. The accounting reforms were easier to accomplish physically because of the computer's capacity for sorting, calculating, and printing information in a variety of formats. The centralization reforms were supported by the computer because it allowed the administrative reformers to meet the departments' claim—that centralization would reduce their operating efficiency through time delays—with the counterclaim that centralized, computerized accounting/finance would provide rapid turnaround for department reports, and instantaneous access to computerized information.

During this early stage, then, computing was used primarily to reinforce the movement toward financial and administrative reform in local governments. The primary beneficiaries of these reforms were finance directors (and, indirectly, chief executives), who gained more information about department expenditures as a result of the reforms. Finance directors, and others who controlled computing, also benefited from having computing under their control. Computing was not only a resource that could be used for improving their own operations, but also one that could be used to influence the activities of other departments if the finance director chose to manipulate the resource. Thus, symbolic and real power accrued to finance directors from their ownership and control of the computing resource.

But the real significance of this first stage was that computing had conquered the local government scene. It had justified itself as a technological innovation in local government. The capability of the technology for rapid computation in large-volume information-processing tasks had proven itself useful enough to justify its continuance. And there were shifts in the distribution of resources during this first stage. Whereas previously data processing had been decentralized, it now was centralized along with the computer and related resources in the finance department. Moreover, power relationships had been set up that had implications for the future. The finance unit had captured the computing resource because finance could best use the technology's computational capability. Therefore future struggles over use of computing resources would be with the finance department. Finance departments gained the power to decide when, at what price, and which others would be given access to computer resources. And finance departments have tended to keep control over computing until recently.[5] In the process, they have also had more computer applications developed and redeveloped than have other departments.[6]

Experimentation and Expansion: The Early-Mid 1960s

By the end of the 1950s, computing was well entrenched in finance departments within the larger local governments; the technological and operational problems of the first decade were under control, and the first applications were implemented. The central issue then became the distribution of expanding computer resources: *how would the benefits of computing be distributed among departments within the government?* As a result of promotion and publicity in professional and popular circles, interest in the use of computing was becoming widespread among all departments. Second-generation computers with larger memories and storage capacities were now available, and many governments upgraded their computer mainframes in order to obtain additional capacity with which to meet growing interest in the application of the technology. Timesharing advances in computer technology also made it possible for some governments to consider decentralizing *access* to computing to the user departments through the use of computer terminals.

This local interest in expansion was matched by federal and state interest and funding support for experimental applications of computing. The federal government in particular stimulated experiments with different computer uses in a wide variety of areas, including routine housekeeping applications in departments other than finance; transportation and land-use data banks; population, land use, and economic models and simulations; and process-control applications for water and electric distribution and traffic signal control (Hearle & Mason 1963; Kraemer 1969, 1971). Only a few governments had such experimental applications, and then usually only one. But collectively these experiments gave the impression that use was extensive, and thereby spurred imitation by other governments. In addition, these experimental applications were widely publicized and frequently reported in professional conferences and magazines before any actual results were available, thereby leading to great expectations from computing, and contributing to a growing desire among department heads and their professional and technical staff to share in the computing bonanza (see, for example, URISA 1963 to 1970).

Although this was a period of computing expansion in local governments, most users still saw computing as a specialized and limited technology with small effects and small stakes. Politically, what was important was that every interested user received some piece of the computing pie. For most departments, this meant their first computer application. Because of lack of knowledge and experience, the departments usually were unable to distinguish between potential applications and currently feasible ones. Although users asked for imitations of popular experiments, they passively accepted what the computing staff provided. This usually was a poor imitation of the idealized, publicized version. User demands were usually easily satisfied by simple stand-alone programs—at least at first.

Each use or application was developed independently. Each had its own model, data, procedures, and report formats. Users in the various departments, or even in the same department, were unaware of and uninterested in one another's activities in computing. Because computing capacity appeared plentiful, decisions about new applications were made without regard to resource limits. Decision making about applications was decentralized by default to the computing unit and the departments. Top management rarely became involved except for its traditional role in deciding on equipment acquisition. Whatever could be negotiated between the computing unit and the departments was justified to higher management. Since top management was not scrutinizing these decisions, this wasn't very difficult.

It was in the interest of both the user departments and finance (the computing unit) to expand their computer applications and their plans for future applications. Departments gained resources from free computing applications, and status from being among the "modern" computer users. Sometimes they even received additional resources, the rationale being that additional expenditures for computing now would curb anticipated large increases in spending by reducing the number of new employees that would otherwise be required as government workload increased. The finance department had another justification for obtaining additional staff, and allies from among the other departments helped convince top management of the need by demanding a greater number of new applications. Since additional computing capacity came only in large blocks, a large, unsatisfied demand was necessary to justify it. Long-range master plans were used to present user demands, implementation schedules, and capacity requirements. This early use of computing master plans was primarily intended to help justify procurement of additional capacity, and to indicate to supportive user departments when their needs would be met. Rarely was it intended to aid serious consideration of whether automation was needed, the order in which development logically should occur, or how the applications might be implemented to constitute a system.

Because computing resources appeared plentiful, there was only infrequent conflict among user departments for computing resources, or between the user departments and the finance department regarding priorities. Political activity centered around the *distribution* of computing resources, and almost every claimant got some share of the computing pie. Resource distribution was characterized by log-rolling. The relative size of each department's share was less important than having a share because this was the first foray into the computing arena for most departments and a small share was all that most could reasonably handle. Each user department had its own interests in automation and was able to pursue them independently, with mutual noninterference.

But the finance department's position was dramatically changed. Once finance had opened the way for other departments to use computing, it also had set up conditions for challenges to, and eventually loss of, its control over computing resources. As computer applications were extended into other areas of government, the department staffs began to see new possibilities and potential benefits in greater computer utilization, and pressed finance for it. Some departments also began to develop an independent computer capability (or at least their own computer analysts and programmers), on the grounds that the finance department was unable to service their demands adequately. Thus, the prospect developed that the finance department might cease to be the sole owner of computing expertise.

Nevertheless, the finance department was still in control.[7] Finance directors had opened the door to other departments in order to create a broad justification for computer use and expansion throughout the government; they closed the door on some departments when allocations were actually made. That is, although additional computing capacity was justified on the basis of government-wide need, its distribution was uneven, and the finance department remained the first and primary beneficiary of the additional capability. For example, time-sharing terminals were used first in the finance department. When the terminals were extended to the other departments, it was usually to enable these departments to prepare data for applications that would extend the finance department's control over revenues and expenditures. Secondarily, they might be used for other departmental purposes.

As the nature of these newer finance applications became apparent, it also became apparent that they led to fundamental changes in existing ways of doing things, with long-term implications for power, jobs, evaluation, and promotion. A new arena for power shifts had been introduced.

Previously, the development of computing in local government was a computer resource issue. Now it also might be an information resource issue—who has access to what information for what purposes, and who controls the access. Thus, a whole new basis by which power shifts might occur was ushered in—information, and control over information.

Those who were close to the new applications, and likely to be in the forefront of their use in a given local government, were excited about the possibilities; others were seriously threatened. Within the finance department, the director and budget staff benefited most directly from the new applications, because of increased control over expenditures, and enhanced capability to estimate cash flows for investment and to present the government's financial standing for bonding purposes. But those whose actions could be more closely monitored felt threatened by computerization. And lower-level, less skilled, and older clerical staff also felt threatened. Some had their jobs eliminated, or had to transfer to similar jobs in other departments, or had to learn new jobs (keypunching, data entry), or were eventually squeezed out of government employment.

Competition and Regulation: The Late 1960s, Early 1970s

By the mid-to-late 1960s, some computing activities were present in nearly every department within the larger local governments, as a result of either the department's own applications or general government applications, such as budget reporting (Kraemer & Howe 1968). Computing tasks grew somewhat more sophisticated, and included storage and retrieval, forecasting, and analysis. These applications brought professionals in the departments and the executive's office into contact with computing, and raised the prospect of a new "information elite" ruling city and county halls. The departments particularly affected by this development were planning, police, finance, the chief executive, and data processing.

Demand for computing was high. The departments seemed to be developing an endless desire for new or modified applications. Now, for the first time, the departments recognized that computing resources were sketchy and limited, and a scramble developed to get access to remaining capacity. Although conflict and competition developed among the departments, it was concealed and indirect. It occurred under the guise of rational decision-making, logical argument, and justifiable "need." Each department tried to establish its claim for a *greater share* in computing, and sought to discount the claims of others. Departments that could demonstrate a clear need (e.g., emergency functions, revenue collections, financial control) formed alliances to support one another's claims and got preference. As yet, few top managers were aware of or involved in the competition.

For development projects, those departments that could create a justification to management for the increased expenditure got top priority. Generally, this meant that the departments that already were powerful in the government also were powerful in the computing resource game. The influx of state and federal moneys to functional departments for various urban programs throughout the 1960s (see Kraemer & King 1978; Kraemer & Perry 1979) changed the balance among departments occasionally, but only temporarily. However, in the late 1960s, the flood of funding from the Law Enforcement Assistance Administration for the "war on crime" gave the clear advantage to police applications, and to a lesser extent to applications for the courts, prosecutor, and other local criminal justice agencies. In the resulting tide of automation, police computing equaled or surpassed finance computing in many governments. In some, it led to the establishment of an independent police or criminal justice computing facility and/or staff (Colton 1972, 1975, 1978).

Since local computing capability was limited, and could be increased only slowly, the rush of police automation displaced many other priorities for computing (Perry & Kraemer 1979). Other departments' projects were delayed, postponed, or abandoned. The significance of this development was that forces outside the local government were introduced for the first time, and they radically changed the rules of the game. Federal and state governments showed that they could be major forces shaping local computing development. Through financial support or mandated reporting requirements, these agencies could, and frequently did, change the basis upon which development and redevelopment priorities were set by the local governments. And of course, they improved the relative power position, in the computing resource game, of the local recipients of federal largesse.

The gap between the "haves" and the "have-nots" in computing began to widen as development became most intensive in the revenue, budgetary, and emergency services. Other services, such as planning, building, public works, libraries, and social welfare received little of the computing resource (Dial et al. 1970). Professionals in these functions recognized the growing gap and their financial inability to play in the same league as the big user departments. By now they also recognized the greater possibilities for computer use in their own areas. Thus, they sought more regulation of the bigger users so there would be some computing capacity left for them.

Pressures created by high demand, departmental competition, and differential preference were reinforced by technical and managerial problems. Computing capacities became overloaded, staff became over-extended, and development project schedules were not met. In efforts to catch up, computing staff took shortcuts in design and programming, which later showed up as operational problems with software and as unmet expectations among users (see, for example, Danziger 1977a; Kraemer & King 1979). User department complaints about computing became wide-spread, increasing the pressures on computing staff.

As the scope and scale of automation and its attendant problems spread, the costs of computing—and *awareness* of the costs—also increased dramatically. Although equipment costs had been decreasing, the costs of the whole computing package had been increasing. Among the elements increasing in cost were computing terminals and other peripherals to support expansion and to deploy computing directly in user departments; software development for the increasingly complex and sophisticated on-line operations;[8] modifications to existing systems wrought by changes from users, the state, and federal agencies; administrative costs internal to data processing for data control, tape library, and backup storage; and administrative costs both within the user departments and between the departments and the computing unit, incurred as a result of dealing with demands and problems.

Although these pressures and trends had been building up for years, the policy issues they generated usually were kept at the department level. Policy was made by a pluralistic process dominated by the large user departments and the computing unit. By the end of the 1960s, however, the problems raised by computing could no longer be contained, and they burst upon the chief executive and the legislative body. The occasion might be the discovery of a dismal system failure or of sharply rising computing costs, vociferous complaints from user-department staff, the need to purchase major new equipment, concerns for data confidentiality, or the burgeoning demands for intergovernmental reporting (see, for example, Anderson 1971; Intergovernmental Task Force on Information Systems 1968; Isaacs 1968; Mendlin 1968).

When this happened, the rules of the game changed once more. Top management stepped in actively for the first time since the establishment of computing and joined the pluralistic competition and conflict over computing resources. From now on, top management would take a major role in setting the regulations, and would no longer merely agree with the computing staff or large user-department recommendations. Top management had acceded to small user demands for regulation of the big users.

As part of the regulation, a wide variety of reforms were instituted, although not all were instituted by all local governments. In some cases, computing was taken out of finance and centralized under the chief executive; in other cases, the finance installation was declared a city-wide resource. Mechanisms were established for priority setting for new development and for current operations. Computing cost records were instituted, and in some cases computing costs were charged back to the user departments. Multidepartment user boards were created to settle disputes among users and the computing department, to determine priorities, and to handle other policy matters. Relationships between users and the computing department were formalized by such devices as feasibility studies, design teams, user testing and acceptance of new systems, formal sign-off on systems, and outside review of the computing unit.

Not all governments instituted all of these reforms, but each usually adopted at least one. Master planning, too, was reintroduced—this time as a means of making hard choices and stabilizing development, rather than merely promoting the expansion of computing. Regardless of all these reforms, when the computing activity was stabilized once again, the chief executives were faced with the hard fact that computing was in the government to stay and that only through commitment to more technology could they get out of the dilemmas created by an expansionistic decade of development.

As the amount of attention executives paid to computing increased, so did their awareness of computing's potential and their desire to have computing serve the executive's needs (see, for example, the symposium on "Managing Data for Decision" 1971). Chief executives generally were satisfied with computing, because their requests for information usually were rare and easily fulfilled. But they also regularly received a considerable amount of computer-based information without requesting it, in the form of financial, operational, personnel, or other reports from the departments. And, as the executives' expectations about computing grew, they became aware of the fact that the computing unit was able to satisfy only their *simplest* requests for information. The primary reason was that with the exception of financial systems, the automated systems in the government had been organized to meet functional/departmental needs for information, rather than city-wide or top-management needs. Since management demands for information were so varied and unpredictable, there seemed to be no easy way to accommodate them in advance through specially designed applications.

The political relationships of this period were characterized by subsurface conflict among competing department interests. There was a highly pluralistic power structure; departments jockeyed for position and coalitions shifted as interests shifted from development priorities, to operations priorities, to user charges for data processing. Policy committees (often dominated by the biggest users) were formed to legislate compromise, to determine who would be indulged and who deprived, and to assure equal treatment in access to computing, user charges, development priorities, and so forth.

The resulting regulations and structures turned out to be very costly in time and money for everyone. Regulation also expanded the computing alternatives for some users and reduced them for others. For example, charging for computing services put computing beyond the reach of many small departments. Other groups, such as planners and analysts in top management, benefited, since they could obtain more computing at lower rates during nonpeak hours. Peak-hour users found their costs increasing, and reevaluated whether all their applications needed to be on-line. All departments found that they must pay for the costs of on-line financial systems that served finance and top management more than they did the individual departments. The competition among departments, and the problems with the computing unit, meant that the departments must develop their own staff capability in order to know what to expect from computers and how to get it from the computing department. The chief executive found a similar need, mainly to deal with the problems created by computing, but also to deal with the issue of satisfying top management information needs.

The threatened takeover of city and county hall by an "information elite" didn't materialize. Urban and regional planners could have become such an information elite—they were a highly trained group of specialists, with a deep philosophical commitment to achieving greater rationality in government decision making, and a voracious appetite for information as the key to achieving that rationality; they felt that if enough information could be collected and analyzed, objective choices would be clear. Their professional emphasis on rationality was, in part, a response to the highly political environment in which planners operate, and to their weakness as a political group. In their naive belief in the power of information per se, and in their enthusiasm for models, analysis, and exotic computing, the planners frequently took on overly ambitious projects, many of which failed to produce the results promised, produced only partial results, or produced them too late—after decision and action had been taken by managers or policy makers. Thus, the planners discredited their efforts, their analyses, and themselves (Brewer 1974; Greenberger, Crenson, & Crissey 1976; Kraemer, forthcoming; Lee 1973; Pack & Pack 1977).

In addition, the takeover by an information elite failed to materialize because the technology couldn't easily support the needs of the planners and other potential information elites. In their attempts to use computer technology, the planners found their efforts confounded by their in-experience with it, by the struggle involved in getting the necessary computing resources in the face of competing demands from more powerful departments, and by the inability of the computer specialists (a technical elite distinguishable from the information elite) to harness the technology effectively for the planners' use, given the rapid change characterizing computer technology and its application. These struggles involved costs and demands that neither the planners nor anyone else had anticipated, and contributed to the failure of the planners' projects. As it turned out, the experience of the planners with computing was being repeated not only with other potential information elites, but also with the operating departments. Computer applications that were purported to be straightforward were not: they generated spiraling costs, delays in project completion time, and unanticipated demands for new data collection. In fact, data-processing departments generated so many unanticipated demands that it truly appeared that the computing specialists were out of control, or at least uncontrolled. As noted earlier, these circumstances brought the power of the chief executive into the computing fray, rather than giving rise to a technological (computing or information) elite.

Reassessment and Consolidation: The Mid-1970s to Early 1980s

The current era of computing might best be characterized as one concerned with the *redistribution* of computing resources. How this will come about is unclear, for local governments are now formulating their responses to two broad developments. The first is technological, the second political.

By the early 1970s, computing was once again being controlled. It had to be, because the costs and performance of computing had become political issues in the bureaucratic politics of local governments. Now top management appeared to be in the process of taking charge. Computing had been moved out of the finance department, into an independent department under the chief executive. The expansionist tendency of the computing department was slowed by user committees with wide representation. Executives began to express some impatience about the failure of computing to provide management information (i.e., organization-wide and comparative information—Danziger 1977a).

In the early 1970s, several technological developments were brought to the market that held high promise for chief executives, on the one hand, and for user departments on the other. The first development was a concept of information management and the associated technology of data-base management software, data dictionary, data administrator, and, of course, larger computer mainframes and mass-storage devices to support these procedural advances. These technological developments seemed to promise chief executives the opportunity to get most of the data they might need for managing the government and for evaluating conditions and needs in the community. They further seemed to suggest that the government might be managed as an integrated whole, rather than as a series of departmental baronies.

The second development, that of minicomputers, trailed behind data-base management and was swamped by it in the larger local governments.[9] But the advent of minicomputers raised, for the first time, the possibility of each user department gaining complete control over its computing by having its own computer and computing staff. The cost of the technology was low and the number of required operators few; only the availability of application programs seemed an obstacle.

These two technological developments have inherent in them the prospect of further centralizing, or of decentralizing, computing in local governments—in effect, of reinforcing, or of fundamentally restructuring, existing arrangements. The information management concept fits well with top management's interests; with departments and groups that are primarily data users rather than data providers; and with the interests of the data-processing department, because it offers justification for doubling computing capacity, thereby offering the possibility of relieving the current computing congestion. Hence, many governments may decide to go the integrated data-base route, and begin to organize for the change.

Department participants seem to be organizing along "class" lines in the debate about integrated data bases. The "computing have-nots" have joined the "data have-nots," top management, and the computing department in favor of integrated systems that would consolidate all data in the government and give everyone equal access to that data. But data providers, who also are major computer users, are concerned about the loss of control over their data, the additional costs they might have to bear in order to collect data for others' information needs, and the misuse of data through lack of understanding or lack of sensitivity. City versus departmental ownership of data, and privacy protection and the need for secrecy versus open access, become issues in the ensuing debates.

In practical terms, an integrated data base means that all data in the government's automated systems, plus all data defined as needed for planning and management, are to be 1) identified; 2) conceived of as though they were in one or more physical data bases; 3) organized conceptually to facilitate interrelation and multiple use; and then 4) located in one or more physical data bases to optimize the anticipated, and some unanticipated, uses. Data are to be separated from the processes and organizations that provide them. Data are conceived in terms of their current and potential *uses* as information for satisfying operational, planning, and management needs, and are organized to facilitate those uses. Specific uses are then embedded in computer programs that can retrieve, organize, process, and report data for a particular use (Kraemer et al. 1974).

Several features of integrated systems are significantly different from the previous independent systems. First, in the past those who performed data collection owned, and decided who could gain access to, the data. With integrated systems, all nonconfidential data could be available to any authorized user. This meant that competing departments, top management, and others in the government could explore the department's operations and use the department's own data against it (see chapters 6 and 7). Thus a strategic advantage might accrue to those departments that were data users but not data providers. Since these data users tend to be groups serving top management, many data-providing departments are potentially threatened.

Second, in the past the data user was also the data provider and bore the full costs of data generation and maintenance. With integrated systems, data users might bear none of the costs for providing the data currently collected. And the data providers might have to bear additional, uncompensated costs for collecting new information defined by some data user as needed. Thus, the data user's resources could be increased at the provider's expense. Third, in the past all data handling was organized around the provider's use, and in such ways as to optimize the provider's operations. But with integrated systems, data and data handling are organized around the requirements of government-wide information management. This may mean that the provider will have to face higher costs of operation and lower operational efficiency, and that the provider's own data needs will be compromised. Moreover, data-providers become legitimately concerned about the "publicness" of their data.

With the advent of integrated systems, it seems that, for the first time, computing's impact on information flows in the government could be substantial, giving a special advantage to those who know how to use data, rather than to those who simply own data. Integrated data bases and their associated technology seem to be solving the data-generation problem and creating potential for the "information-rich" world forecast by Simon (1973) and others. The prospect that an information elite could gain increased power, that various kinds of power shifts could occur, appears increasingly realistic. But even currently, such impacts are extremely subtle, difficult to discern, and far less dramatic and widespread than early predictions suggested (chapter 7).

POLITICAL REASSESSMENT

Political developments of the 1970s are likely to influence the evolution of computing as much as, if not more than, technological developments. Most of these political developments arise from the growing fiscal crisis faced by local governments. In the past, computing often was viewed as a tool for improving efficiency and economy. While this is still a major claim of data-processing professionals, it is being questioned, mainly by elected officials. In part, these questions arise because the size and fiscal responsibilities of local governments have continued to escalate rapidly despite the greater use of computing. Moreover, some critics cite computing as a contributor to the fiscal crisis, as the costs of computing personnel and software continue to escalate, and the expected savings from computing are not evident. In short, the failure of computing to achieve clear and widespread cost savings creates a great deal of uncertainty over its future development in an era of increasing public concern over the growth and expense of local government. As elected officials search for mechanisms to decrease the size and expenditures of local governments without eliminating services, computing budgets might be reduced.

Such cost concerns could reverse the current trend toward advanced technology. And potentially, more far-reaching cost concerns could cause many local governments to reconsider the wisdom of in-house operations as the method for procurement of computing services.[10] Local governments currently show increased interest in various modes of sharing computer facilities, and in private computer services—facilities management organizations, service bureaus, and nonprofit corporations.[11] The significance of this development is that each arrangement has implications for both the demands that the government can place on computing services, and the demands that these services place on the government.

In all of these outside arrangements, the local government has only general control over the data-processing services it receives. And, by the same token, the outside data-processing service provider is not in the same relation to the government as an in-house computing arrangement, in terms of dependence and responsiveness. When a government contracts for a share of another government's computer installation, its use of the installation frequently will take a back seat to the other's local demands for computer services; more complex sharing arrangements among multiple governments only increase the problems of gaining priority access, and add others as well (e.g., standardization, governance). While private service providers are somewhat more responsive to the individual government's demands, such private providers also must balance multiple service commitments. And if any single service bureau takes over the whole of the government's information system, a serious dependency situation can develop, since withdrawal of the bureau's cooperation could produce chaos.[12] More important, the government will have lost its own capability to deal with computing problems and issues.

Historically, it was not surprising that most local governments, responding to various real and symbolic imperatives, developed in-house capabilities for at least their basic computing service needs. This tendency was facilitated by the decreasing cost and greater flexibility of hardware, and by the availability of skilled staff and generalized software (see chapter 2).

However, the changing political climate of local governments may reverse this long-term trend toward in-house computing. The costs of computing personnel and software are increasing, the availability of skilled staff is decreasing, and the political dividends of reducing costs are now great. Thus, the use of private computing services is viewed more favorably.

Given these technological and political developments, the potential for power shifts during this fourth stage is both different and greater than in previous stages. In the first stage such shifts were limited. Computing development mainly involved introducing the technology into the government, setting up the rules of the game, and determining the major constituency. Few local officials perceived that computing might be a power resource over which there might be competition. The second stage was a resource-rich period, during which computing was introduced to the operating departments, the departments recognized its potential, and, consequently, competition for the resource was born. Now that there was more than one interested computing user, there was the potential for power shifts resulting from differential access to computing resources. By the third stage—competition and regulation—these power shifts had materialized, with the advantage going to the already powerful departments in the government. But many departments had become true believers in the technology—so much so that pluralistic competition and conflict erupted among them, and computing had to be regulated. Chief executives stepped in and became not only regulators but interested users of the technology. The addition of chief executives to the participants introduced the government hierarchy into the computing and information resources game. Although chief executives were latecomers to the computing scene, when they did enter influence shifted to them and their management and planning analysts almost automatically because of their formal position and authority within the government.

This shift set the scene for the fourth stage of computing development. Increasingly, computing and information are viewed by top management as "organization-wide" resources (Kling 1978b). And departmental perspectives about cost, ownership, control, access, and use of information are judged from top management's viewpoint. Now, providers of information resources, as well as providers of computing resources, try to protect their ownership and control, whereas most data users try to separate data collection from data ownership, control, and use, opting for "free" information resources to all. Moreover, the *use* of information now becomes paramount. Those who are able to use information stand to gain over those who are not, staff groups that are already influential stand to gain over the less influential, and those in top hierarchical positions stand to gain over those in lower positions. In short, power potentially shifts as a result of information, and the dominant, though not the only, pattern of power shifts is toward reinforcement of existing patterns of power and influence within the government (Kraemer & Dutton 1979; see also chapter 7). Now the stage is finally set for the kinds of impacts Downs (1967) predicted would result from the information in urban data systems.

PERSPECTIVES ON THE POLITICAL CONSEQUENCES OF COMPUTING

Looking at the development of computing in the larger local governments over nearly three decades, we may make three major conclusions. 1. Due to the political context of computing innovation, the primary beneficiaries of computing have been those who own and control the technology. 2. Political activity has been characterized more by "resource" politics than by "information" politics. 3. The political consequences have been dynamic rather than static, with perceptible differences in power allocation between stages.

The Political Context and Beneficiaries

To date, computing has been used by politicians, executives, and federal and state agencies to reinforce political reforms, or to supplant them. Computing is a political instrument rather than simply a neutral tool. Not only does computing have political consequences, but it is deliberately used precisely to achieve such consequences. And these consequences do stem largely from the way it is used, the way it is introduced.[13] This can be illustrated by several examples. Computing was first introduced into local governments during the 1950s, which were years of financial reform in many of these governments. In some cases, computing was deliberately used to reinforce budgeting and accounting reforms such as PPB systems; in many other cases it was not consciously used for this purpose, but had the same effect. Together, these reforms strengthened the control of centralized finance departments over department budgets and expenditures.

Similarly, computing was promoted in the 1960s for social service information and referral systems which were part of a "services integration" strategy in local governments, promulgated by federal and state health and welfare agencies (Kling 1978a; Quinn 1976). Other elements of the strategy included consolidation of social service units within the government, granting of department status to the consolidated units, government coordination of its activity with private service agencies, and uniform activity reporting systems. The manifest role of information and referral systems in the midst of these reforms was providing a common information base about clients and services, unifying public and private social service agencies, and achieving greater coordination in the handling of social service clients. The latent role was to reinforce several centralizing reforms that gave greater control over public and private social service agencies to local chief executives, and better performance monitoring capability to federal and state agencies.

More specifically, our historical analysis indicates that the predicted rise of a new technological elite did not occur in the experimental stage of the 1960s, and also might not occur in the consolidation stage of the 1970s. For example, professional planners are among the prime candidates for becoming an information elite, but the analysis indicates that although they are involved in a highly politicized activity, they are an extremely weak political group within the government. There have been efforts to bolster their position with data-based arguments using models, simulation, data banks, and social indicators; but professional planners have remained politically weak. In fact, because many of their efforts have been overly ambitious, planners have often been discredited.

The computer specialists have not been very successful in gaining power and influence either. Because of their monopoly on computing expertise, they generally have been able to maintain some autonomy and freedom from outside control (Danziger 1979a; see also chapter 4). Some have so successfully promoted the expansion of computer use that they have obtained the status of independent departments. But computer specialists handled the opportunity to gain regulatory power so ineffectively that the chief executive stepped in. Furthermore, because computer specialists are not themselves users of computer-based information, they have not been able to benefit from the true power shifts of the information politics game. Analysis groups serving high-level officials (top management or departments) appear to have been more successful, but their effectiveness in using data-based arguments appears to be integrally related to the power of their (or their superiors') position in the government, at least as much as to the power of their information and rational argument. From these instances it seems that, given a position of power, data-based arguments may offer symbolic value by adding legitimacy and rationality to decision processes, but they do not in themselves convey power to otherwise weak groups or individuals, especially in highly contested disputes (chapters 6 and 7).

While information analysts and computing specialists per se have benefited relatively little from computing, higher level officials, particularly chief executives, could have benefited from computing throughout all stages of its development in local governments, but have rarely done so. Even when computing uses were primitive and limited to financial applications, they provided the information for somewhat greater management control over budgets and expenditures. Yet most chief executives failed to utilize this advantage. Furthermore, when computing uses expanded to other support services, such as personnel and purchasing, the chief executive's control was potentially extended over the details of department procurement and staffing. And when computing was extended to the departments' operations, the executive could have benefited again, by having direct access to information about department operations that previously had been "filtered" by department and division heads. But chief executives rarely took steps to ensure that such capabilities were present in the applications. The current trend toward consolidation of operational data from all departments provides further potential advantage to chief executives, because the greatly increased capacity of data-management technology permits flexible use of integrated data bases for a wide variety of information searches, analyses, models, and evaluations. Only recently have chief executives begun to recognize the potential of modern data management for serving their information and control needs. And although they are latecomers to computer utilization, they have the advantage of previously automated operations that can serve their interests, and the added advantage of their formal positions.

In addition, several other features have increased the amount, frequency, content, and value of information flows to top executives. These include the desire of lower level officials to share information with the executive as a means of influencing decisions, and the desire of the computing staff to ensure that the executives' information needs are met (Dutton & Kraemer 1978a, 1978b). Consequently, it is likely that benefits of information to chief executives will increase at a greater rate than benefits to local legislatures, department heads, and lower level staff. But there is little evidence that *many* chief executives have achieved greater political benefits to this point. Few are organized to use the vast information-related capabilities available to them; few have the policy-making, political, and analytical staffs to make greater use of this information (see chapter 7).

It seems clear that those who have controlled computing have benefited considerably over those who have not. Control usually has meant "ownership" as well—that departments that owned the computer usually could direct its use to their purposes. Even when use was extended to other departments, ownership usually meant the right to determine how, when, and where extended use would be made. Thus, each extended use could be viewed from the standpoint of its potential benefit to the "owning" department; those uses which might entail benefits for the owners would be supported, whereas the others would be rejected. The benefits to the owners have included additional resources for the computing enterprise, the status and prestige associated with modern technology, the uses actually made of the technology, including new uses not feasible before, and monopoly of computing expertise within the government. Yet the *direct* control and "ownership" of computing is not a necessary condition for shaping the interests served by the technology. As this historical account suggests, and as chapter 7 will show, those who control computing often have used this resource to serve the interests of those who head the organization as a whole. In this way, the controllers have strategically used computing resources to maintain and enhance their organizational positions.

Resource versus Information Politics

The historical development of computing also sheds light on the kinds of political shifts associated with computing. Downs (1967) predicted that the political impacts of computing would result from the "information" contained in computerized systems. Yet our analysis indicates that computing has been primarily characterized by resource politics, and that political impacts have resulted from ownership and control of computing resources. But the analysis also indicates that in the future, computing will be increasingly characterized by information politics.

Most political impacts to date have resulted from ownership and control of the computing resource per se. That is, those who have controlled computing have been able to obtain other resources (staff, space, equipment) needed to apply it, as well as status and prestige. Also, they have garnered a monopoly on expertise in computing; they have been able to justify computing broadly while using it narrowly, for their own purposes; and they have been able to retain control of computing over several decades by serving the agendas of those who control the broader organization.

The current information politics is similar to the politics of computing resources, but it also is significantly different in several regards. When computing was a new resource in the government, it was potentially available to all, and generally without strong prior claims. But the current distribution of information resources in the government represents established claims, resulting from past legal assignments of responsibility, and from past political struggles over functional responsibilities and information needs. The new data-base technology holds the potential for major redistribution of information resources, and therefore for renewal of those struggles. The redistribution of information raises the further possibility that power shifts might result from new uses of information as well as from changes in who controls information resources (Kling 1978b, 1978c). But what kinds of uses, and whose use, of information is facilitated? The major uses of information facilitated by consolidation and redistribution of data are those that cross departmental and neighborhood boundaries. Such uses include, for example, monitoring department operations, evaluating departmental performance, and controlling department expenditures or staff, identifying community-wide problems or needs, evaluating proposed solutions to problems, and assessing the political feasibility of various proposals (Danziger 1979b; Dutton & Kraemer 1978a, 1978b). The prime beneficiaries of these kinds of information uses are top managers, their staffs, and the various planners and analysts who serve them. We may assume that this trend will continue.

DYNAMIC VERSUS STATIC POLITICS

Finally, this history of the development of computing in local politics indicates that the politics of computing is dynamic and changing. These dynamics are important because they illustrate that there is no certainty in power, and that the use of computing shapes its impact considerably. As the rules of the game change and the participants change, the uses change, and therefore the impacts on power also change. The introduction of computing to local government created rules for its use, with the finance department as the prime beneficiary; but the expansion of computing outside finance changed the rules, brought in other participants, and diminished the finance department's control over computing resources.

The use of computing for law enforcement, aided by financial support from federal agencies, dramatically changed local priorities for development and brought police agencies to the forefront of computing power and politics. Given these dynamics, chief executives, department heads, computing managers, and others concerned with computing need to recognize that they cannot base expectations on past experience. They must learn to adapt their expectations to the continually changing power relations generated by computing.

This review also indicates that Downs' (1967) analysis primarily characterizes the latest stage in computing's historical development. Yet each of the three earlier stages had important political consequences. For example, the introduction and conquest stage, while not involving high political controversy, nevertheless was important politically because it defined the relevant constituency of computing, set the institutional framework for the computer unit, and prescribed the rules within which computing evolved over several decades. And when computing issues became explicitly political, the definite advantage was in the hands of its first constituency—the finance department. The rationale for computer use was defined in terms advantageous to finance department uses, the expertise in computing was concentrated in the finance department, and the finance department was in a position to review other departments' uses of computing, both as an agent in control of computing and as an agent for budget and expenditure control in the government.

These structural consequences, and later outcomes of resource politics, have been far more characteristic of computing in local government to date than have power shifts from the information contained in computerized systems. The example of the finance department's historical advantage, and other variations in political stakes and relationships during the four stages, suggest that hypotheses about the information politics of computing might be appropriate to the current stage of computing, but clearly fail to account adequately for the resource politics of earlier stages. Even in the current stage, it is unclear whether the predicted effects will actually occur, because they are extremely subtle and difficult to discern, and frequently are swamped by other political conditions in the environment. And now, resource politics might predominate again as local elected officials turn more toward private computer services, in order to cut costs and thereby gain public support. It seems that computing can serve a variety of agendas. In fact, its very malleability makes it an important resource in the bureaucratic politics of American local governments.

CHAPTER SIX

COMPUTERS IN THE POLICY PROCESS

James N. Danziger and Rob Kling

INFORMATION AND THE POLICY PROCESS

SINCE World War II, many analysts have become interested in the processes by which the policies of public agencies at all levels of government are developed. The group politics (pluralist) accounts emphasize the way in which public officials establish policy on issues where there are various groups with various special interests, public and private (Dahl 1961; Latham 1964). Such accounts focus on the political relationships among the different participants, and on the institutional constraints within which policy agendas are formulated and developed (Lindblom 1968).

Banfield's (1961) classic case studies of Cook County, Illinois illustrate the predominance of "politics" in the pluralist perspective on local government policy making. For example, his analysis of the attempt by city and county politicians to locate a new public hospital emphasizes the complex relations among, and varied interests of, many institutional and informal groups. Ultimately, Banfield accounts for the hospital decision in terms of the clash of interests among these participants and the way in which they mobilized support among elites and bargained with each other, producing an outcome desired by almost no one. As Lindblom (1968) notes, "At one time or another almost everyone complains about 'politics' in policy-making."

In the last two decades, some analysts have argued that "politics" can be taken out of the policy-making process (Bell 1958). In this view, systems analysis, analytical decision methods based on operations research and statistical inference, and large data bases that can be manipulated by computers are developments that promise major increases in the "rationality" of policy making. Some notable successes of these kinds of techniques, particularly in space and weapons engineering ventures, have added to the excitement.

Some studies argue that modest and carefully specified computerized models are gaining acceptance and having an effect on certain policy processes (Dutton & Kraemer 1979; Pack & Pack 1977). But such techniques may not be well suited to "depoliticize" the policy-making process in public agencies—frequently cited studies indicate that some elaborate models and large data bases have been of little utility to urban policy makers (Brewer 1974; Lee 1973). Such cases suggest that the methods of management science have been tried and found inadequate or impolitic in public agencies where policies are formulated.

Thus, in this chapter we shall examine when and how the information in computerized systems (which will be treated as synonymous with "automated information systems") seems to affect the policy process of local governments. Our fieldwork in the 42 cities indicated that most governments with any automated applications do have some computerized systems that generate policy-relevant data. And in a substantial number of these cities, there are working computerized models and analytical systems. It is clear that in most local governments, there is more and more computer-based information that could be used in making policy.

However, the fact that a computer-based information system exists may not be especially meaningful. More important questions concern *whether* and *how* the policy maker uses such a system. As an illustration, what is the significance of a claim that a city manager has "used" an automated system in deciding whether and where to close fire stations? Did automated information systems help shape the policy agenda? For example, did they help transform a general concern for saving money into a focus on the fire department and, finally, into a review of the utility of many small neighborhood fire stations? Were automated data files primarily helpful in dealing with some aspects of the evaluation of policies rather than others? For example, did data help the city manager more in identifying the costs of operating fire stations than in evaluating the effects of station location on response times to fire calls, or on public trust in the fire department? It is important to determine whether automated systems are more appropriate, and more likely to be used, in some stages of policy making than in others.

In addition to the ways in which automated systems are used by policy-makers, we are also interested in the *impact* of such systems. Do automated information systems alter the process of policy making in any substantial way? Do they alter the kind or quality of policy decisions that are reached? These questions about the *uses* and *impacts* of automated systems in local government policy making will occupy our attention in this chapter and in chapter 7.

Perspectives

Throughout this book we have contrasted four alternative viewpoints as frameworks for studying the ways in which computing and information resources are allocated in public agencies, and the consequences of these resources for the participants. These four perspectives—managerial rationality, technocratic elitism, organizational ("elite") pluralism, and reinforcement politics—were used in chapter 4 to help specify those in the computing milieu who are involved in decisions about the distribution of computing resources. In this chapter, we will use them to help us understand how computerized information fits into, or alters, the process of policy making in local government.

For *managerial rationalists* computerized information serves to increase the rationality of the policy process (Fuller 1970; Simon 1975, 1976). In this view, use of computer technology leads to both qualitative and quantitative improvements in the information environment. First, it is generally assumed that the very availability of, and ease of access to, large amounts of automated information will lead to greater use than would be the case if the information were available only through manual systems. Second, the technology is assumed to liberate policy personnel from their own cognitive limitations, since it facilitates the handling of larger amounts of information at rates of speed and levels of sophistication that far exceed human capacity. And third, automated information is presumed to be less subject to certain major "information pathologies," such as filtering and distortion, since there are fewer human intermediaries between the data and the user of data-based information.

The notion that computerized information will enhance the rationality of the policy process is held by many scholars in "rational" disciplines such as management science, economics, and engineering. Herbert Simon (1975), for example, observes that

> The most important organizational requirement for handling energy policy in an intelligent way is the creation of one or more models— either of an optimizing or a simulation type—to provide coherence to the simulation process. . . . The mere existence of the models, wherever located, cannot but have a major impact on energy policy decisions.

In its most extreme form, the rationalist view claims that information systems can and should dominate the policy process. One of the strongest statements of this view comes from Buckminster Fuller (1970:120), for whom the computerized decision system becomes worldwide:

> You may very appropriately want to ask me how we are going to resolve the ever-acceleratingly dangerous impasse of world-opposed politicians and ideological dogmas. I answer, *it will be resolved by the computer.* Man has ever-increasing confidence in the computer; witness his unconcerned landings as air-transport passengers coming in for a landing in the combined invisibility of fog and night. While no politician or political system can ever afford to yield understandably and enthusiastically to their adversaries and opposers, *all politicians can and will yield enthusiastically to the computer's safe flight-controlling capabilities in bringing all of humanity in for a safe landing.* (emphasis added)

In contrast, the central assumption of *technocratic elitism* is that the technology is *not* controlled by the policy makers. This perspective shares with managerial rationalism a sense of the tremendous potency of automated information systems; but it assumes that the technology is either uncontrolled, or controlled primarily by technocrats. This corresponds to Winner's (1977) notion of "autonomous technology" which was introduced in chapter 1. Minimally, analysts holding this perspective believe that the handling and application of information technology is controlled by a technological elite, composed primarily of the professionals in the computing unit. As characterized in chapter 4, this computer elite is not responsive primarily to the information needs of policy makers. Thus, improvements in the information environment owing to new information-processing technologies are limited, or at least far more incidental than is predicted by analysts holding the rationalist perspective.

From this second perspective, the entire policy process becomes fundamentally dependent upon the characteristics of the computerized information systems—the kinds of data they contain, their mechanisms for comparing alternatives, their techniques for measuring policy impacts, and the orientations of the computer elite and information elite. Those critical of technocratic elitism insist that such use of automated information reinforces the primacy of technological values and of "instrumental reason," even if the technological elite is relatively benign. Thus Weizenbaum (1976:251–257) argues that the mystique of problem-solving by computers, and the reliance on instrumental reason, have converted genuine ethical, moral, and political dilemmas into what appear to be mere technical problems that can be solved by simplistic criteria and by the application of logical calculations. And Winner (1977:237) observes: "One locates the political essence of technology in its total formative impact on all of nature and human culture. . . . Political reality becomes a set of institutions and practices shaped by the domination of technical requirements."

Analysts who adopt either *reinforcement politics* or *organizational pluralism* as their perspective contend that the mere fact that information is produced by an automated system does not make it significantly different from other forms of information utilized in the policy process. As is other information in a political environment, automated information is generated through institutionalized channels, modified through standard operating procedures, and employed selectively to serve the agendas of those who are dominant in the organization. In this view, automated information is merely one resource in the decision struggle which Allison (1971) has termed "bureaucratic politics" (see also Greenberger, Crenson, & Crissey 1976; Laudon 1974). And computer-based data and analyses are often tailored to serve certain political agendas rather than to increase the rationality of the policy process.

However, the pluralist perspective differs from the reinforcement politics perspective in its beliefs about whether *one group* can exploit computerized information systems so successfully that they can usually get their way on the many subtle issues that underlie the policy process—the questions that will appear on the agenda for formal action, the terms in which these questions will be framed, and the kinds of arguments that will be admissible. Technocratic elitist analysts contend that one group often dominates these decisions—technical experts. Reinforcement politics implies that one group in any given government will dominate—those who are already powerful. For example, in small strong-mayor cities, the "controlling coalition" might center around the mayor; but in large cities with strong departments, those departments would tend to dominate the control and use of automated data. In contrast, organizational pluralists would argue that single groups might dominate on specific issues (e.g., tax rate, industrial development, library services), but no one group will dominate on all issues.

Stages of Policy Making

We may distinguish four stages in the policy-making process: 1) a predecision stage—finding and defining the problem; 2) a decision stage—specifying goals, identifying alternatives, gathering relevant information, and selecting preferred policy action; 3) a rationalization stage; and 4) a postdecision stage—implementing and evaluating the action. Clearly, such a stage typology separates continuous and interactive phenomena in a somewhat arbitrary manner; but it seems useful for assessing the instrumental role of computerized information in the policy process (Dutton, Danziger, & Kraemer 1980).

Symbolic, Instrumental, and Conceptual Information

All stages of the policy process are based on information, particularly if one accepts the broad definition, proposed by Claude Shannon, of information as "whatever reduces uncertainty" (Danziger 1979b). By this definition, "organizational intelligence" is protean and extensive. As a consequence, it is virtually impossible to specify with precision the array of information which is used in the policy process or even in a given stage of the policy process. In order to evaluate the roles and possible effects of automated information systems, we must simplify our view of policy making and focus on specific forms of automated information and strategies for its use.

This broad conception of information ensures that some sorts of "information" will be central to virtually every policy-making process. And, in order to make sense of the role of *automated* information, we shall identify domains of behavior during which automated information *might* be (that is, it has the potential to be) a significant component in the policy-maker's considerations. In fact, most actual decision situations in current local governments do not involve extensive use of automated information systems. As we shall suggest below, this is due to many factors, including the inadequacies of current automated systems, the perceived irrelevance of the data to many decisions, and the incapacity or unwillingness of policy makers to utilize automated information under various circumstances.

Several distinctions about the utilization of information in the decision process are noteworthy. One useful distinction is that between "symbolic" and "instrumental" uses of information. Instrumental use occurs when a decision maker such as a city councilman actually bases some decision, at least in part, on the data *content* of a report or presentation. In symbolic use, the decision maker relates his or her decision to the *presence* or *form* of a report or presentation. Social scientists have shown clearly that virtually all social life has symbolic as well as instrumental elements. The implementation of a major public policy program, and even the logo on the government's letterhead, serve *both* symbolic and instrumental purposes. Some analysts suggest that much of political life is primarily symbolic (Edelman 1974), and the symbolic uses of research, whether or not they rely upon automated data analysis, are often readily apparent (Greenberger, Crenson, & Crissey 1976; Knorr 1977).

A related distinction is that between "instrumental" and "conceptual" uses of information. Some analysts observe that even when one has no explicit awareness of the instrumental use of certain information, it could be unconsciously integrated into one's thinking or it could be a factor in structuring one's general understanding of the issue (Caplan, Morrison, & Stambaugh 1975; Lindblom & Cohen 1979; Rich, 1978). For example, Carol Weiss (1980:381) has argued that systematic information tends to "creep" into the decision-making process:

(K)nowledge that derives from systematic research and analysis is not often "utilized" in direct and instrumental fashion in the formulation of policy. Only occasionally does it supply an "answer" that policy actors employ to solve a policy problem. Instead, research knowledge usually affects the development and modification of policy in diffuse ways. It provides a background of empirical generalizations and ideas that *creep* into policy deliberations. (emphasis in original)

The data in automated systems and the kinds of analyses that can be generated from such data tend to affect the local government policy process in this conceptual mode, making it difficult to specify precise use and impact. Nonetheless, we believe that one can gain considerable insight about the integration of automated data into policy making by examining empirical data about patterns of computer use by local government officials. Thus we shall attempt to characterize the instrumental, conceptual, and symbolic uses of automated information in the policy process, sensitive to the subtleties involved.

USE AND IMPACT OF COMPUTERIZED INFORMATION

Two general types of automated data are available for use in the policy process: *urban databanks*, that measure characteristics of the government's environment, and *operational data systems*, that capture information about the internal operations of the government. We shall explore the distinctive uses of each type in chapter 7. In this chapter, we examine the relative validity of the four alternative assessments of the instrumental role of all such automated information in the policy process by examining levels of use and impacts.

We have noted that there are many information sources available to a policy maker and that the policy-making process is highly complex. The social scientist can observe the outward characteristics of this complex process, but it is impossible to determine how the protean array of bits of information is actually used by any policy maker. So, in the attempt to assess the use and impact of any type of information upon policy decisions, it is best to rely on multiple measures—both from the policy makers themselves and from the researcher's assessment of the policy process (Kraemer, Danziger & Dutton 1978). This is the strategy employed here in order to analyze the role of automated information.

Table 6.1 shows how often various policy makers receive computer-based reports. Among chief administrative officials, 50 percent receive basic reports, and 73 percent receive special analyses based on computer data at least a few times per year. Department heads are the most frequent recipients of special reports, with 78 percent receiving special analyses at least a few times per year, although only 31 percent of them receive basic reports this often. In general, most top policy makers do receive some sort of computer-based reports at least a few times per year. However, data in the table do not indicate that top policy makers are being inundated by computer printouts. Rather, most receive basic reports infrequently, and in none of the official categories does a majority receive special analyses as

Table 6.1   Frequency Computer-Based Reports Are Sent to Officials

	Official			
Type of Report	Manager ($N=20$)	Mayor ($N=18$)	Council ($N=69$)	Department head ($N=256$)
Basic				
Monthly or weekly	20%	13%	10%	7%
Several times per year	30	28	24	24
Once per year or less	43	51	63	61
Never	7	8	2	7
Special Analyses				
Monthly or weekly	27	24	15	46
Several times per year	46	42	34	32
Once per year or less	27	34	51	22

often as monthly. In many cases, such automated information is probably reaching these personnel indirectly, in the form of manually prepared summaries from subordinate staff and analysts.

Measures of the quantity of such reports do not indicate their quality. These same officials were asked about the accuracy and objectivity of reports based on automated data banks. Their answers are given in table 6.2. The assessments are complex. On one hand, only 3 percent to 18 percent expressed "little" or "no confidence" in the accuracy and validity of the analyses. On the other hand, between 24 percent and 54 percent felt the analyses were "somewhat" or "quite biased." It is clear that a considerable proportion had reservations about these reports. This may reflect a generalized lack of confidence in dealing with the products of high

Table 6.2   Perceived Accuracy, Validity, and Objectivity of Data Bank Reports

	Percentage of cities in which official(s)	
Official	Have little or no confidence in the accuracy and validity of analysis	View the analyses as somewhat or quite biased
Council and Council Staff ($N=40$)	18%	54%
Mayor and Staff ($N=37$)	11	49
Manager and Staff ($N=30$)	17	24
Planners and Analysts ($N=40$)	3	25

technology, or it may indicate a suspicion that the technological elite was manipulating the data to serve its own agendas. It could also be that the policy makers were correct—that the quality of the basic data was poor (e.g., out-of-date, invalid, inaccurate), that the analyses had been poorly done, or that the data were essentially irrelevant to their purposes.

To what extent does computerized information affect the policy process? In what ways does such information serve various policy makers? Is computerized information used more extensively in certain stages of the policy process? Given the complex and often subtle impacts that such information might have on a particular policy-maker and the diversity of roles and policy domains, we marshal various types of data and observations in the attempt to produce valid generalizations.

We asked policy makers about the use and utility of automated information for various activities. Most of the activities were specified generically, such as "leading to new or clear perceptions of community problems" and "determining the political acceptability of a policy action," and some of the activities were specified substantively, such as use of automated information during the annual budget cycle. Table 6.3 summarizes (at the city-level of analysis) our assessments of the responses

ble 6.3   Uses of Automated Information by Policy Makers

		Level of use by:		
Kind of Use	Level of Use	Manager	Mayor	Council
edecision				
Lead to new or clear	Not used[a]	27%	40%	41%
perceptions of	Exceptional use	63	49	46
community problems[c]	General use	10	11	13
	Mean[b]	.83	.71	.72
cision making				
Policy development[c]	Not used	40%	47%	54%
	Exceptional use	50	50	38
	General use	10	3	8
	Mean	.70	.56	.54
Provide surprising	Not used	57%	72%	67%
results[c]	Exceptional use	43	25	23
	General use	0	3	0
	Mean	.43	.31	.23
Determine political	Not used	76%	78%	77%

Table 6.3 (Continued)

Kind of Use	Level of Use	Level of use by:		
		Manager	Mayor	Council
acceptability of	Exceptional use	17	22	18
actions[c]	General use	7	0	5
	Mean	.34	.22	.28
E. Change or affect	Not used	18%	38%	46%
decisions[d]	Exceptional use	32	34	27
	General use	50	28	27
	Mean	1.32	.90	.81
Rationalization				
F. Document policy	Not used	26%	28%	47%
positions[d]	Exceptional use	30	36	36
	General use	44	36	17
	Mean	1.18	1.08	.70
G. Gain publicity[c]	Not used	40%	47%	54%
	Exceptional use	50	50	38
	General use	10	3	8
	Mean	.70	.56	.54
H. Legitimize existing	Not used	40%	33%	36%
positions[c]	Exceptional use	43	33	51
	General use	17	33	13
	Mean	.77	1.00	.77
Postdecision				
I. Monitor and control	Not used	18%	20%	24%
departments and	Exceptional use	33	63	61
agencies[d]	General use	49	17	15
	Mean	1.31	.97	.91

SOURCE: Adapted from Dutton, Danziger and Kraemer (1980: Table 2). Data are from the 42 cities in Phase II.
[a]Percentage of cities where operational data are automated, but not used, by role-type.
[b]Scored: 0 = not used in this way, 1 = exceptional use, 2 = general use.
[c]Based on the use of urban data banks only.
[d]Based on the use of operational files only.
[e]Based on the use of both urban data banks and operational data files.

of various policy makers during interviews when specific examples were discussed. Table 6.4 reports responses of policy makers (aggregated by role) to questionnaire items. We also conducted interviews about the role of automated information in selected policy domains, particularly fiscal planning and land-use planning. In the remainder of this chapter and in chapter 7 we shall see what conclusions can be drawn from these data and

Table 6.4 Usefulness Attributed to Computer-Based Data

Kind of Use	Level of Usefulness	Mayors (N=18)	Councilors (N=69)	Managers (N=20)	Top Staff (N=68)	Dep't Heads (N=256)	Analysts (N=79)
					Level of Usefulness to:		
Predecision							
A. Identifying city problems	Not at all useful	10%	14%	15%	25%	37%	14%
	Somewhat useful	80	64	75	63	48	49
	Useful	10	13	10	9	12	22
	Very useful	0	9	0	7	7	15
	Mean[a]	1.00	1.16	0.95	0.89	0.81	1.38
Decision							
B. Determining solutions to city problems	Not at all useful	11%	13%	5%	24%	24%	25%
	Somewhat useful	72	56	85	57	55	54
	Useful	17	22	10	12	14	18
	Very useful	0	9	0	7	7	3
	Mean	1.06	1.26	1.05	1.03	1.04	0.99
C. During the annual budget cycle	Not at all useful	0%	9%	0%	9%	6%	13%
	Somewhat useful	24	37	5	31	41	28
	Useful	29	29	45	31	32	33
	Very useful	48	25	50	28	22	27
	Mean	2.24	1.70	2.45	1.78	1.68	1.73
D. Day-to-day expenditure decisions	Not at all useful	22%	21%	5%	22%	20%	18%
	Somewhat useful	22	41	26	46	38	38
	Useful	28	22	42	18	24	22
	Very useful	28	16	26	15	17	22
	Mean	1.61	1.33	1.89	1.25	1.38	1.47

Table 6.4 (Continued)

Kind of Use	Level of Usefulness	Mayors (N = 18)	Councilors (N = 69)	Managers (N = 20)	Top Staff (N = 68)	Dep't Heads (N = 256)	Analysts (N = 79)
					Level of Usefulness to:		
Postdecision							
E. Providing the real costs of programs and activities	No, it does not	20%	27%	16%	24%	32%	42%
	In a few	35	36	47	50	40	23
	For many	40	23	21	20	17	20
	For nearly all	5	14	16	5	11	14
	Mean	1.30	1.23	1.37	1.07	1.06	1.07

[a]Scored: 0 = not at all useful; 1 = somewhat useful; 2 = useful; 3 = very useful.

from our field research. This chapter uses the previously mentioned stages in the decision-making process as a framework for analysis.

Predecision Stage
PROBLEM FINDING

Computerized information systems are at least potentially good at finding problems. A highly automated problem-finding system would require 1) the collection of data that indicate the current and/or future state of an activity amenable to policy intervention; and 2) the specification of criteria that indicate that the current and/or future state is unacceptable. Many local governments collect data that indicate current conditions, but it is uncommon for policy makers to have specified those conditions that would constitute a "problem."

Some governments do have automated systems that identify significantly nontypical conditions through some kind of exception report. But such systems differ in the extent to which aspects of the search for exceptions are automated. For example, most local governments have some automated accounting applications. Typical automated systems periodically report the amount authorized, and the expenditures and encumbrances, for each line-item in the budget. A budget analyst can then examine these line-items to assess whether any are likely to involve substantial overspending or underspending during the remainder of the fiscal year. In the case of overspending, the financial control unit may, given sufficient time, freeze spending on certain activities such as the hiring of new or replacement personnel or the purchase of equipment. Where an account is projected to underspend, there may be action to transfer the funds to another account where additional resources are desired.

Automated accounting systems that have problem-finding capabilities "flag" those budget categories in which there is more than a specified level (e.g., 10 percent) of difference between the authorized and the expended-encumbered figures. The more sophisticated budget-monitoring systems project existing spending patterns forward to the end of the fiscal year, compare this figure with the authorized figure, and thus provide early warning of a nontypical pattern. A few leading-edge automated budget monitoring systems even account for "lumpy" spending patterns by projecting the expenditure through the fiscal year on the basis of spending patterns from prior years (Danziger 1978a; Kraemer, Dutton, & Northrop 1980b). In general, as problem-finding capabilities are increasingly automated, more comprehensive analyses and more timely information can be provided to policy makers.

Most of the problem-finding uses of automated information systems are by means of ad hoc examinations of data rather than by routinized systems of exception reporting. In these cases, the policy maker notices a problem during the examination of a computer-based report or requests a special analysis to identify or document a problem. For example, one city manager requested a printout that rank-ordered the total wages paid to each city employee during the previous quarter. He was surprised to discover that the two employees at the top of the list were police officers. This prompted an examination of police overtime pay policies and led, ultimately, to an alteration in those policies.

Table 6.4 indicates that a large proportion of managers and mayors feel that computerized information is "somewhat useful" in identifying city problems. A larger proportion of analysts and department heads make more extreme assessments, attributing greater usefulness or uselessness to such information. These differing evaluations may be due to the different perspectives of the personnel. Managers and mayors probably consider the full range of problems and find some instances where automated information is useful; but department heads and analysts are more or less positive, depending upon how well the automated information systems in their cities serve their particular functions.

PROBLEM DEFINITION

Problem identification focuses upon the question "Is there a problem?" The problem-definition stage is primarily concerned with the question "What is the nature of the problem?" At a broad level, this involves the development of a perspective within which the problem can be understood and considered. In the above example of the city manager and the wage levels, the discovery that police personnel were receiving such high wages prompted the manager to explore how and why this was occurring. The problem-definition stage involved a discussion between the manager and the police chief, revealing that a few officers were being allowed to obtain extraordinary amounts of overtime work at two to three times their regular wage rate. This information provided the framework within which an alteration of policy could be considered. Table 6.3 indicates that only about one in ten managers, mayors, or council members find that automated information generally leads them to new or clearer perceptions of community problems. More than two in five of the elected policy makers claim that automated information never assists in problem-definition. Only about one-fourth of the top appointed officials offer such a totally negative assessment.

It is especially difficult to determine the extent of the role of automated information in problem definition. We have noted that Rich (1978; 1979) and Weiss (1980), in studying the uses of social-science research by policy makers, argue that most such uses are "conceptual"—that is, providing a broad understanding of the nature of the problem and/or solution—rather than "instrumental"—that is, specifying the dimensions of the problem or its solution. Thus it is possible that automated information does affect the policy maker's conceptualization of the problem, even when the policy maker is not consciously aware of this.

Decision Stage

The heart of the policy process is the decision phase. Once a problem has been identified and defined, effort must center upon deciding whether there is a policy intervention that will alleviate the problem or enhance the achievement of policy goals. The decision phase includes three general activities: 1) designing alternatives—the policy maker must devise one or more potential policy responses appropriate to the policy problem; 2) gathering of intelligence—information on each alternative must be collected to guide the problem-solving process and reduce any uncertainties; and 3) choosing among alternatives—the policy maker must determine which, if any, of the potential responses best deals with the problem, and then must authorize the enactment of this policy response.

Accounts of "rational" policy making treat these stages as sequential. In practice, different processes tend to occur simultaneously and to influence each other in an interactive manner. For example, the rationales that policy makers know will be acceptable often limit the array of policies devised during the design stage. Even when policy makers are faced with a quite limited set of alternatives, these can generate new options, based upon compromises or upon new opportunities that arise at any point before the final decision is to be made. Thus discussions of choice may reopen discussions of design that were supposedly resolved before the intelligence phase. Nevertheless, these three categories denote distinct kinds of activities and these distinctions are useful for understanding the role of automated information in policy formation.

DESIGNING ALTERNATIVES

In some instances, the identification and definition of a problem make the appropriate response obvious. But public policies typically involve tradeoffs, and there usually are alternative responses that are possible. For example, congestion on a roadway could lead to a decision to expand the road, to build additional roads, or to develop an alternative mode of transportation. Or the policy makers might decide to accept the congestion either as a means to deter further development in the area or because the costs of any response would be too high. Thus the design phase typically allows for the specification of *multiple* alternative policy responses.

Usually, the key criteria regarding acceptable alternatives relate to *political* feasibility, and thus only a few policy interventions are realistic options. But automated systems, in the generation of possible alternatives, are usually constrained only by considerations of *technical* feasibility. As a consequence, automated information systems rarely have more than an ancillary role in the specification of policy alternatives. As reflected in table 6.3, computer-based data are credited with general use in policy development by only 10 percent of the managers, 8 percent of councils, and 3 percent of the mayors. It is also noteworthy that less than 10 percent of the policy makers (and none of the mayors) indicate general use of automated information to establish the political acceptability of courses of policy action. Only 10 percent of the managers or mayors indicate that automated information is "useful" in determining solutions to city problems, and not one manager or mayor feels that such information is "very useful" (table 6.4). Similarly, only about one-fifth of the department heads or analysts report that automated information is useful or very useful in the design phase of the policy process. These data clearly support the position that computerized information has only limited utility in the development of alternative solutions to policy problems.

Automated information systems are rarely more significant than the policy makers' experiences and insights. Table 6.5 reveals that for both identifying problems and determining solutions the great majority of policy makers attribute greater importance to personal information and experience than to automated information. In fact, only among administrators do as many as one-third cite automated information as more important than personal information and experience. Interestingly, however, it is possible to turn the conventional wisdom reflected in this table on its head: about one-fourth of the policy makers acknowledge that computer-based

Table 6.5 Personal Observation and Experience Versus Computer-Based Information

Kind of Use	Personal observation and experience is more important than computer-based information:	Opinion of:						
		Mayors (N=20)	Councilors (N = 91)	Managers (N=21)	Top Staff (N=79)	Dept. Heads (N=277)	Upper Level Administrators (N=127)	All (N=620)
In determining solutions to city problems	Never	5%	3%	0%	2%	6%	3%	5%
	In a few cases	20	23	24	16	22	32	23
	In many cases	30	33	48	42	36	32	35
	In nearly all cases	45	41	29	39	36	32	36
	Average Score[a]	2.15	2.11	2.05	2.18	2.02	1.94	2.00
In identifying city problems	Never	0%	2%	0%	1%	4%	3%	3%
	In a few cases	21	24	25	21	20	33	23
	In many cases	53	34	60	36	43	39	40
	In nearly all cases	26	40	15	42	32	25	32
	Average Score	2.05	2.12	1.90	2.18	2.04	1.86	1.97

SOURCE: Adapted from Danziger (1979b: Table 3).

[a]Scored: 0 = never; 1 = in a few cases; 2 = in many cases; 3 = in nearly all cases.

information is sometimes more important than their personal insights in identifying problems and determining policy solutions; and only about one-third indicate that personal insight is nearly always more important than automated information. At least, these responses show that computer-based information is not completely ignored.

PROVIDING INFORMATION REGARDING ALTERNATIVES

Information regarding alternative policy choices could be supplied through computers, and indeed automated information currently tends to have considerable impact in this area. At this point in the process, policy makers have a reasonably clear sense of the kinds of information they may need—information on the characteristics or needs of a population to be served by a policy, on the financial and other costs of providing the policy, on projections of the future effects and implications of the policy, and so on. The data available in urban data banks and in operational data systems are often relevant to these concerns. And because computer systems are capable of performing such information-processing tasks as record-restructuring and sophisticated analytics with relative ease, it is feasible to make many such information requests.

Thus more than four-fifths of the appointed officials and three-fifths of the elected officials indicate that automated information has led to programmatic recommendations (table 6.6). Two-fifths (43 percent) of the appointed officials even acknowledge that such automated information has at least occasionally provided them with surprising results, although most elected officials (72 percent of mayors and 67 percent of councilors) deny that they have been surprised by such data. It is the data in operational data systems that policy makers seem to find most useful and to rely upon most extensively. Fifty percent of the managers indicate that it is generally the case that the automated information in operational data systems has changed or affected policy decisions, and 82 percent of the managers note

Table 6.6   Effects of Automated Information

Have computer-based data and reports led to programmatic recommendations?	Manager/CAO ($N=28$)	Mayor and Staff ($N=34$)	Council and Staff ($N=37$)
No	21.4%	41.2%	40.5%
Yes	79.6	59.8	59.5

that this occurs at least occasionally (table 6.3). Top policy makers—managers, mayors, council—say that automated information has been particularly useful during the annual budgeting cycle and during the ongoing decisions concerning resource allocation (table 6.4).

Clearly, there are limits to the value of the automated information currently available during the decision process. For example, more than three-fourths of managers, department heads, and analysts do not believe that automated information provides useful data about the political feasibility of policy actions (table 6.3). Fundamentally, many policy makers seem to have some ambivalence about the value of the data in their automated systems. On one hand, 88 percent of the chief executives in (560) municipal and county governments agree that "in general, computers provide information which is helpful to me in making decisions." But on the other hand, only 29 percent of these executives agreed with the statement that "much of the data gathered by this government in its daily operations is currently organized to provide useful information" (Danziger 1975).

Thus it seems that many local policy makers suffer from a syndrome that has been termed "policy-maker's complaint" (Dutton, Danziger, & Kraemer 1980). They sense that the appropriate and necessary data do exist, and that they are probably in the government's information systems; but they believe that these data are not readily available to them when they must gather information and when they must make a policy decision.

SELECTING AMONG ALTERNATIVES

In Fuller's vision, computerized information systems will not only be designed to identify problems, formulate alternatives, and provide information relevant to those alternatives, they will also perform the actual choice of the preferred policy action. Policy makers specify decision parameters and hierarchies of values, and then the automated information system makes the optimal choice. There are currently a few computerized systems in local governments that approximate cybernetic systems, but these tend to be in highly technical and limited domains of operations. For example, some cities have automated traffic control systems that regulate the flow of vehicles by means of a real-time monitoring and controlling system for traffic signals.

However, there are almost no current systems that actually select the best alternative in significant policy matters. Basic to the policy maker's power is his or her capacity to determine the policy choice. The capacity to choose is one of the fundamental determinants of power. Thus the policy maker will not usually yield this capacity to an automated system unless he or she is utterly indifferent to the alternative choices, or unless the costs of choice are enormous. While the former situation is rare, the latter situation does occasionally occur. For example, a major southern city was obliged to select certain neighborhoods for Community Development Bloc Grants. There were considerably more "deserving" neighborhoods than there were available grants and most neighborhoods had substantial political clout. The city's policy makers persuaded all competing groups to accept a set of specific criteria (and the relative importance of each criterion) for selection of the neighborhoods to receive grants. The relevant social-indicators data were then assessed by an automated system, which selected the most "deserving" neighborhoods. The virture of this procedure was that, since all competitors accepted the policy choices produced, the decision makers escaped the wrath of the losers. While this example does correspond to Fuller's scenario, there are currently very few instances when political decision makers are willing to yield the crucial power of making choices, even to the "neutrality" of an automated system.

Rationalization Stage

POLICY ARGUMENT

There is a transitional stage of the policy process which begins during the decision phase and continues in the postdecision phase. Both before and after a preferred policy position has been selected, there is a need to develop and communicate potent evidence that reflects favorably on the logic of the particular policy choice. Majone (1978) has termed this phase "policy argument." It has been common to interpret these activities as a rather transparent attempt to rationalize the policy, and to characterize the use of information here as merely "political ammunition" (Weiss 1978:14–15). But Majone observes that policy argument is a positive and valuable activity, during which information is used to clarify the policy and to mobilize consent for its effective implementation. Many policy arguments are in part grounded in automated information, which becomes a key source of *evidence*—that is, " . . . information selected from the available stock and introduced at a specific point in the argument in order to persuade a particular audience of the truth or falsity of a statement of fact" (Majone 1978).

Policy makers acknowledge the use of computerized information in the policy argument or rationalization phase. Table 6.3 indicates that a large majority use automated information to legitimize the existence of problems, which then merit and justify a policy response, and then to document policy positions. About half of the elected policy makers and two-fifths of the appointed ones use automated information at least occasionally in order to generate publicity for policies and programs. It is evident that, where relevant information is available from an automated system, such information has a significant role in explaining, justifying, and clarifying the policy choice.

Postdecision Stage

MONITORING IMPLEMENTATION

Implementation involves the actions undertaken to carry out and achieve policy goals. Computer systems have nearly unlimited capacity to capture data as a by-product of recording basic operations (primarily in operational data systems). These data can then be restructured by the automated system to illuminate many aspects of policy implementation. Automated information systems are especially valuable as control devices, providing data that indicate whether resources (e.g., budgetary allocations, personnel activity, capital equipment, and so on) are actually applied to the programs for which those resources were authorized. Systems used to identify significantly abnormal levels of spending by means of exception reports are one of the more sophisticated applications of this type. Some systems also assess the performance of personnel, typically using various quantitative measures of workload or output (e.g., number of cases handled by each social welfare worker, number of parcels appraised by each field assessor, number of parking tickets processed by each clerk, and so on).

Chapter 8 will document more fully the extensive use of automated policy-monitoring applications as a set of bureaucratic control activities. Since elected policy makers typically devote sporadic rather than sustained attention to policy implementation, most of this effort is undertaken by top administrators. This fact is reflected in the use of automated information in this phase of the policy process. Half of the managers, but only about 15 percent of the mayors or councilors, make general use of automated information to monitor and control departments and agencies (table 6.3). But about four-fifths of all top policy makers report at least occasional use of automated data for these activities.

EVALUATING POLICY

Policy evaluation includes those activities that explicitly assess the impacts of the applied policies. Automated information is well suited to evaluative uses. In particular, the data in operational data systems can be aggregated, compared, and analyzed in a variety of more and less sophisticated ways to generate such evaluative data as unit cost measures, cost-benefit indicators, and program effectiveness measures. Such data always have imperfect correspondence to actual effects, and are subject to inevitable concerns about validity and reliability, but they can provide illuminating information about the nature of policies. Table 6.4 indicates that 45 percent of the mayors and 37 percent of the managers and councilors believe that computer-based data provide them with the "real costs" of programs in most cases. Department heads, top staff, and analysts attribute somewhat less utility to such data, although the majority of each group thinks automated information reveals the real costs of at least some programs.

Despite considerable rhetoric about the desirability of policy evaluation, few local governments currently utilize this capacity of computer systems extensively. In part, this is because many policy makers believe that there are insufficient and/or inadequate data to undertake valid policy assessment (Caplan, Morrison, & Stambaugh 1975). But it also seems that, in general, policy makers do not want objective information that allows a critical and public evaluation of policies. The political costs of an evaluation which indicates that a policy has been a "failure" or even a "partial success" are very high relative to the political capital to be gained by a policy "success" (Dutton, Danziger, & Kraemer 1980). Therefore, such evaluation data are used only very selectively, when the policy makers are quite certain of unambiguous and positive information and interpretation. Automated information is particularly suspect in this context, since its application is more mechanical and subject to more interpretations than are data developed and presented from the manual file systems of the policy maker. Thus the most common use of automated information systems in this phase of the policy process is in quasi-evaluation procedures (rather like the policy argument uses), through which administrators and technocrats generate data and reports that justify the continuation or extension of current programs.

SYMBOLIC USES OF COMPUTERIZED INFORMATION

The preceding discussion reveals that automated information systems have some instrumental value for the policy makers in local government. But it is important to stress that most of these uses of computer-based data, reports, and analyses can also serve a variety of symbolic functions. Political analysts have become aware that certain policy actions are more symbolic than real (Edelman 1964; Knorr 1977). For example, the decision to study a problem might serve as a delaying tactic, in the hope that by the time the study is done, the problem will be forgotten.

The capabilities of computer technology allow policy makers to be more confident that the government's staff can indeed come up with a credible study in such a case. Computers and automated data analyses have become one hallmark of rationality. Many people place more credibility, other things being equal, in the "hard facts" that emerge from a computer-based analysis than in the "opinions" in a report produced manually. As chapter 7 will document more fully, such computer-based analyses can be extremely biased (see also Dutton, Danziger, & Kraemer 1980). Indeed, such uses of automated systems can bury political decisions within a technical system of analysis that is unfathomable to outsiders. There are an increasing number of instances when automated information systems are used to "make" policy decisions, as in the case of the southern city's Community Development Bloc Grant allocations. But the choice and weighting of key variables and decision parameters, and the selection of decision algorithms in such computerized reports and analyses, are seldom genuinely apolitical. In a revealing example in a large western county, policy analysts were repeatedly instructed to readjust the parameters in their estimates for county population growth until the model's estimates were consistent with the estimates desired by the county's most powerful politician (Kling 1978c).

Thus, the use of automated information systems can transmit various messages to the "interested public" of the local government. For example, messages from the generation of a computer-based report on a policy issue might include: "the government is concerned"; "calm down, something is being done"; "the government makes rational policy decisions"; "this particular policy decision is rational"; and "this policy decision is appropriate/necessary/unavoidable, given the facts." It should be obvious that these kinds of images are invaluable to the policy maker who can effectively manipulate the symbols of computer use.

THE LIMITS OF COMPUTERS

At the beginning of this chapter, and previously in this book, we delineated four broad perspectives that offer alternative explanations for the use and effects of automated information systems in the policy process. The subsequent discussion and data indicated that there is some utilization of automated information in the policy process and variable use in phases of that process. Does any perspective explain the limits on the use of automated information? Our discussion provides a basis from which to assess the adequacy of each of these explanatory approaches. Broadly, it seems that this is a research issue, like many examined by social scientists, for which no single approach provides a complete and accurate explanation; rather, all four approaches provide some insights into the role of automated information.

Computers as a Rationalizing Force

For managerial rationalists, automated information is by definition a rationalizing force in the policy process. It is seen to be axiomatic that the availability of more extensive, more quickly accessible, less filtered, and more fully analyzed data and information will necessarily increase the rationality of most stages of the policy process. To date, the most widespread improvements in organizational rationality derived from automated information systems have come primarily from the more routine information-processing tasks on basic operations, leading to cost and staff efficiencies, improved record-keeping, and so on; but it is also true that in many local governments automated information systems have provided improved information for the policy process.

However, one obvious limit to the role of automated information is that the mere availability of more and better information does not ensure that automated data will be used "rationally" or even that the data will be used at all. In fact, it is not unreasonable to intrepret much of the data in this chapter as suggesting that there has been considerably less use and utility of automated information than one might expect. Few policy makers have yielded decision discretion to ". . . the computer's safe flight-controlling capabilities."

In most local governments, the current rationalizing impacts of auto-mated information vary across different aspects of the policy process. As one might expect, automated information systems are employed most and are attributed the greatest current utility in providing basic data. This is most notable in the generation of information about policy alternatives, in the development of data to support policy argument, and, to a lesser extent, in problem definition. It is these "intelligence" functions, broadly con-strued, for which a richer data base is viewed by policy makers as a valuable resource. The role of computerized information in policy monitoring, although less extensive, has a similar configuration of uses and utility. But a recurrent theme in this chapter (and in chapter 7) is that many impacts of computerized information are arational or nonrational—contrary to the expectations of the managerial rationalists. This has been especially evident in design of alternatives, policy choice, and policy evaluation, as well as in the many symbolic uses of automated information.

Computers and the Technocratic Elite

There is no question that certain technical experts—the computer elite—have a major role in the development and operation of automated information systems, and that other technical experts—the information elite—carry out the detailed analyses of population shifts, housing forecasts, cost estimates, and other quantitative analyses in American local governments. In seeking fine-grained data about housing or municipal expenditures, urban planners or budget analysts are tempted to use computerized files, so that alternative analyses of large data sets may be made with relative ease. A fortiori, when quantitative analyses are automated, more experts—computing specialists—enter the arena, and the resulting proliferation of technical details typically becomes even more intimidating to inexpert actors, public officials, municipal staff, or citizens.

However, the central questions are not whether automated analyses and technical experts go hand in hand, but whether the involvement of technical experts in local governments' policy analyses manifestly alters the policy, or whether it allows technical experts to dominate the policy process. Our field studies did not indicate that technical experts had "taken over" the shaping and setting of public policy. Chapter 5 indicates that the computer elite do have major impacts on aspects of the application and use of automated information systems, and suggests some of the effects of a relatively autonomous technological elite—poorly designed systems, squandered resources, and shortcomings in the quality of computing-service delivery.

But most of the linkages between these effects and the dynamics of the policy process are subtle and quite indirect. One important mitigating factor is the very ideology of the computer elite itself. Although they are not totally apolitical, these technical experts are generally indifferent to the uses to which automated information is put and to the impacts of that information on the political system (Danziger 1979:384–86). For example, the computer professional is usually much more concerned about elegant design and data quality in a computer simulation of the amount of sewage to be produced by different land-use policies than about the final zoning decision or even about the impact of the simulation on the decision process. At present, the computer professionals become politicized primarily on issues of *computer resources* (e.g., the allocation of financial resources to support the computing operation) and *computer operations* (e.g., the location of skilled personnel, the ownership of, and access to, the government's data resources), but are not especially active in the politics of *information resources.*

Although the technical elite connected directly with the computer unit is relatively apolitical, others with computing expertise do have political agendas which they attempt to serve by the use of automated information. These information elites might be involved in the politics of information resources because of their interest either in strategic planning (e.g., policy analysts for the executive, land-use planners) or in departmental operations (e.g., police manpower allocation analysts, traffic engineers). It is evident that these kinds of technical experts attempt to introduce more sophisticated analytic techniques and more empirical data into the policy process. But the underlying issue is whether such uses of "technique" (in Ellul's sense) produce a technocracy dominated by instrumental reason.

We have some systematic survey data to answer this question, although our field studies provide a richer basis for answering it. Based on data in tables 6.2 and 6.4, members of the information elite (specifically, planners and analysts) seem more likely than elected officials to rely upon automated data sets to identify city problems and to legitimize their perceptions. Moreover, they have markedly greater confidence in their analyses than do elected officials, and they are considerably less likely to view the analyses as biased. But do such analyses dominate? Most respondents report that automated analyses are "somewhat useful" in identifying city problems and in determining solutions for them (table 6.4). "Somewhat useful" is a weak indication of support. It seems to show that the technical elites who control automated analyses are neither utterly powerless nor a determining influence on the process or content of public policy.

In local governments, the introduction of such rational-technical innovations as automated information systems, program budgeting, systems analysis, and management by objectives, have altered some standard operating procedures. But the evidence also suggests that, in general, such innovations have produced limited rather than pervasive effects and have not dramatically altered the nature of the policy process (Brewer 1974; Wildavsky 1976). Again, the reality of bureaucratic politics seems to mitigate the overall effect of techniques such as the use of automated information systems. Information does tend to be of higher quality and greater quantity; but it is clearly not a dominating resource in most interactions among players with competing agendas. In cities where urban planners seemed to have considerable influence and high morale, their values were usually aligned with the agendas of the most powerful top policy makers in the government. In this situation, simple reports tended to receive more attention and there seemed to be greater support for analytical studies. In contrast, in cities where the planners favored lines of action that were rejected by top policy makers, the planners often seemed ignored and dejected. Clearly, these patterns suggest that the information elite's influence in such cases was not independent, but was primarily contingent on their capacity to serve the agendas of powerful actors.

Organizational Pluralism and Reinforcement Politics

The organizational pluralist and the reinforcement politics perspectives are further specifications of bureaucratic politics as developed by Allison (1971). That explanation is based on a game metaphor, involving the behavior of players in positions (Allison 1971:162–81). The players' actions are guided by parochial priorities, goals, and perceptions, and their bargaining and overlapping actions constitute the organizational activity producing policy decisions. In such a setting, characterized by interactions among players with competing agendas, information—including automated information—is likely to be a powerful resource. But the use of such information is contingent on the agendas of the players and on the dynamics of their competitive behavior. As we have noted in the previous sections, it is this bureaucratic politics perspective that seems to best explain the limits on the role of automated information in the policy process.

The fundamental value of information to the policy maker is its capacity to reduce uncertainty—about the nature of the environment, the implications of alternatives, the likely effects of an action. But paradoxically, *automated* information, more than most other information available to the policy maker, can *increase* rather than reduce uncertainty (Danziger 1979b:376–78). This increased uncertainty is due to concerns about control of automated information—control of access, manipulation, and application. As Crozier (1964) and others have argued persuasively, a critical goal of organizational actors is to reduce the uncertainty of action in their domains. Thus if they are not confident that they can control automated information in order to reduce their uncertainty, they are likely to limit its use in the policy process.

Control of *access* to automated information is often problematical. Most data held by local governments are assumed to be "owned" by the government as a whole. Manual file systems are typically held by the data-generating agency, which has considerable de facto control over access to its data by outsiders. When such files are automated, however, most data are actually held by the computer unit, whose organizational position and technical expertise provide it with considerable control over access. Indeed, even the data-generating agency is often dependent upon the skilled staff of the computing unit to provide the agency with access to its own data. We noted in chapter 5 that, as bureaucratic politics approaches would suggest, data ownership is among the issues rated as most important for the computing function. Thus, except where files are "dedicated" or where an agency has its own automated system, the automation of data will tend to reduce a unit's capacity to control outsider access to that data.

The corollary of reduced control over access to automated information is reduced control over the *manipulation* of that information. There are two important ways in which automated information systems facilitate the manipulation of data by a larger number of people. First, the automated system typically contains a full data set as well as the necessary information about the meanings of the data elements. Second, all who have access to the computer, and to computer experts, are in a position to undertake an extraordinary range of record-restructuring and sophisticated analytics activities. In contrast, when the data are available only in manual files, the owner agency generally dominates these aspects of data manipulation—it can control the information and insight necessary to "de-code" the data base, and thus it tends to have a relative monopoly of expertise in how to massage the data appropriately.

Similarly, where access to and manipulation of automated information have been broadened, the resulting *application* of the information in the political process is considerably expanded. Information-in-use is the essential resource to those in a bureaucratic politics setting (whether seen from an organizational pluralist or reinforcement politics perspective). Rich (1979) has noted that public officials are extremely conscious of the possibility that information could embarrass them. This influences their reactions to information provided to them by others, as well as to the data that they control. The "knowledge utilization" literature indicates that the organizational actor tends to be biased against information which he or she has not produced and cannot control (Feller et al. 1979; Rich 1979:399).

With the expanded applications of automated information, most actors can, at least theoretically, obtain the kinds of high-quality information available through computerized data systems. This, in turn, means that most will feel obliged to employ data-based arguments more extensively, for self-protection if not for enhancement of their bargaining positions (Kling 1978b). But since everyone has more data-based evidence, and because a number of positions can usually be supported by credible automated information, there tends to be an increased number of plausible alternative policy positions. This expands the arena of potential disagreement and conflict on a given policy issue and increases the likelihood that a "data war" will erupt. The infusion of data-based evidence can improve the quality of the decision process and/or the ultimate policy choice by increasing the rationality of the policy process; but such an advocacy process can also exacerbate the competitive aspects of bureaucratic politics, producing outcomes desired by none of the players. That is, data wars can be embarrassing because they often result in an ambiguous truce in which no one's original position seems tenable and no one's credibility seems enhanced (Danziger 1979b).

In a representative example, the transportation department in an urban eastern county presented a computer analysis which projected the need for a substantial expansion in the area's arterial road system. The planning department in the county's major city then countered with a reanalysis of the same data, making different assumptions about the changes in population movement and economic development, and concluded that no additional roads were necessary. Ultimately, the different assumptions were not resolvable and this data-based debate ended in a confused stalemate (Danziger 1979b; see also Brewer 1974; Greenberger, Crenson & Crissey 1976).

These uncertainty-producing characteristics seem important in explaining the selective use of automated information in the policy process. First, it will tend to be used where the policy maker believes that he or she can control the access to, manipulation, and application of such information. This is especially evident in the intelligence-gathering phases of the policy process, since the policy maker searches selectively for information that reduces uncertainty about alternatives, but is also prevalent in the phase of policy monitoring, since those who control resources need information to assure themselves that those resources are being used appropriately. Except where information quality is poor, or where there is information overload, policy monitoring usually benefits from increased automated information.

A second general point about computerized information and uncertainty is that such information is employed least where its use most clearly increases the risk or reduces the control of the policy maker. The policy maker will only rarely yield discretion over agenda setting (that is, problem finding and problem definition) to automated information systems. Nor will the policy maker willingly yield the fundamental right to choose among policy alternatives. And, due to the risks involved, there is little enthusiasm for rigorous computer-based evaluation of policies among those in any way responsible for the policies in question.

This line of analysis differs markedly from that advanced by managerial rationalists. These differences are most clearly evident in the rationalist's assumption that "politics" can be removed from policy making by providing better data or improved technologies for gaining access to or manipulating data. The bureaucratic politics perspective suggests that when new data resources are provided, they will be exploited to enhance the control of "political" actors. For example, rationalists might suggest that policy agendas could be set more rationally if the bases of each actor's choices were made public. Moreover, accessible and improved data about municipal conditions would help (and could not hurt) more rational agenda setting. In contrast, the bureaucratic politics approach suggests that political actors will attempt to maximize their control over agenda-setting and will avoid the use of any data that they do not understand or cannot control.

Thus far we have emphasized the points of convergence between organizational pluralism and reinforcement politics. But these two per-spectives differ on the important matter of which group, if any, is especially benefited by the use of automated data. Organizational ("elite") pluralists would argue that no one group is advantaged. In different policy contexts (e.g., policing, personnel policy, parks, schools), different groups will dominate. In contrast, the reinforcement politics perspective suggests that those groups who are already powerful in a given political system (e.g., mayor, planners, department heads) will gain further power by exploiting automated data analysis.

Computerized information will tend to be used where the policy maker believes that he or she will suffer a competitive disadvantage by not using it. This is especially evident in the policy argument phase, and is also a factor when the attractiveness and feasibility of policy alternatives are being considered. Although there may be added uncertainty owing to the broadened access to information which is automated, it can be extremely hazardous to ignore such information. Indeed, the first casualties of a data war are likely to be those with few or no data resources. And because of the general credibility attached to information from automated systems, any individual, group, or agency that does not have such data—other things being equal—must operate from a weakened position. This observation supports the reinforcement politics perspective more than the organ-izational pluralist perspective. It is all the more telling in that automated data systems are relatively expensive to acquire, operate, and exploit effectively (Kling 1974). Thus extant inequities in financial and staff resources are likely to be translated into corresponding inequities in data resources.

Although automated data are important, the "other things being equal" qualification raised in the preceding paragraph is significant. We have stressed above that in the bureaucratic politics setting, many other resources in addition to the kinds of data in automated systems are of critical importance. An actor's position and political skills, the configuration of competing actors, and the history of the relevant policy arena are some of the more obvious forces that can overcome the impact of information resources in a given policy process. Nonetheless, the symbolic value attributed to a more rational, properly managed policy process means that there will be organizational biases toward the more effective and extensive use of automated information in this process.

CONCLUDING OBSERVATIONS

While most of the current efficiency and effectiveness benefits of automated information systems in local governments are in routine and basic operations, it is evident that computerized information can also enhance the information environment of the policy process. This chapter has shown that computerized information is used and is significant in certain stages of the policy process, particularly in the generation of information regarding alternative policy choices, the development of policy arguments, and the monitoring of policy implementation. To a lesser extent, there is evidence of the conceptual and instrumental use of computerized information in other stages of the policy process. Moreover, automated information systems serve important symbolic functions, particularly in promoting the image of rational decision making and in validating certain policy choices.

But an intriguing irony is that although information in general tends to reduce uncertainty, many of the possible uses of *computerized* information in the policy process might actually *increase* uncertainty. Because automated information systems tend to expand various actors' access to, and capacity to manipulate, information resources, the uses and impacts of such resources become less controllable for any particular actor. Moreover, there are stages of the policy process during which such information could reduce the discretionary range of the policy maker. These factors, in addition to the initial premise that formal information is only one resource among many in the various stages of the policy process, underpin our general conclusion that *there are currently selective utilization and limited impacts of computerized information in the policy process of local governments.*

The data and inferences in this chapter do not provide generalized support for either the managerial rationalism or the technocratic elitism perspectives. Although aspects of the policy process have benefited from improvements in the information environment owing to computerized information, such benefits are not widespread, and there are instances where computerized information supports organizational biases rather than a more abstract notion of rational decision making. And although the information elite is sometimes effective in using computerized information, there is little evidence to support the view that the technical experts have emerged as the dominant force in the policy process, or that the process itself is now driven by instrumental reason.

The data and inferences in this chapter do seem to support the perspectives of organizational pluralism and reinforcement politics. Various actors do use computerized information as a resource in the struggles of bureaucratic politics, and no one group seems to have unilateral control over computerized information resources in the process. We have not provided a critical test that discriminates between these two perspectives. It is reasonable to infer from the arguments above that the selective utilization of computerized information is contingent primarily on the relative power of those actors for whom the information is relevant. This implies that computerized information is reinforcing; it will rarely serve as the stone in David's sling against the policy-making Goliaths. But automated information systems may have a more telling impact in those cases where relatively equal actors engage in competition over policy. In those cases, the notion of elite pluralism may be appropriate. To explore this issue more fully, chapter 7 analyzes the power payoffs and the possible power shifts among organizational actors resulting from the use of computerized information.

CHAPTER SEVEN

THE AUTOMATION OF BIAS

Kenneth L. Kraemer and William H. Dutton

MANAGERIAL RATIONALISM suggests that computers are, manifestly, tools for enhancing service delivery, operational performance, and the quality of information in local governments. The prominence of this perspective in the computing literature (Nolan 1973; Simon 1971) has led most officials to view computer technology as "distributive" in its impacts—as providing new information resources without significantly altering the current arrangements of power, influence, and prestige. However, in earlier chapters we have argued that the functions of computing make it a *political* tool for influencing the relative power and autonomy of particular actors and interests in the governmental system. These functions involve the "redistribution" of resources (information, prestige, money, legitimacy) that can affect the decisional effectiveness of people in organizations.

This chapter investigates the interests served by computing. Specifically, it examines the power shifts that result from governmental computer use, and the interests served by these power shifts. First, we assess four alternative hypotheses about the direction of power shifts by empirically examining our 42-city survey and case-study data. Second, these findings are elaborated by a more intensive examination of the use and impacts of a new type of computer model—the Fiscal Impact Budgeting System—in the local budgetary decision-making process.

COMPUTERS AND POWER SHIFTS[1]

There is a considerable debate, in the research literature on computing, concerning both the existence and the direction of power shifts. Many people believe that computing is an apolitical technology and that it does not produce power shifts. For some (Blum 1972; Evans & Knisely 1970; Weiner 1969), this belief is tied to an assessment that computer-based information is only minimally relevant to decision making in local governments. In this view, such information is seen as unsophisticated, of low quality, often conflicting, one of many sources of information, easily ignored by decision makers, often irrelevant, and, even if relevant to decisions, subject to variable interpretations. In sum, decision makers would seldom develop, or change, their positions on the basis of computer printouts.

On the other hand, some view information as a political resource within organizations, much like expertise, status, or positional authority (Kling 1974; Lawler & Rhode 1976; Weber 1970). Earlier chapters have noted that because computers can change the character of information flows within organizations, including their speed, direction, content, and pattern of circulation, computers might influence the relative effectiveness of different participants in decisions, and therefore the relative influence of different interests in the governmental system.[2] Furthermore, those who control the technology might use that control to enhance their decision-making effectiveness and interests within the organization.[3] That is, computing is likely to entail certain power payoffs or "power shifts." These power shifts are "gains to one person's decision-making effectiveness made at the expense of another person's. They are redistributions of the benefits of decision-making" (Downs 1967). The most prominent expectations about the interests served by computing—the managerial rationalism, technocratic elitism, organizational pluralism, and reinforcement politics perspectives—were outlined in chapter 1 and restated, in relation to the policy process, in chapter 6. Here we note the elements of these perspectives relevant to the distribution of benefits and power payoffs of computing.

Managerial Rationalism

As we have seen, from this viewpoint computing is a tool of managerial rationalism and supports the economy and efficiency goals of the administrative reform movement for the organization as a whole. Computing serves "organizational interests" because it is controlled by professional bureaucrats through central administrative structures; and it is used to improve their ability to manage operations and subordinates, and to marshal information that supports the recommendations they make to top elected officials (Bell 1973; Downs 1967; Dutton & Kraemer 1978b; Ghere 1977; Laudon 1974). Managerial rationalism suggests that computing tends to shift power to top managers (e.g., shift more power to the city manager in the smaller council-manager cities, and to the mayor and one or two major department heads in the larger mayor-council cities).[4]

Technocratic Elitism

From this perspective, computing, like most high technologies, will be controlled by technical experts (Danziger 1979a; Downs 1967; Ellul 1964; Lowi 1972b).[5] Technocratic elitism suggests that computing tends to shift more power to an information elite—the "new urban planners," the modern counterpart of Taylor's (1911) "new class of urban managers," trained in the techniques of scientific management. In contrast to the traditional planner, skilled in zoning and land-use planning, the new urban planner is skilled in the use of computer-based analytical tools such as statistical analysis, urban modeling, and simulation. Often such planners are located in the research division of local planning departments, but they are also found in the chief executive's office, and in the urban renewal, community development, and community analysis agencies.

Organizational Pluralism

This prominent rival hypothesis suggests that no single interest controls computer technology. Rather, pluralistic interests—those of bureaucrats, technicians, and politicians—participate in the variety of governmental decisions that shape the adoption and use of computing (Cyert & March 1963; Pettigrew 1973, 1975). In local governments, organizational pluralism suggests that computing will benefit elected officials, managers, and planners, all of whom influence the use of computer-based information systems.

Reinforcement Politics

The reinforcement politics perspective suggests an additional hypothesis, which is a refinement of the pluralist position. At the broadest level, reinforcement politics suggests that computer-based systems tend to follow and reinforce the existing pattern of power relationships, whether that pattern be pluralistic or centralized in bureaucrats, technocrats, or politicians. Computing tends to be used or not used to the degree that it supports the position or interests of those who control the governmental organization. It reallocates power or influence only in the sense that it accentuates existing inequalities of influence (Dutton & Kraemer 1978b, 1979a; Hoffman 1973, 1977; Kling 1978c; Kraemer & Dutton 1979). Computing simply enhances and extends the organization's capability to serve the interests of those who control the organization. In local governments reinforcement politics suggests that computing will increase the decision-making effectiveness of managers in reform governments, and of departments and planners in governments with departmental autonomy.

COMPUTER-BASED INFORMATION SYSTEMS AND POWER SHIFTS

Our strategy for empirically assessing the power shift hypothesis is to focus on those kinds of computer-based information systems that are most likely to affect the power relationships among organizational elites in American cities. Although nearly any use of computer-based information can be viewed as increasing the effectiveness of some official or agency in the government,[6] those systems that are most likely to affect the balance of power among bureaucrats, technicians, and politicians are those that better enable any of these officials to:

Manage—control events by getting rapid and correct feedback about operations in progress
Plan—anticipate future uncontrollable events by getting analyses of current trends and predictions
Persuade or coerce—control decision situations by getting superior or sensitive information which is perceived as compelling.

Systems that serve these purposes fall into two groups, according to whether their primary orientation is toward data about the environment, or data about the day-to-day operations, of the government (Dutton & Kraemer 1978a). Table 7.1 arrays various illustrative systems that are likely to affect the decisional effectiveness of bureaucrats, technicians and politicians both by the purpose (management, planning and politics), and by the kind of information system (data bank versus operational) that supports their use.[7]

Table 7.1 A Typology of Computer-Based Systems

Purpose	Kind of Information System	
	Data Banks (Contain data about the population/ clientele and their environment)	Operational Systems (Contain data about government personnel and operating departments)
Management	*Intergovernmental reporting:* Uses: Completing grant applications; preparing proposals; meeting intergovernmental reporting requirements. Ex: U.S. Census of population; housing survey; land-use inventory.	*Governmental reporting:* Uses: Monitoring the activities of individuals and the operations of departments; monitoring revenues and expenditures, equipment and supplies. Ex: Budget-monitoring systems; inventory-control systems; activity reporting systems; accounting systems.
Planning	*Environmental analysis:* Uses: Analyzing socioeconomic characteristics of populations, geographic areas, and political districts; forecasting demand. Ex: Population, land use, traffic and economic inventory systems; urban development models; fiscal impact models.	*Governmental analysis:* Uses: Allocating resources and manpower; scheduling activities; forecasting revenues and expenditures; forecasting cash flows; optimizing routes. Ex: Manpower allocation models; emergency vehicle dispatch models; routing models; revenue and expenditure forecasting models.
Politics	*Client persuasion:* Uses: Legitimation of policy positions to clients; political assessment of development plans; analysis of political constituency; analysis of distribution of costs and benefits of government services. Ex: Social indicator systems; planning models and analyses (above); political analyses.	*Client and intragovernmental persuasion:* Uses: Handle client requests and complaints; document policy positions. Ex. Complaint-monitoring systems; collective bargaining models; performance analyses.

SOURCE: Adapted from Kraemer and Dutton (1979: table 1).

Data Banks

Data banks pool facts about people and their environment (e.g., a jurisdiction's demography and its economy). In turn, this new information is aggregated and analyzed to determine environmental conditions (e.g., social indicators of the welfare of citizens and the health of the economy). These analyses can be used as a guide to public officials in identifying problems, determining needs, developing remedies, and applying for outside assistance. In some cases, information is fed into simulations and other models that mimic the behavior of some aspect of the environment (e.g., population growth and economic development). These analyses and models can be used to pretest the effects of various public actions in order to guide public officials in deciding among alternative policies. And information about people (their demographic characteristics, likes and dislikes, etc.) can be used to assess the political feasibility of development and financial plans.[8] As these examples illustrate, such data banks serve management, planning, and political purposes.

Operational Data Systems

Operational data systems are the computer systems that serve the day-to-day operations of the government and that contain data about government employees and departmental operations. This information is variously aggregated and analyzed to determine revenue and expenditure patterns, personnel vacancies, turnover, vacations or sick leave, individual and departmental workloads, and to evaluate selected indicators of performance. These analyses can be used by public officials in monitoring expenditures, identifying personnel problems, determining work assignments, and scheduling or rearranging departmental operations to improve performance. Sometimes, data are fed into computer models that imitate some operation of a department, such as handling emergency calls, dispatching vehicles, assigning personnel, or predicting cash flow. These analyses and models can be used to predict the effects of various departmental actions in order to guide public officials in deciding among alternative operational priorities and procedures. Also, individual and aggregated data from the operational systems can be used in support of particular policy positions, personnel actions, collective bargaining negotiations, or citizen requests and complaints. Consequently, operational data systems can serve management, planning, and political purposes, as can their data bank counterparts.

Given the different types of computer-based information systems in government, and the different purposes they can serve, our strategy is first to describe empirically the use of data banks and operational data systems by each type of decision maker, for management, planning, and political purposes. Thus we may specify the ways that computers are used by bureaucrats (city managers and administrators), technicians (new urban planners), and politicians (elected mayors and councils). These patterns of use can enable us to speculate about the likely magnitude and direction of power shifts, because the use of computing might be a necessary (although not a sufficient) condition for the occurrence of power shifts in a computer-oriented bureaucracy. Second, we explore the magnitude and direction of power shifts more directly, through an analysis of systematically coded case-study observations regarding those officials whose influence was affected by the use of computing in the 42 cities studied.

USE OF COMPUTERIZED INFORMATION SYSTEMS

The frequency and magnitude of power shifts are likely to depend on the degree and kind of use made of computers by bureaucrats, technocrats, and politicians (Kraemer, Danziger, & Dutton 1978). We began an analysis of the use of computerized information systems in chapter 6. In this section, in order to describe the use of data banks and operational systems, we indicate whether each kind of public official used either data banks, in each of six tasks displayed in table 7.2, or operational data systems, in each of four tasks displayed in table 7.3. Public officials were asked for examples and evidence of this use and responses were used to determine whether, for each role-type (management, planning, politics), computing was *not used, used only in exceptional cases*, or *generally used* (not just in isolated or nonspecific cases) for each task.[9]

Use of Data Banks

There are three broad conclusions based on the patterns of data bank use (table 7.2). First, while each kind of official tends to use data banks, the overall use of data banks is low (also see Kraemer, Danziger, & Dutton 1978). In only about 10 percent of the cities does any given kind of public official *generally* use data banks for most activities. In about half the cities, any particular type of official uses data banks only in exceptional cases. Officials in over 20 percent of the cities tend to use data banks for only two tasks—policy development and problem legitimation.

Second, there are more similarities than differences in use by role. Planners are the major users of data banks—their median level of use is highest on five of the six tasks. The planners are followed by the managers, mayors, and council, respectively. But the total difference among roles on

Table 7.2 Levels of Use of Urban Data Banks

Kind of Use	Level of Use	Level of Use by:			
		Manager	Mayor	Council	Planners/ Analysts
Planning					
Problem finding—					
lead to new or	(0) Not used[a]	27%	40%	41%	18%
clear perceptions	(1) Exceptional use	63	49	46	60
of community	(2) Generally used	10	11	13	22
problems	Median[b]	.87	.69	.69	1.04
Change or	(0) Not used	57	72	67	57
affect decisions	(1) Exceptional use	43	25	33	38
	(2) Generally used	0	3	0	5
	Median	.38	.19	.25	.37
Policy	(0) Not used	21	41	40	21
development	(1) Exceptional use	4	0	0	3
	(2) Generally used	75	59	60	76
	Median	1.83	1.30	1.32	1.84
Politics					
Legitimize	(0) Not used	40	33	36	26
existing	(1) Exceptional use	43	33	51	38
problems	(2) Generally used	17	33	13	36
	Median	.73	1.00	.78	1.13
Gain publicity	(0) Not used	40	47	54	38
	(1) Exceptional use	50	50	38	50
	(2) Generally used	10	3	8	12
	Median	.70	.56	.43	.75
Determine the	(0) Not used	76	78	77	73
political accept-	(1) Exceptional use	17	22	18	22
ability of actions	(2) Generally used	7	0	5	5
	Median	.15	.14	.15	.19

SOURCE: Adapted from Kraemer and Dutton (1979: table 2).
[a]Percentage of cities where one or more data banks are automated, but not used in this way by role-type.
[b]Scored: 0 = not used; 1 = exceptional use; 2 = generally used.

Table 7.3   Levels of Use of Operational Data Systems

Kind of Use	Level of Use	Manager	Mayor	Council
		Level of Use by:		
Management				
Monitor and control	(0) Not used[a]	18%	20%	24%
	(1) Exceptional use	33	63	61
	(2) General use	49	17	15
	Median[b]	1.44	.97	.93
Planning				
Change or affect	(0) Not used	18	38	46
decisions	(1) Exceptional use	32	34	27
	(2) General use	50	28	27
	Median	1.50	.85	.67
Politics				
Respond to citizen	(0) Not used	35	55	59
requests and	(1) Exceptional use	38	19	22
complaints	(2) General use	27	26	19
	Median	.90	.41	.34
Document policy	(0) Not used	26	28	47
positions	(1) Exceptional use	30	36	36
	(2) General use	44	36	17
	Median	1.31	1.09	.58

SOURCE: Adapted from Kraemer and Dutton (1979: table 3).
[a]Percentage of cities where operational data are automated, but not used in this way by role-type.
[b]Scored: 0 = not used in this way; 1 = exceptional use; 2 = general use.

any task is less than 20 percent; most frequently it is around 10 percent. This small difference in use among officials is unexpected, given the predictions in much of the power-shift literature that some set of actors will dominate the use of automated information.

Third, each kind of official tends to use data banks in a somewhat different way. Our field research indicates that planners focus on planning and administrative purposes; managers focus on administrative and planning purposes; and elected officials focus on planning and political purposes.[10] Table 7.2 further indicates that while managers are more likely to use data banks for planning purposes (problem finding, decision making, and policy development), they are about as likely as are the elected officials to use data banks for political purposes (legitimizing their position, gaining publicity, and determining the political feasibility of different actions). Thus, while there is some specialization of purpose within each of the three roles, no one kind of official seems to monopolize computing in a specific area.

Use of Operational Data Systems

The relatively low use of data banks by public officials may be due to the fact that data banks play a minor role in urban decision making, as compared to operational data systems (Kraemer, Danziger, & Dutton 1978). Operational data systems are, in fact, used more extensively than data banks, but overall use remains moderate (table 7.3). In more than three-fourths of the cities, operational systems are used for management, planning, and political purposes. Also, there are somewhat greater differences in use by role. The managers' use of operational systems clearly exceeds the use made of them by elected officials.

In about one-half of the cities, the managers make general use of operational data systems for monitoring subunits, making decisions, and documenting policy positions. The only use that ranks low for the managers is responding to citizen complaints. In contrast, mayors most often use operational data for documenting policy positions and monitoring subunits. Councils most often use operational systems to monitor subunits. Thus our general inference from these patterns of computer use remains the same: power shifts appear quite possible, but are not likely to be dramatic in their intensity.

POWER SHIFTS FROM USE OF COMPUTERIZED SYSTEMS

The direction of power shifts is likely to be sensitive to the degree and kind of use made of computers by bureaucrats, technocrats, and politicians. Assuming that information can enhance decision-making effectiveness, we consider the relative frequency with which each kind of official tends to use computing, and develop a loose hierarchy of officials who are more likely to gain in effectiveness. Tables 7.2 and 7.3 show that planners tend to dominate in the use of data banks, and that managers tend to dominate in the use of operational data systems. This suggests that managers and planners might gain somewhat more decision-making effectiveness than elected mayors or councils. Consequently, these data are supportive of managerial rationalism and technocratic elitism. However, the fact that there is often little difference among the various public officials in their frequency of use is equally suggestive of patterns expected by the organizational pluralism interpretation.

Patterns of Use

The foregoing loose hierarchy of officials with relatively greater and lesser gain from computing is based on the percentage of cities in which a particular type of official rated high or low in the use of computing. It may be that in cities where the manager gains, the mayor and council do not, and vice versa. In other words, the data could support the power-shift hypothesis, if a tendency for high levels of use by one subset of officials is associated with low levels of use by other subsets of officials. But, as shown in table 7.4, this is not the pattern.

In cities where one kind of official tends toward a high level of use—of either type of system—all other kinds of officials also tend to have a high level of use. Rather than being distinguished by having one of the three types of officials dominate the use of computerized information, cities are largely distinguished by having either a high or a low use of computing by all three types—planners, bureaucrats, and politicians. Thus the simple frequencies presented above do not seem to mask more differentiated patterns of utilization. This finding tends to cast further doubt on the

Table 7.4   Relationships Among Indicators of the Use of
Computer-Based Information

Indicators	Manager Use	Mayor Use	Council Use	Planner/ Analyst Use
		Operational Data[a]		
Manager use		.36*	.34*	—
Mayor use	.51*		.43*	—
Council use	.46*	.60*		—
Planner/ Analyst use	.41*	.60*	.46*	
		Data Banks[a]		

SOURCE: Adapted from Kraemer and Dutton (1979: table 4).
[a]Pearson correlations among role-types for use of operational data are presented in upper right and correlations for use of data banks are presented in lower left.
*$P < .05$

managerial rationalism and technocratic elitism hypotheses. However, it tends to support the organizational pluralism hypothesis.

Frequency of Power Shifts

While the frequency of utilization of computerized information systems is suggestive of power shifts, a more direct measurement is available in the form of ratings made on the basis of our case-study observations within each of the 42 cities. Table 7.5 shows the degree to which each type of public official was judged to gain, or lose, influence as a result of the use of information systems in the government. These ratings provide support for the existence of power shifts, and for the loose hierarchy of beneficiaries described above. Computerized information systems are judged to have had *some effect* on the relative influence of at least one kind of official in about 80 percent of the cities. Where there is an effect, the information systems have tended to increase, rather than decrease, the influence of public officials. Whereas computerized systems have decreased the influence of at least some officials in 27 percent of the cities, they have increased the influence of some official in 54 percent of the cities. Those who tend most often to gain influence are the planners (the information elite), followed by the top managers and department heads (the bureaucrats), and the mayor and council (the politicians).

However, these rankings are less pronounced than suggested by either the technocratic-elitist or managerial-rationalist formulations of the power-shift hypothesis. Planners are not major beneficiaries of computing,

Table 7.5 Use of Computer-Based Data and Influence Shifts

	Effect on Official[a]		
Official Affected	Decreased Influence	No Effect	Increased Influence
		(% of cities)	
Data bank custodians and planners	0	68	32
Manager, CAO and staff	3	70	27
Departments	10	72	18
Mayor and staff	14	67	19
Council and staff	20	75	5
Any of the above officials	27	19	54

SOURCE: Adapted from Kraemer and Dutton (1979: table 5) and Kling (1978: table 10).
[a]Investigators' judgmental ratings based on all interviews.

for they have tended to gain influence as a result of computerized systems in only about 32 percent of the cities. Likewise, managers have gained influence in only about 27 percent of the cities, and department heads and mayors in 18 and 19 percent. Only the councils generally have tended to lose influence (20%) more often than gain it (5%). Thus, no single official appears to be a substantial, or sole, beneficiary of power shifts from data banks and operational data systems in cities. The shifts that occur are mainly gains, rather than losses, in the influence of officials, but the gains appear to be shared among nearly *all* officials.

Patterns of Power Shifts

While the marginal values reported in table 7.5 support organizational pluralism, they are susceptible to a problem common to the aggregation of cross-sectional data. The same marginals could result from either pluralistic patterns characterizing some subset of cities, or the operation of different models of power shifts in different cities. Thus it is important to evaluate the foregoing support for the pluralist interpretation by testing whether power gains on the part of one official are positively associated with power gains on the part of other officials—as would be the case if organizational pluralism were actually present.

Surprisingly, the patterns of power shifts are opposite to those that would be expected from the viewpoint of organizational pluralism (table 7.6). The power gains of one official are not positively associated with gains by other officials. Instead, there is a great deal of independence, as evidenced by the low and sometimes negative correlations in table 7.6.

Table 7.6   Relationships Among Power Shift Ratings

Power Shifts to:	Manager	Mayor	Council	Planner/ Analyst	Departments
			Pearson Correlations[a]		
Manager		.05	.10	−.13	−.19
Mayor	27		.04	.36*	−.19
Council	30	37		−.23	−.05
Planner/ Analyst	30	37	40		.21
Departments	30	37	40	40	
			Sample Size[a]		

SOURCE: Adapted from Kraemer and Dutton (1979: table 6).
[a]Pearson correlations are presented in upper right and sample sizes are presented in the lower left.
*$P < .05$

Apparently, different kinds of power shifts operate in different cities, and the marginal values reported in table 7.5 do not result from pluralistic patterns operating in a subset of cities.

Power Reinforcement from Computer Use

The reinforcement politics perspective provides a plausible explanation for the variation in the nature of power shifts among cities. It may be that computing tends to reinforce the influence of those officials in control, rather than to shift influence to a particular type of official. If this is the case, then because the influence structures of local governments vary from city to city, so will the nature of power shifts. In order to test the reinforcement hypothesis, we must explore this relationship. If the reinforcement hypothesis is valid, then those in control should gain (and certainly not lose) power as a result of computerized information systems.

We have approached the measurement of organizational control from two perspectives. First, we have developed indicators of *direct control of computing decisions.* These measures indicate whether top management, mayors, council members, and department heads have a major input into decisions related to data processing, such as that of introducing computers to help perform a specific task. It may be that those officials with direct control over the development of computer-based information systems shape the systems to serve their interests. And because the direct control over computer-based information systems tends to be somewhat pluralistic in most local governments (chapter 4), a rather pluralistic array of interests may also tend to be served.

Second, we have developed indicators of *indirect control over computing decisions.* These represent structural attributes of local governments that affect control over the organization as a whole, rather than merely control over computing as a particular activity. For example, the manager is likely to achieve greater control over local governments with a council-manager form of government than with a mayor-council form. And departments are likely to have greater organizational autonomy in large cities than in small.

Our hypothesis is that computer-based systems might be shaped to serve the interests of those who control the organization as a whole, regardless of whether direct control over those systems is highly centralized or highly pluralistic. The assumptions behind this expectation are that those who directly control the development of computer-based information systems will know and anticipate the needs and interests of those who control the organization (Dahl 1961; Schumpeter 1947), and will more or less deliberately shape information systems and their use to serve those needs and interests (Dutton & Kraemer 1978a, 1978b). This behavior is both a strategy for maintaining and enhancing their own position within the organization, and an automatic response that stems from their subordinate and supportive roles (Northrop & Dutton 1978). By the same token, most organizational elites have little direct involvement in computerized information systems; they assume that subordinates will guard their (the "organization's") interests.

Table 7.7 describes the relationship between power shifts and direct control over computer-based information systems by managers, mayors, councils, or departments. In cities where top managers are very influential in computing decisions, they are somewhat less—not more—likely to have gained decisional influence as a result of computer-based information. Similarly, neither mayors nor councils are likely to have been major beneficiaries of power shifts as a result of direct influence over computing decisions. Only for departments is there a weak association suggesting that power shifts may correspond to direct influence over computer-based information systems. Generally, the relationships between direct control and power shifts are weak and mixed. Direct control does not systematically affect the direction of power shifts!

One weakness with this interpretation is that both direct influence and power shifts are measured at a particular point in time. It could be that

Table 7.7   Correlations Between Control Over Computing Decisions and Power Shifts

	Power Shifts to:[a]				
Control Variable[b]	Managers	Mayors	Councils	Planner/ Analysts	Depart- ments
Top manager influence	−.21	.25*	−.24*	.04	−.29*
Mayor influence	−.49*	.10	−.16	.04	−.12
Council influence	−.34*	−.04	−.16	−.12	−.03
Department head influence	−.11	−.32*	−.19	−.16	.20

SOURCE: Adapted from Kraemer and Dutton (1979: table 7).
[a]Marginals for these dependent variables are presented in table 7.5.
[b]Two or more informants in each city were aksed "Consider a decision related to data processing, such as introducing computers to help perform a task. How often has each of the following officials had a major input into the final decision?"
*$p < .05$

some officials exercise direct control over computing only when they believe they are not being served currently by computer-based information systems. Direct control could translate into gains in decisional effectiveness at some future date. However, a more plausible explanation is suggested by the reinforcement politics perspective. That is, subordinates regularly participate in computing decisions and serve the interests of those controling the broader organization. Thus we turn to those indicators of organizational control that might indicate indirect control over computing.

In order to test the reinforcement hypothesis, we will assume that in strong mayor cities the mayor will gain over the manager (CAO), council, planners, and department heads. We will also assume that in city-manager cities the manager will gain over the other roles. We will further assume that in larger cities, where there is traditionally greater fragmentation and pluralism, power will be distributed and therefore planners and departments will gain.

Table 7.8 describes the relationship between power shifts and those independent variables that tend to reflect the general influence structure of local governments. The most striking relationship in the table is the perfect negative symmetry between the structural variables and power shifts to mayors and managers. In strong mayor cities, computing tends to shift greater influence to the mayor, whereas in council-manager cities, computing tends to shift greater influence to the manager. And in both cases, there were no gains by councils, planners, or departments. However, as cities become larger and more complex, managers, mayors and council *all* lose power because the governmental environment is more fragmented and differentiated. And computing tends to shift power to planners and the operating departments, who are able to work more effectively in a decentralized environment (table 7.8).

These findings are significant because they refute the organizational pluralism perspective and support the reinforcement politics perspective. Organizational pluralism would have predicted that, over time, everyone gains and loses in any given environment. The rationale is that because everyone has an opportunity to use computer-based information systems and everyone has a variety of resources to bring to bear on the decisions considered crucial, the distribution of power shifts among roles would be about equal. But this is not the case. There are clearly different patterns of power shifts in different cities. And these patterns indicate that power shifts tend to conform to the general structure of influence in the city, as predicted by the reinforcement politics interpretation.

Table 7.8 Correlations Between Organizational Control Variables and Power Shifts

| | Power Shifts to:[a] | | | | |
| | | | | Planner/ | Depart- |
Independent Variables	Managers	Mayors	Councils	Analysts	ments
Structure					
Strong mayor city	−.22	.38*	−.03	.12	−.13
Council-manager city	.22	−.37*	.09	−.23	.05
Size and Complexity					
Total population	−.31*	−.03	−.20	.39*	.41*
Government expenditures	−.26*	−.15	.03	.29*	.46*

SOURCE: Adapted from Kraemer and Dutton (1979: table 7) and Kling (1978c: table 11).
[a]Marginals for these dependent variables are presented in table 7.5.
*$p < .05$

THE INTERESTS SERVED BY COMPUTING

We have examined the use of data banks and operational data systems, and the power shifts to which they can be linked. We can now review our findings concerning the magnitude and direction of those power shifts, and draw some conclusions as to the explanatory power of the four perspectives.

Power shifts attributable to computerized information systems occur in most local governments with computer technology, but they tend to be subtle, limited, and complex in their patterns. Such shifts were judged to occur in over 75 percent of the cities investigated, but the generally low or moderate use of computing for management, planning, or politics tends to limit the relevance of computing to the power relationships among bureaucrats, technocrats, and politicians. No single type of official's relative decision-making effectiveness is powerfully enhanced.

Managerial rationalism suggests that managers will be major benefi-ciaries of power shifts. We did find that managers are the most frequent users of operational data systems, and that managers were judged to have gained some influence in about one-fourth of the cities. However, managers are not the most frequent users of data banks, and although they are some-what more likely to gain as a result of computing in the smaller cities and the city-manager cities, they are not the dominant beneficiaries in general. Consequently, managerial rationalism does not accurately predict the nature of power shifts.

Technocratic elitism suggests that the new urban planners—the information elite—will be the major beneficiaries of power shifts. We did find that planners use data banks more than other officials for nearly every purpose investigated, and that planners are the most likely beneficiaries of power shifts. However, they do not monopolize the use of data banks; they are minimally involved in the use of operational systems; and they tend to gain influence in only about one-third of the cities investigated. Furthermore, where planners tend to gain, so do mayors and operating department heads (generally in the larger cities). Thus while technocratic elitism correctly predicts the relative dominance of the planners, it fails to explain the overall pattern of power shifts, which includes many shifts in favor of other officials.

Organizational pluralism suggests that no single kind of official predominantly gains in decision-making effectiveness. This hypothesis finds substantial support in that each kind of official uses computer-based data, and all appear to gain influence, occasionally, as a result. Further support is provided by the fact that where one kind of official tends to use computer-based data, other kinds of officials also use these data. However, organizational pluralism is inconsistent with the patterns of power shifts. Gains for a given role are independent, or even negatively linked with gains for other roles, suggesting the operation of different power shifts in different cities.

Finally, reinforcement politics predicts that computer-based systems tend to follow and reinforce the existing pattern of power relationships. This hypothesis is most consistent with our findings, and it explains why the nature of power shifts varies among governments. Each of the other models might be found to operate in some cities, depending on the existing structure of influence. And reinforcement politics explains why technocrats might be dominant participants in the pluralistic processes surrounding computing decisions, but not be more dominant beneficiaries of power shifts—technical experts serve their organizational interests best by anticipating and serving the interests of those who control the broader organization.

We do find that *technocrats and managers often tend to be relative gainers.* However, their gains are less likely to result from their direct control over computing resources than from their increasing importance in the politics and administration of local governments. In many cities the new urban planner is taking on a more significant role with the increased importance of federal grants, needs assessments, evaluations, and more stringent reporting requirements. In the larger cities, these factors come into play within an organizational setting that is more decentralized. Within such a system, the new urban planners have some autonomy, and gain relatively more influence than they might have without the computing resource.

Likewise, managers clearly gain influence in relation to their subordinates by using computing to monitor and control departmental operations. Yet computing does not tend to shift greater influence to the manager in those cities where departments and agencies have a great deal of political autonomy from the manager—that is, in the larger, strong-mayor cities. In contrast, computing tends to reinforce the power of the manager in the smaller, city-manager cities in which the mayor and council are less active and influential.

THE DYNAMICS OF REINFORCEMENT POLITICS

The dynamics of reinforcement politics can be better understood if we explain how they act within specific local governments. One medium-sized southern city, for example, was especially illustrative. Before our fieldwork in the city, the dominant power there had shifted from a group of old-style politicians to reform-minded businessmen. The first major action of the businessmen was to successfully support the structural reform of the city's administration from a mayor-council to a council-manager form of government. Once the city manager was hired, the dominant coalition was composed of the majority members of the city council, the mayor, the city manager, and two department heads, the police chief and fire chief. This coalition then used computing as a strategy for reinforcing their influence and reform goals.

First, the city manager hired an extremely skilled data processing manager from a California-based consulting firm that had consulted with the manager on the redesign of the city's computing operations. In addition, he hired a new financial analyst-administrator to work under (and around) an entrenched old-style finance director. The city then launched an aggressive effort to implement two major computing systems. The first was a city-wide system, but was, in fact, dedicated to finance and, more specifically, to the development of an integrated financial information system headed by the manager's new financial analyst. This system was used to aid the manager in controlling the spending activities of the various city departments that had previously enjoyed a great deal of autonomy under the mayor-council form of government.

The second system was dedicated to the police department and was focused on the development of a police information system supporting patrol officers and detectives. The police system served the manager in that it gave the manager's only potential opponent within the dominant coalition what he wanted. Thus, the manager could pursue his financial system without the opposition of the police department. Similarly, he gave the fire chief what he wanted, which was no computing. The police system also served the police chief by permitting him to develop the most advanced police computing system in the region, which enabled him to obtain even more resources. For example, he was able to acquire the county-wide Prosecutor's Management Information System and implement it on his system. By such actions, the police chief was becoming a major force in the politics of law enforcement within the region. While other city departments were hopeful of expanding their computing, they were well aware of the city's priorities and they realized that their own plans had to await the development of the police and finance systems.

Although reinforcement politics is the norm, it is not the universal pattern in the politics of computing. For example, the dominant coalition of one large city in the north central United States was composed of the mayor, his director of budget and management, and his director of the law department. The mayor and law director were extremely skilled political entrepreneurs; but they concentrated their attention on community and council politics, leaving the management of the city to the director of budget and management. In effect, however, this left the city bureaucracy nearly unmanaged, because of the functional limitations of this director and his staff. In this milieu, an otherwise powerless department, city planning, was able to use computer-based analyses to influence city policy. The planning department did sophisticated studies supporting liberal social policies directly in conflict with the conservative policies of the mayor's coalition. And the analyses gained influence by being leaked to the press and to the mayor's political opponents. As a consequence, in several major cases the policies advocated privately by the planning department prevailed over policies advocated by the mayor and supported publicly by planning. In this case, a relatively powerless group was able to use computing to undermine the influence of the dominant coalition of the organization.

Another exception was found in a small midwestern city. The dominant coalition was clearly composed of the majority members of the council and the mayor. This coalition opposed, as an unnecessary expense, a city data-processing facility, and the city never acquired one. However, the utility department, which generated its own revenues, acquired its own computer installation and data-processing specialists. Then, as problems developed in the operations of other city departments (such as a major parking ticket scandal involving the theft of fines), widespread demand arose for computing services. The utility department found itself in an especially attractive bargaining position, because of its monopoly of computing resources, and it was able to exert considerable influence on computing priorities and on the speed at which computing services were provided to other city departments. This case indicates how a department outside the dominant coalition can use its control of the computer elite and of computing resources to create an independent base of influence within the organization.

Despite these exceptions, the pattern of reinforcement by means of computer technology is widely evident. The organizational processes that underlie the role of computer technology in reinforcement politics can be broadly illustrated by a more intensive analysis of the use and impacts of Fiscal Impact Budgeting Systems (FIBS) in American local governments.[11] FIBS are large-scale computer models that forecast local government service needs, expenditure levels, and revenues for the coming fiscal year(s). Such forecasts are based on previous expenditure and revenue data, community land use, housing and demographic data, governmental characteristics, and intergovernmental funding relationships, and on projected changes in all of these characteristics. The models define the relationships among these elements by means of sets of mathematical equations and instructions. Due to their level of detail, the projections from the models can be directly applicable to governmental budgeting decisions.

FIBS are a classic management-science response to a fundamental policy problem—that of developing more rational control by elected officials and the general public over decisions that affect the fiscal position of government.[12] They are promoted as leading to improvements in information processing, content, and flows, and as such, they represent a potential tool for managerial rationalism.

However, our case studies of the uses and impacts of FIBS suggest that they are employed more often as a political tool to reinforce the prevailing biases of the model-using organization than as a rational tool to enhance public control. First, local officials normally limit the number of alternative policies assessed by FIBS models, in part to lessen uncertainty regarding the recommendations based on the models. Governmental budgets are traditionally developed on the basis of a very limited search of alternative taxing, spending, and development policies. This occurs both because of the incremental nature of budgetary decision making (Crecine 1968; Wildavsky 1964), and because of the complexity of evaluating the budgetary implications of alternative decisions (Simon 1957:198–99). Fiscal impact budgeting systems are thought to provide participants in the budgeting process with the technical capability to evaluate the budgetary impacts of a broader array of alternative taxing, spending, and development decisions. The consequences of slight variations in model assumptions can be rapidly computed with most computerized FIBS—an impossible calculating task without them. In practice, however, local government officials place severe restrictions on the number of alternative scenarios that are evaluated with a FIBS. For example, one southwestern city utilized a FIBS model to compare only two policy alternatives—a "managed growth" plan promoted by the mayor, and continuation of "urban sprawl." Not surprisingly, the fiscal analysis supported the greater fiscal profitability of the managed growth plan, because it reduced the need for future capital investments.

Second, FIBS often reinforce the biases of traditional, decentralized budgetary decision making in local governments. Traditionally, major budgetary decisions are largely fragmented and decentralized among the various departments and agencies of local governments. They are therefore highly dependent on internal information developed by the departments, and on behavioral factors such as the forcefulness of department heads (Danziger 1978b; Hale & Douglas 1977). In contrast, fiscal impact budgeting systems are designed to assess taxing and spending policy by using information about the community environment as the basis for budget forecasts, and by having an independent group (the FIBS modelers) prepare the forecasts. Thus, the forecasts might be less subject to manipulation by departments and agencies seeking to maintain and enhance their resources during the annual budget cycle. However, the implementation of FIBS requires that the modelers make literally hundreds of estimates of such factors as the number of patrol officers required per capita, the rate of inflation, the revenue capacity of single-family housing, and so forth. And these estimates are generally not made by the top elected officials. Rather, as in traditional budgeting, such technical decisions are made by department and agency heads who usually are the only people that have the necessary data and the experience. Consequently, FIBS produce outputs that appear far more objective and independent of departmental influence than they necessarily are. Since elected officials and the public are rarely able to discern this fact, let alone trace through the bases of all the estimates, their understanding and control is lessened.

Third, embedded within every fiscal impact budgeting system are assumptions and theories that can systematically influence the model outputs in ways that benefit certain interests more than others. For example, FIBS can be developed to exhibit a progrowth bias by over-weighing the short-term revenue gains and underweighing the long-term carrying costs of population growth. Such systems are likely to bias decisions in favor of fiscal profitability (as opposed to other goals, such as maximization of urban amenities, redistribution of wealth, or an increase in the quality of social services), by suggesting that fiscal impacts are to be considered important criteria for decision making. Also, decision makers will be more likely to take fiscal effects into account because the model makes such information available and lessens the importance of other decision criteria.

Fourth, as in the case of other models, FIBS are employed to serve political functions contrary to the rational functions used to justify their adoption. These political functions of models include their use to block or delay decisions (Brewer 1974), to provide a symbolic response to problems (Greenberger, Crenson, & Crissey 1976), to legitimize policy positions already taken (Pack & Pack 1977), or to gain credibility and publicity in order to persuade others to support a given policy (Brewer 1974). To give an example, a western city sought to annex some adjacent lands. Stymied by residents who sought to incorporate as a city rather than be annexed, planners for the city used a fiscal impact model to overwhelm the residents with evidence that incorporation was not economically feasible. After the local agency formation commission approved the annexation, the city manager privately admitted that the model also showed that annexation was no more efficient than was incorporation.

SUMMARY AND DISCUSSION

Governmental structures and processes are not politically neutral—they tend to favor some interests over others (Schattschneider 1960). This chapter suggests that computers tend to extend and reinforce the prevailing biases of governmental structures and processes. Those who control local government decisions have adapted computer technology to serve existing structures of influence and control, by determining the kinds of applications adopted, and by selectively utilizing available computer-based information.

Computing can be viewed as a malleable (but certainly not as an apolitical) technology, for it often serves the interests of those who control the organization. The computing package (the equipment, technique, and people) is a means, a tool, for accomplishing the ends of organizational elites. As such a tool, its impacts are not neutral—it tends to serve some interests more than others. Most generally, computing supports the status quo. Specifically, urban data systems have been shaped to serve the interests of planners, top managers, and department managers over those of elected officials. In large part, this bias is a reflection of the success of prior structural reforms in local government. Reformers may have been so successful in raising the influence of technocrats and bureaucrats that those officials can now in many cases shape organizational change and innovation to suit their own needs.

This reinforcement of prevailing biases was illustrated through an examination of the use and impacts of Fiscal Impact Budgeting Systems. Ironically, fiscal impact budgeting systems have been promoted as a tool for reforming the budgetary processes of local governments—for achieving managerial rationality. However, rather than being a tool for reform, FIBS tend to automate the existing biases of the budgetary process, and might even exaggerate these biases, because the complexity and mystique of computer-based models make it harder for outsiders to oppose those who control the use of these models in order to support their own interests and values.

CHAPTER EIGHT

COMPUTING AND URBAN SERVICES

Rob Kling and Kenneth L. Kraemer

WHEREAS PREVIOUS CHAPTERS showed how political, managerial, and professional elites within the government use computing to carry out their own agendas, this chapter focuses on how citizens' interests are dealt with and mediated by means of computer technology. Computing in local government can be applied to such diverse activities as creating urban data banks for support of local policy making by top officials, keeping maintenance records on vehicles in the motor pool, and providing lists of wanted persons and stolen property to police officers in the field. Computing in support of these activities ranges from, for example, on-line, real-time systems to help fire dispatchers locate the fire hydrants near a burning building, to batch systems that produce thousands of tax bills a year. In this chapter, we examine the distribution of computing resources to different government activities and, indirectly, to different client groups. We assess the extent to which the patterns of computer use reflect stable patterns of choice favoring some uses over others and, therefore, some client groups over others. And we ask whether computing has a different impact on citizens than it does within the government.

Two political perspectives are considered in this chapter: managerial rationalism and reinforcement politics.[1] Many descriptions of local government computing label the technology as one that "serves citizens" (ACM 1973; Blum 1972; Evans & Knisely 1970; Nanus 1972; Sackman & Boehm 1972; URISA 1977; USAC 1976; Weiner 1969). Implicit in this labeling is the managerial rationalist notion that computing provides an important means to:

1. increase revenues;
2. reduce service costs;
3. improve the quality and effectiveness of important current services;
4. provide kinds or qualities of services not now available, particularly those highly esteemed; and
5. achieve highly valued principles—for example, by improving equity in the distribution of service cost and benefits, or by making municipal government more adaptive and responsive to changing citizen needs and desires (Blum 1972:48).

It is important to note the difference between this application of the concept of managerial rationalism, and the within-government application of the concept discussed in previous chapters. *Inside the government*, managerial rationalism is essentially concerned with questions of efficiency—increased revenue collection, reduced service costs, and improved decision making about the quality and effectiveness of current services. Some writers (Evans & Knisely 1970; Weiner 1969) even conceive of computing as a means of effecting changes in administrative organization, practices, and behavior. When managerial rationalism is considered *in relation to the community*, as it is in this chapter, additional dimensions become prominent. Computing is conceived not only as a means of enhancing efficiency, but also as a means of providing new services and achieving greater equity in the distribution of services. Moreover, the technology is perceived as providing citizens with additional choices, rather than limiting or coercing them in any way.

Managerial rationalists seldom conceive of these objectives for computer use as potentially conflicting, but they frequently are (Levy, Mettsner, & Wildavsky 1974). A commitment to reduced costs, for example, can preclude the provision of new services or increased responsiveness to citizens' needs and desires, and achievement of some objectives may serve some groups but not others. For example, achieving greater equity in service provision without increasing costs would require a greater reduction in services to advantaged groups in order to increase services to disadvantaged groups.

If the managerial rationalist emphasis on service to citizens does, in fact, characterize computing decisions, we would expect to see most computing used in those activities that provide direct services and make more choices available to citizens. But given the conflict among objectives, it is not at all clear that those using computing within the government actually use it in this way.

Reinforcement politics offers an alternative viewpoint. This perspective suggests that computing is a tool of whatever social forces are dominant in organizational settings. If that setting is benign, then computing will be used to increase choice; if the setting is coercive, then computing will be used to limit choice. In the context of local government vis-à-vis citizens, the reinforcement politics perspective suggests that computing is used primarily to support those government activities that serve the traditional and dominant values and interests of citizens in the community—concerns for efficiency in government operations, provision of basic services such as police, fire, and public works, and prevention of fraud and abuse in government programs. If this perspective indeed characterizes computing decisions, we would expect to see computing used in support of routine administrative activities, basic local government services, bureaucratic control over government departments and agencies, and social control over the recipients of social services such as welfare, health, and recreation.

Is computing a radical change agent, bringing about new services and new distributions of the benefits and costs of services? Or is it a conservative instrument, merely reinforcing the existing dominant distribution of values and services within the community? These are the central questions of this chapter.

Many current applications of local government computing do indeed "serve citizens," in that they support routine activities through which a government agency serves its public. But some activities, such as fire truck dispatching, have a more direct effect on citizens than do other activities, such as maintenance of a municipal motor pool. Moreover, in some activities, such as law enforcement, public employees exert a *high* degree of control over citizens, whereas in others, such as library circulation, they exert a relatively *low* degree of control.

These distinctions raise questions about what it really means to say that computer applications "support services to citizens." To what extent do computer applications in local governments support *direct services* such as dispatching police or fire vehicles to an emergency, rather than *administrative activities* such as eliminating city fleet vehicles that are costly to repair? To what extent do they tend to enhance *social control* of government agencies over citizens, and *bureaucratic control* over employees?

These questions assume that computing is a resource that can be applied to a variety of situations for a variety of purposes. *How* it is applied is a matter of the *choices* made by particular administrators and elected officials. What are the *patterns* of choices that have been made in city and county governments during the past few decades? What dynamics of computing development or local government operations seem to produce these patterns? And, in the end, which perspective of the technology— managerial rationalism or reinforcement politics—seems to account for these patterns?

This chapter examines the evidence for each perspective by first looking at the extent to which computing is applied to different government functions. We suggest that computing tends to reinforce the traditional emphases of local governments on internal administrative efficiency, and on basic government functions, especially finance and police. We then classify local government computing applications as to whether they provide direct services to citizens as opposed to indirect support, and whether they facilitate social control of "targeted" citizen groups as opposed to bureaucratic control of government departments, agencies, and employees. These findings are used to assess how well the managerial rationalist and reinforcement politics perspectives predict and explain the current distribution of computing resources among different activities in local government.

AREAS OF USE

As indicated in chapter 2, computing is important to a wide variety of government functions. It is used as more than simply an accounting machine, and its use is likely to span most major functional areas of local government services and administration. However, distribution is uneven.

Figures 8.1 and 8.2 characterize the level of automation both within and between functional areas of local governments in 1975. The vertical scale in the figures ("commonality") indicates the percentage of local governments that have applied computing to a specific function. The horizontal scale ("intensity") indicates, for each specific function, the average number of automated applications per site in those cities and counties with at least one application in that functional area. Thus location higher in the figure reflects an area where computing has been widely used, and location farther to the right in the figure indicates a function that tends to be more intensively automated.

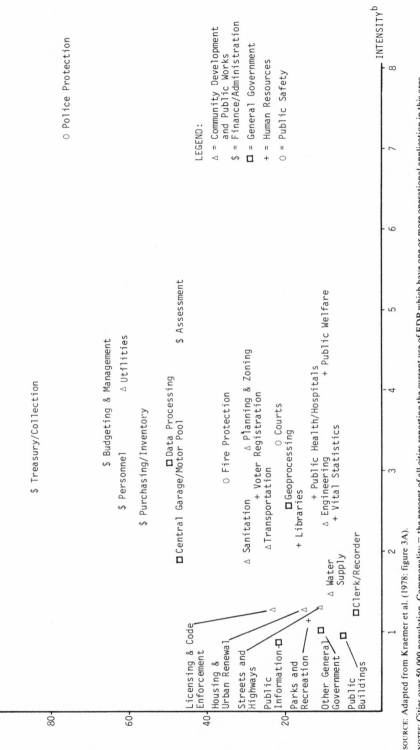

SOURCE: Adapted from Kraemer et al. (1978: figure 3A).

NOTES: Cities over 50,000 population. Commonality = the percent of all cities reporting the current use of EDP which have one or more operational application in this area. Intensity = the average number of operational applications in the functional area for all cities with one or more applications operational in this area.

Figure 8.1 Commonality and Intensity of Automation—Cities

COMMONALITY[a]

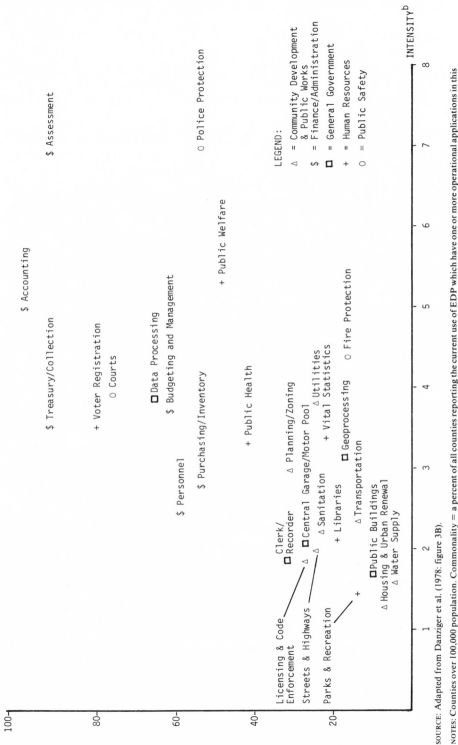

SOURCE: Adapted from Danziger et al. (1978: figure 3B).

NOTES: Counties over 100,000 population. Commonality = a percent of all counties reporting the current use of EDP which have one or more operational applications in this area. Intensity = the average number of operational applications in the functional area for all counties with one or more applications in this area.

Figure 8.2 Commonality and Intensity of Automation—Counties

In both city and county governments, finance and police are most commonly and intensively automated. Within finance, the accounting, treasury and collections, and budgeting and management functions are highly automated in both cities and counties. The assessment function also shows a high level of automation in counties and in those cities that perform assessment. Certain record-keeping functions, particularly personnel, purchasing, and inventory records, reflect high levels of computer application in both cities and counties. Computer use is also high for some record-keeping functions that are usually responsibilities of counties, such as voter registration and administration of the court system. And where public welfare activities have been automated (usually counties), the number of computer applications is quite high. Among city functions, moderate levels of computer use are found in the area of utilities.

Generally, the data in figures 8.1 and 8.2 suggest that the primary emphases of computer use in local governments have been on the revenue-producing and expenditure-controlling activities, on police activities, and on some administrative housekeeping activities. In other words, it appears that the functional bias in local government automation has led to the technology's being applied primarily to facilitate administrative and social control and routine administration. There are relatively few applications of automation to functions for planning and maintaining the physical environment, or with providing human services. Moreover, in 1975 the applications most commonly scheduled for development over the subsequent two years were revenue and expenditure forecasting; cash control; expenditure monitoring; police service and facility planning; and police manpower allocation. Thus, current kinds of use are likely to continue to dominate.

CHARACTERIZATION OF USE

The pattern suggested above—the reinforcement by computing of the prevailing biases in local government activities—can be examined more closely by characterizing the distribution of computing applications in terms of support of service delivery to citizens versus administration, and social control versus bureaucratic control. In order to do this, we must first develop a characterization of local government activities.

Service Administrative

The activities of local governments may be characterized by features of the service provider (e.g., whether it is a public, private, or voluntary agency), and the level of government providing the service (e.g., regional versus local, or centralized versus decentralized) (Ostrom 1975; Savas 1978; Sonenblum, Kirlin, & Ries 1975). Usually, a further distinction is made between direct services to citizens and indirect services (which we call administrative activities). The aim of these characterizations usually has been to see whether different structural arrangements for these activities have any effect on the quality of governmental performance. They also can be used to show the ways in which government resources are distributed.

When local government agencies educate children, collect garbage, fight fires, and circulate library books, they are engaged in service delivery to citizens. These examples typify those activities whereby a tangible good or service is provided directly to some person, organization, or group in the local government's jurisdiction. Increases in the effectiveness, efficiency, or equity of these activities directly benefit some of the public.

Other government activities do not directly deliver services to citizens. Rather, they support the administration of services (e.g., operation of the motor pool) and of the government as an institution (e.g., control of government spending). Administrative activities provide a tangible good or service to some person or organization within the government, or to the government as a whole. Increases in the effectiveness, efficiency, or equity of these services indirectly benefit the public through their effects on the operation of specific services and, more broadly, of the whole government.

Control

In addition to the service-administrative distinction, every government activity can be characterized by a control dimension—namely, the extent to which recipients of direct services or administrative support have their activities controlled by the staff of a public agency. *Social control* is exerted over citizens in delivering public services; *bureaucratic control* is exerted over employees in providing administrative support. Moreover, our concept of control focuses on the "primary modality" or "typical pattern" of an activity. This approach is very different from one that focuses on the "potential capacity" of an activity for enhancing control (e.g., Rule 1974).[2]

Clearly, some government activities are more "control-oriented" than others. Most direct services to citizens involve a low level of social control. That is, in the course of providing goods and services, local government officials exercise some control over the public use of the resources entrusted to their care. For example, library books are lent for a specific time and perhaps in a limited number per patron. Some service departments, exerting higher levels of social control, engage in mandated programs to control specific behaviors of some segment of the public as a major part of their activity. For example, fire departments send inspectors to check the fire safety of theaters, restaurants, department stores, and other business establishments serving the public. And finally, some agencies exert high levels of social control—such as the police, both in catching lawbreakers and in maintaining civic order (Wilson 1968).[3]

Government administrative activities—purchasing light bulbs, repairing trucks in the city fleet, distributing the payroll—may also be more or less control-oriented. Many administrative activities involve a low degree of bureaucratic control. For example, if a local government purchasing department keeps a card file listing the addresses of common vendors, those records largely support internal administrative routines rather than bureaucratic control. However, every organization develops means to control the behavior of its members as well as the resources that they allocate (Blau 1955; Friedson 1970; Perrow 1972). For example, records such as monthly expense summaries by department are used by authorized officials to control expenditures. Potentially, any record might be used by some staff member for controlling the work of others and the resources that they use; but in practice, such records are also frequently used to control the activities of an agency's staff.

Characterizing Computer Applications

As can other governmental activities, computer applications can be characterized in terms of their service-administrative orientation and level of social or bureaucratic control. Some computer applications, such as payroll processing, primarily serve as aids to administrators, while other applications, such as police wants and warrants files, assist patrolmen in providing services to the public. We call this a *service-administrative* support dimension. For example, the processing of traffic tickets and the dispatching of fire trucks *directly* influence citizens who have received a parking ticket or whose homes are on fire. When done properly, one of these activities (dispatching) helps deliver a service (fire fighters) to a

	Service Support	Administrative Support
High Social/Bureaucratic Control	*Examples:* Traffic ticket processing, police wants and warrants, child support records (courts), firearms registration file, library circulation records. *Criteria:* The application supports a government activity which is designed to limit the choices of citizens or institutions that are the "targets" of the activity. (Other people or institutions may be served when the targets are controlled). *Illustrative Rationale:* Police wants and warrants applications are explicitly designed for social control, i.e., to aid in the location, identification, and apprehension of criminals.	*Examples:* Motor vehicle maintenance records, courtroom scheduling, budget monitoring, cost accounting, personnel, position control. *Criteria:* The application supports an administrative activity in which government resources such as space, goods, money, or staff are allocated or such allocations are monitored. *Illustrative Rationale:* Budget monitoring is explicitly aimed at bureaucratic control—limiting and rationing the expenditures of government departments and agencies.
Low Social/Bureaucratic Control	*Examples:* Check processing in welfare, information and referral systems in welfare, emergency vehicle dispatch, vital statistics records, neighborhood social data analysis. *Criteria:* The application supports a government activity in which a citizen or institution receives a direct service from a government agency and there is little or no attempt to limit the choices of the targets of the activity. *Illustrative Rationale:* Check processing in social welfare is mainly concerned with delivering payments to individual welfare recipients. Although the application might check for a valid payee before printing the check, it is not designed to support social control, e.g., determine the eligibility of an individual for welfare payments or to catch welfare cheaters. Other applications might do this, however.	*Examples:* Media mailing list, payroll processing, purchase order file, street inventory, census data file. *Criteria:* The application supports an administrative activity in which there is little or no effort to allocate or monitor resources. *Illustrative Rationale:* Payroll processing is mainly concerned with calculation and printing payroll checks for government employees. It involves no bureaucratic control; however, other personnel/payroll applications such as position control are aimed at bureaucratic control over hiring by the departments.

person or business in distress. In contrast, the traffic ticket processing system is often designed to notify citizens that a fine is due; but it is also designed to catch those who fail to pay and, consequently, it supports the control that police and courts exert over the public. Thus each computer application can be additionally characterized by a *control* dimension—the extent to which it *tends* to increase the degree of social or bureaucratic control exercised by a public agency over its clientele, or over some segment of the public.

Computer applications that exemplify each of these categories appear in table 8.1, along with the criteria used to classify them and illustrative rationales. In classifying each application, we focused on the way in which the application is typically used in local government operations. Clearly, the service-administrative support and the high-low social control dimensions are continuous, unlike the simple dichotomous classifications presented here. Moreover, many computer applications, like many government activities, have aspects of both service and administrative support, and both high and low social control. However, in our classification we have attempted to focus on the primary modality of an application.

Thus we classify computer applications as *mainly* supporting service or administrative activities and as high *or* low control. For example, a purchase order file is coded as administrative support / low control because it is typically used to expedite invoice processing. Some staff could use it to analyze which departments are making especially frequent or add-on purchases; thus it has an inherent "surveillance capacity" that could enhance bureaucratic control. However, such dramatic uses of a purchase order file for internal surveillance are rare, and our coding reflects only the dominant uses.[4]

DISTRIBUTION OF COMPUTER USE

We would like to understand how American local governments invest in computing activities, in terms of the characteristics discussed above (i.e., degree of social control, service vs. administrative orientation). How can we measure these investments? Perhaps the amount of money spent each year to develop and operate computer applications, sampled from each of the four cells of table 8.1, would provide the best measure. Unfortunately, such expenditures are difficult to estimate for even single applications developed and used by an organization, let alone the dozens of applications used by many cities and counties. Another set of measures could be based on the number of computer applications that local governments adopt.

An analogy can help clarify our choices of measurements. Suppose we were interested in learning what genres of film (e.g., science fiction, disaster, tragedy) the American public viewed each year. Different measures could be used to answer this question. One is the number of films in each genre that were available for distribution to theatre owners in a given year. But some kinds of films (e.g., disaster) might have been disproportionately popular. A second measure, the number of theatres actually showing films of each genre, would emphasize the popularity of films; and we could determine the number of tickets sold to film showings of each genre as an even better measure. Actually, each of these measures taps something different. The films available for distribution indicate a pool of choices from which theatre owners can select with relative ease. Their actual choices are a much better measure of what the public actually sees.

In the case of computer applications in local governments, we are asking a similar question. If the four categories of applications in table 8.1 are treated as "genres" of computing, we are interested in what selections were made by local government officials. One measure, like the films available for distribution, is the set of applications known to be automated in at least one local government. A second measure would tap the extent to which local governments actually developed and operated applications in each "genre."

Distribution of Known Computer Uses

We first characterized an inventory of 264 "known" computer uses in local governments by their service-administrative orientation, and by their level of social or bureaucratic control.[5] We refer to these computer uses as "known," because they had previously appeared in other surveys of computing, were offered by federal agencies or private vendors as prototypes, or were discussed in the literature of professional conferences. Generally, at least one local government had automated each application. Moreover, many of these applications were prominent in the occupational networks of information-processing specialists in local governments. If one believes the managerial rationalists, who say that computing provides service to citizens and enhances their choices, one would expect that the distribution of "known" computer applications would be oriented toward

Table 8.2   Orientation of Known Computing Applications

Type of Support	Computer Orientation (%)
Service	36% ($N=96$)
Administrative	64 ($N=169$)
Total	100 ($N=264$)

service delivery and toward low social or bureaucratic control, even if the "selected" distribution is not.

Based on the distribution of applications according to our categories (tables 8.2 and 8.3), a city that selected its applications in proportion to those that were "known" would select approximately:

1. 21% of its applications to support high social control in service delivery;
2. 15% of its applications to support low social control in service delivery;
3. 22% of its applications to support high bureaucratic control in administration; and
4. 42% of its applications to support low bureaucratic control in administration.

Of course we don't expect local governments actually to choose applications simply based upon those that were known to exist somewhere in the United States. However, these patterns of known uses provide us a baseline against which to contrast the computer uses selected by local governments. Thus if cities were to select, on the average, 30 percent of their applications supporting services with low social control, then we could conclude that they were especially disposed to supporting service delivery. We would conclude this because, based on our "known" distribution, we had expected only 15 percent of the cities' applications to be supporting services with low social control. Conversely, if, on the average, only one percent of municipal applications supported services with low social

Table 8.3   Level of Control in Known Computer Applications

Degree of Control	Orientation (%)	
	Social Support	Administrative Support
High Control	58% ($N=56$)	34% ($N=57$)
Low Control	42 ($N=40$)	66 ($N=112$)
Total	100 ($N=96$)	100 ($N=169$)

Table 8.4 Distribution of Selected Computing Applications

| Type of Government | Orientation of Applications (Average No.) | |
	Citizens	Administrators
Cities	9.0	23.0
Counties	11.5	20.0

control, we could conlude that cities were biased against such computer uses.

Local governments have been under tremendous pressures during the last decade to increase, or at least maintain, the quality of urban services without increasing costs. We should expect that these service-cost pressures would lead local governments to emphasize services to citizens, on the one hand, and internal bureaucratic control on the other. And we should expect that local governments have used computing in support of these objectives. Next we shall examine the computer uses they have "selected."

Patterns of Computer Use Selected

Tables 8.4 and 8.5 present the distributions of different kinds of computer applications selected by cities and counties. Our data indicate that city and county investments in computing generally parallel the "known" distribution of possible applications. However, there are four variations:

1. Local governments invest somewhat more in applications to support administrative activity than one finds in the inventory (68% versus 60%).

Table 8.5 Distribution of Application Support Toward Known and Selected Uses

| | Service Support | | Administrative Support | |
	Low Social Control	High Social Control	High Bureaucratic Control	Low Bureaucratic Control
Known Distribution	19.35%	20.07%	20.43%	40.14%
Selected Distribution				
Cities	9.83%	19.97%	18.87%	51.40%
Counties	16.20%	19.50%	14.30%	49.97%
City and County	11.66%	20.04%	17.27%	51.03%

2. Of those applications that support services, a somewhat smaller fraction support social control than one finds in the inventory (31% versus 39%).
3. County governments provide a larger number of computer applications to support services with low social control than do municipal governments (16% versus 12%).
4. Local governments invest somewhat more in applications to support low bureaucratic control than one finds in the inventory (51% versus 40%).

This parallel between known and selected uses stems partly from the fact that potential uses of computing in local governments are nearly always defined as marginal extensions of current uses. It is very rare for totally new computer uses to be proposed or to be imported (e.g., from private vendors or federal and state agencies); or for research leading to development of new uses to be conducted by local governments themselves.

The parallel may also stem from other, more subtle pressures. Chief among these is the fact that even potential uses to which computing might be put are highly constrained by local government's emphasis on certain traditional functions, values, and interests. Theoretically, computing could be applied to the full array of local government functions and services, and even, as suggested by the managerial rationalists, to new services and activities not possible without the computer; but such uses might conflict with traditional emphasis on automating those activities that are easiest to automate and that produce cost-efficiency payoffs. Providing new services also could increase costs rather than reduce them, and it could reduce efficiency in government operations, reduce political control, and have unanticipated consequences. Thus the conservative bias of local governments tends to limit the scope of uses selected for adoption and development.

In addition to the parallel between known and selected computer applications, several other patterns can be discerned in the data in table 8.5. Sixty-eight percent of local government computing is oriented toward administration; about 37 percent of the applications in a typical local government serve to enhance control within the bureaucracy and within the community; and about 12 percent are devoted to serving the public without manifest increases in social control. These patterns differ from those that we would expect from the managerial rationalist viewpoint, and from consideration of the cost-service pressures placed upon urban governments during the last decade.

The most significant finding from the data is that computer applications that support service to citizens without increasing social control are the exception rather than the rule. We shall examine the reasons for these patterns in the next section.

FACTORS UNDERLYING THE PATTERNS OF COMPUTER USE

The foregoing analysis provides little support for the managerial rationalist perspective, which assumes that computing is used by local governments to support service delivery to citizens and to enhance the choices available to citizens. Does this mean that the reinforcement politics perspective is supported?

Clearly, the data support reinforcement politics as an explanation for the patterns of computer use more than they do managerial rationalism. At the most general level, the data indicate that local government computing reflects the dominant character of local government activity, and allows local governments to do more efficiently what they are already doing. Thus it reinforces current biases. Four features of the current pattern of computer use lend support to the reinforcement politics perspective.

The Traditional Service Bias

The use of computing by local governments tends to reflect the traditional allocation of public expenditures to certain government activities and, indirectly, to certain community values. These governments provide a wide variety of services, and, consequently, no one service usually commands more than ten percent of the total budget; but various studies indicate that they traditionally have devoted most of their resources to certain *basic* governmental activities (Lineberry & Sharkansky 1978). According to statistics from the 1975–1976 census of city government finances (U.S. Bureau of the Census, 1976), these basic activities include police protection, public welfare, highways, fire protection, sewerage, and hospitals (table 8.6).

Budgets indicate relative priorities among public choices. Masotti and Bowen (1965) have noted that "the community budget can be viewed as public policy spelled out in dollars and cents, and . . . budget decisions represent the allocations of certain kinds of values." Decisions about computer use similarly represent allocations of certain kinds of values, and

Table 8.6   Local Government Expenditures, 1974–1975

Function	Amount (Millions of Dollars)	Percent
Total general expenditure	41,514	100
Police protection	5,281	12.7
Public welfare	3,846	9.3
Highways	3,861	9.3
Fire protection	2,901	7.0
Sewerage	3,415	8.2
Hospitals	2,735	6.6
Parks and recreation	2,274	5.5
Interest on general debt	2,294	5.5
Housing and urban renewal	1,752	4.2
Sanitation other than sewerage	1,763	4.2
General control	1,440	3.5
Financial administration	819	2.0
General public buildings	845	2.0
All other functions	8,288	20.0

SOURCE: U.S. Bureau of Census; *City Government Finances in 1974–75* (Washington, D.C.: U.S. Government Printing Office, 1976), p. 2.
NOTE: Excludes education.

mainly are used in support of traditional activities, such as police, finance and administration, fire, sanitation and utilities, and (in counties) public health and public welfare (table 8.7). The allocation of computing resources to police activities is particularly interesting in this regard. Police computing is the single largest use of computing outside of finance and administration in local governments, and reflects not only traditional concerns of citizens for order maintenance, but also the recent rise in the "fear of crime." Most cities (72%) and counties (97%) have at least one computer application supporting police; and, on the average, cities have seven such applications and counties have five (table 8.7).[6]

The Efficiency Bias

The use of computing reflects traditional concerns of citizens with economy and efficiency in government and, more recently, with the urban fiscal crisis. Local government revenues have lagged, but citizen demands have not. Indeed, demands have often been increasing in response to problems of urban growth and urban deterioration. So have the demands of municipal workers who, hit by inflation and erosion of their purchasing power, have demanded a fair share of local government budgets. And just as inflation has eroded the personal purchasing power of government employees, so has it eroded the purchasing power of local governments (Lineberry & Sharkansky 1978).

In this context, computing has been viewed by local governments as a major means of achieving cost efficiency. Local governments historically have given priority to those computer uses that emphasize efficient revenue generation, cost saving, cost avoidance, and expenditure control, over those that involve provision of new services. This "efficiency bias" in local government computing has been evident since the first introduction of computers into the finance function (chapter 2).[7] And it has continued as computer uses have been extended not only to other finance and administration activities, but to the operating departments as well.

The legacy of finance computing also helps to explain why the assumption of the managerial rationalists—that computing would be oriented primarily toward service delivery rather than toward administration—is invalid. First, the centralization of computing in the finance department has made if difficult for other departments that serve the public more directly to gain access to computing equipment and staff, either for developing new applications or for gaining adequate priorities for their computerized operations. The departments generally lack the required expertise to know what applications could be developed, with what costs and what payoffs. Even when they have the expertise, they must deal with a finance-oriented computing staff who may not have the inclination to support development. And the operating departments are dependent on the finance department not only for computing support and the resources for computing development, but also for support of their annual non-computing budgetary requests. Thus they have been reluctant to push too hard on the finance department for greater access. This influence has been particularly strong in cities (Table 8.8).

Second, the practice of justifying computer technology by arguments of "cost savings" and "cost avoidance" has made it difficult to justify applications that involve the provision of new services to citizens. The easiest targets for such cost-saving attempts have been those that entailed a large volume of routine processing. The net effect has been to use automation to support routine printing, calculating, or record-keeping activities. If staff reduction and greater efficiency in revenue generation could be combined, then the case for computing as a technology that could pay for itself could be made stronger. Thus utility, tax, and other billing

Table 8.7 Average Applications by Function in 1975

Functional area	Cities			Counties		
	No. with application(s)	% of total	Average no. of applications	No. with application(s)	% of total	Average no. of applications
Total cities/counties reporting	305	100	31.32	190	100	32.31
Public safety						
Police protection	221	72	7.18	97	51	5.46
Fire protection	104	34	2.72	19	10	3.36
Courts	65	21	3.21	137	72	3.24
Emergency preparedness	3	1	1.66	2	1	2.00
Public finance and administration						
Accounting	281	92	4.00	174	92	3.99
Treasury and collection	253	83	2.85	165	87	2.80
Assessment	135	44	4.80	166	87	5.18
Budget and management	188	62	3.20	166	61	3.00
Purchasing and inventory	170	56	2.26	98	52	2.37
General government						
Personnel	182	60	2.46	110	58	2.12
Data processing	153	50	2.94	123	65	3.14
Geoprocessing	57	19	2.64	28	15	2.50
Public information	55	18	1.14	26	14	1.00
Public buildings	33	11	1.21	12	6	1.41
Clerk recorder	17	6	1.35	46	24	1.52
Central garage, motor pool	139	46	1.84	43	23	1.60
Other general government	36	12	1.13	20	11	1.20

Community development and public works						
Planning and zoning	94	31	3.27	43	23	2.46
Housing and urban renewal	44	14	1.54	9	5	1.00
Licensing and code enforcement	70	23	1.55	36	19	1.38
Engineering	26	9	2.50	27	14	1.92
Transportation	58	19	2.17	17	9	1.88
Streets and highways	49	16	1.53	31	16	1.51
Sanitation	87	28	2.06	35	18	1.74
Water supply	35	11	1.68	5	3	1.40
Utilities	191	63	4.44	36	19	3.08
Human resources						
Public health	37	12	2.64	64	34	3.00
Public welfare	24	8	4.45	79	42	4.34
Parks and recreation	49	16	1.35	17	9	1.29
Vital statistics	21	7	2.52	37	20	2.89
Libraries	54	18	2.11	32	17	1.90
Voter registration	90	30	2.64	143	76	2.79

NOTES: Cities over 50,000 population; counties over 100,000. Total N varies from 375 to 410; average $N = 400$.

Table 8.8   Service Delivery Applications, by Location of Computing Unit

	Location	
Service Delivery Applications	Finance Department	Independent Department
In cities	7.6%($N=142$)[a]	10.3%($N=59$)
In counties	13.8 ($N=26$)	15.3 ($N=86$)

[a]T-test is significant at the .01 level for cities but not for counties.

operations were particularly attractive to local officials. When computing was extended to the operating departments, the applications to be automated had to be justified in these same terms. For example, when libraries adopted computer applications, they were encouraged to automate overdue book notices rather than book lists.

Third, this logic for automating applications continues today in the use of computing for small cities, and in justifying the first applications in specific departments. For example, we have found that county assessors who use mass-appraisal techniques that are based on regression analyses are able to increase the equity of taxation for the class of single-family property owners. However, these appraisal techniques do not result in net decreases in the appraisal workload. In most cases, although the effort required to appraise each property decreases relative to that required in traditional methods, the net workload has increased, because with mass-appraisal techniques, whole counties are assessed annually rather than every four or six years. Assessors who have adopted mass-appraisal techniques have had a difficult time obtaining additional staff to support the increased workload, because many county supervisors believe that automation of appraisal should automatically lead to reduction of staff. Thus the managerial rationalist assumption that local officials value equity as a goal of automation runs into trouble when the achievement of equity conflicts with the traditional goals of cost reduction.

The Regulatory Bias

Many local government "services" are inherently regulatory; that is, they are *intended* to enhance social control.[8] This is obvious in such activities as law enforcement, code enforcement (building codes, fire codes, zoning ordinances, health and sanitary codes, and pollution codes), licensing and franchising activities, and housing regulation (rent control, occupancy control, and purchasing and contracting activities). By definition, these services are aimed at controlling the behavior of some targeted individuals, groups, or organizations. But more subtle forms of control have been found by scholars who have studied services without manifest control objectives, such as welfare (Handler 1972; Piven & Cloward 1976).

Again, computing tends to be used to reinforce the dominant character of local government activity—in this case, the regulatory bias. It was noted earlier that 60 percent of the applications that support services to citizens also are supportive of high social control. Much of the citizen-oriented computing in local governments is, in fact, police computing. Local government computing grew out of financial applications developed internally, but in the late 1960s and early 1970s it received substantial federal funding for local police computing (Colton 1978). By 1975, police applications constituted one of the largest clusters of computer use in local governments (table 8.7). For example, approximately 72 percent of the cities over 50,000 population in the United States had at least one police computer application in 1975, and on average, cities with police automation had eight such computer applications, primarily in areas such as criminal offense files, arrest records, parking tickets, traffic accident records, traffic violations, wants/warrants, stolen vehicles, and service data. These applications, and most police applications, are oriented primarily toward law enforcement (patrol and detective work), rather than toward crime prevention or other police activities (table 8.9).

Moreover, while studies show that police spend 50 percent of their time on service calls (Wilson 1968), most police training—and pride—focuses on law enforcement. Most of the rookie's training in the police academy is devoted to target practice, ways of collecting physical evidence and preparing a case, and so forth; much less time is devoted to such matters as deescalating family disputes. Law enforcement is not the only role of the local police, but is the aim of most police computing (table 8.9).

Taken together, these tendencies suggest that a good deal of local government computing is in support of regulation—and thus of control. Even when agencies, such as the police, have many activities available to them they tend to concentrate on social control, and automation of police activities reinforce that regulatory bias.

Operations of both the regulatory bias and efficiency bias indicate the inadequacy of managerial rationalism for understanding the patterns of computer use in local governments. After local government officials have

Table 8.9 Distribution of Police Applications

Police Applications	%	$(N=400)$[a]
Law Enforcement Activities		
Field interrogation report file	10%	(41)
Intelligence compilations	4	(17)
Modus operandi (criminal patterns file)	8	(31)
Criminal offense file	31	(126)
Arrest records	11	(45)
Juvenile criminal offense file	17	(69)
Fingerprint file	6	(26)
Alias name file	18	(74)
Parking ticket file	44	(182)
Traffic accident file	36	(143)
Traffic violations file	37	(153)
Wants/warrants file	33	(135)
Stolen vehicles file	25	(102)
Stolen property file	21	(84)
Dispatching	13	(51)
Other Police Activities (crime prevention, administration, reporting, etc.)		
Jail population/custody file	11	(45)
Uniform crime reporting (UCR)	36	(147)
Other crime reporting system	28	(104)
Law Enforcement Manpower Resource Allocation System (LEMRAS)	5	(21)
Other manpower allocation systems	14	(54)
Service data (type of call, location, time, response, etc.)	35	(143)
Vehicle maintenance records	25	(101)
Civil offense file	8	(29)
Firearms registration file	7	(28)
Motor vehicle registration file	25	(100)
Bicycle registration file	11	(45)

[a]N varies from 375 to 410; average $N=400$.

made commitments to invest heavily in computer applications that support finance and other housekeeping activities, and that enhance social control through law enforcement, there are few computing resources (particularly staff) left to invest in other kinds of services. We view this low level of support granted to public services that do not enhance social control as the product of a *nondecision*. Local officials are not opposed to such investments; rather, because of the demands of their work, their professional ideologies, and the kinds of resources that are available for computing, they do not actively promote them. For example, even though planning-oriented data banks, and social service information and referral systems, were built (as were the police applications) during the late 1960s and early 1970s with federal funding assistance, these kinds of applications were outside the mainstream of local government priority interests and concerns; and when the federal funding disappeared, they were seldom maintained locally. Other kinds of applications, that reflect the dominant biases of local government, dominate local computing investments.

The Reform Bias

The use of computing also reinforces the reform orientation of many local governments. As noted earlier (chapter 5), computing has historically been used as a tool of financial and other administrative reforms aimed at achieving greater efficiency in local government operations. Various analyses of local computing have argued that the managerial philosophy of reform governments leads to computing strategies that emphasize "efficiency rather than equity" and "administration rather than service delivery" (Dutton & Kraemer 1978a; Laudon 1974).

Our findings support these earlier studies. Table 8.10 provides some correlations of selected governmental, administrative, and technical characteristics with the orientation of computing in local governments. It shows that although larger governments provide a larger fraction of citizen-oriented applications, they provide proportionately fewer administration-oriented applications. The primary reason for this relationship is that larger cities are more likely to provide more services (e.g., hospitals, museums), and on a scale sufficiently large that their administrators can argue for computing support.

However, reform governments show the opposite pattern: their computer applications support fewer services to citizens, and more admin-

Table 8.10   Correlation of Environmental Factors with Orientation of Computing

	Orientation			
Environmental Factors	Service delivery	Administrative support	High social control	High bureaucratic control
Reform government	−.22*	.23*	−.02	.08
Log of total population	.30*	−.10	.10	−.24*

*Significant at .001 level

istrative activities. And as might be expected, most of these administrative applications involve large-volume record-keeping, printing, and calculating tasks whereby efficiency gains can be realized.

Table 8.10 also shows that bureaucratic control is negatively related to larger governments, and that it has no relation to reform governments. The negative relationship between larger cities and bureaucratic control fits the findings of much research: that the pluralism of large cities leads to lack of control (Yates 1977). The orientation of computing, by itself, is simply inadequate to overcome the fragmentation of these larger governments. Computers supposedly should be more helpful in large cities as a means of control. In fact, however, they don't seem to be. The orientation of computing does not counteract the pluralistic tendencies of large bureaucracies to resist control by top managers. On the other hand, the reform governments, which also tend to be smaller governments, may not have extensive need for computing that is oriented toward bureaucratic control. Here, top managers may be able to exert control through their close contact with government operations, and through their informal, frequent contacts with department heads and staff.

In the smaller cities, it is also possible that communication between the top managers and data-processing personnel is more direct, and leads to the informal adaptation of routine administrative applications to serve the interests of top administrators even though the computer applications are not explicitly control-oriented. For example, in their study of management-oriented computing in local governments Dutton and Kraemer (1978a) indicate that routine administrative applications usually serve the operations of the government *and* generate information useful to top managers. They note that these applications are a unique adaptation to the decision agenda, and available technology, of many local governments:

> Most decisions made by top managers are *routine* in the sense that they recur frequently, *incremental* in the sense that they involve small changes from current conditions, and *remedial* in the sense that the changes are movements away from some undesirable condition rather than movements towards some desired condition. . . . In making these decisions, managers tend to use data which reflect current and near past conditions and projections of the near past into the near future. These kinds of data are frequently found in the automated applications serving the operations of various local agencies or derived therefrom. And as one data processing manager put it, "Top managers who want computer reports will generally get them." (Dutton & Kraemer 1978a:209)

The benefits from administrative applications are not simply that managers are provided with more and better information faster. Rather:

> The benefits evolve from the complex interactions between top management and computing professionals, wherein existing operations-based information is brought to bear on the manager's decision problems, with each interaction producing small marginal benefits to the decisions. Taken together, however, these many small benefits can make a substantial difference. (Dutton & Kraemer 1978a:216).

Thus the heavy emphasis on administrative applications, especially in reform governments, reinforces the decision-making capabilities of top-level administrators even though they may not have been originally designed specifically for this. To the extent that bureaucratic control or decision-making effectiveness is important to professional administrators, they will find a way to use administrative applications to fit these additional purposes.

SUMMARY AND CONCLUSION

We have shown that managerial rationalist conceptions do not fit well with the reality of computing development in most local governments. Rather than being oriented toward service delivery to citizens and toward enhancing the choices of citizens, computing appears to be oriented toward governmental efficiency and toward enhancing the choices of top-level administrators. The data indicate that reinforcement politics is operative— that computing reinforces the prevailing biases in local government activities. Specifically, the analysis has demonstrated that computing tends to be used primarily to: 1) support *basic* government services (police, fire, highways, sanitation), rather than newer and more socially oriented services; 2) achieve efficiency payoffs rather than equity, effectiveness, or other possible payoffs; and 3) enhance social control through support of inherently regulatory services like law enforcement and various kinds of code enforcement. Clearly these uses of computing serve a wide variety of citizen interests; indeed, they serve what many believe the public has always most wanted from its local government—basic services, efficiency, and law enforcement. In a broad sense, computing has served to reinforce prevailing community biases.

More narrowly, and within the government itself, computing has been used to serve the interests of central administrators in reform governments. The reform administrators' values of efficiency, control, and decision-making effectiveness have been served as a by-product of routine administrative automation in finance, in general administration, and in the operating departments of the government. Thus even where computing appears to have been broadly applied to a wide variety of government functions and departments, it has in fact been narrowly applied to generate efficiencies in large data-handling operations of the departments, and to produce rudimentary data that top managers can use for the many decisions they face in managing the government. Thus computing has served to reinforce the biases of reform administrators.

CHAPTER NINE

POLICY, POLITICS, AND COMPUTERS

The Authors

IN THIS BOOK we have undertaken an analysis of the politics of computing as it is, not as it should be. We have not been primarily concerned with arguing how computing should be organized, how computing resources should be allocated, and whose interests computing should serve, but rather with understanding whether computer use in local governments can be said to have a systematic politics. To sharpen our analysis, we have developed four alternative perspectives on the politics of computing. The dominant conceptual framework within which computing developments have been framed and considered, managerial rationalism, has seen computing as apolitical (Chartrand 1971; Simon 1977). We have consistently found that computing *does* have a distinctive politics and that managerial rationalism is a misleading approach. In general, we have found that the reinforcement politics perspective offers the best overall description of this process. Consequently, we have used the reinforcement politics perspective as a tool for understanding the current pattern of values and interests served by computing.

The dynamics of the impacts of computer technology implied by our empirical analysis is disturbing at a normative level. Therefore, it seems appropriate, as we conclude this study, to explore the normative implications of our research and findings. Broadly, we are disturbed by the tendency for computing to be used to reinforce the dominant political coalition in a local government. First, it is inherently undemocratic—many legitimate interests are excluded, both from the process of control and from a share in the direct benefits of computing. Second, while such computer use has somewhat improved the work conditions of government employees, it has also led to a situation where problems with computing are found throughout the operations of many governments (Dutton & Pearson 1975; Kling 1978d; Kling & Scacchi 1979). Third, it has led to computing's application for internal administrative support and for increasing bureaucratic and social control rather than for service delivery to citizens. Fourth, although we did not directly investigate effects of local government computing on citizens in our research, there is mounting evidence from other research that those effects generally have been negative—increased cost and inconvenience, greater inequality of access to services, and decreased responsiveness to citizens being among them (Kraemer 1980). We believe that these negative effects stem from the conservative and elite-dominated politics of computing in organizations. Finally, we are disturbed because the dominant political coalitions have failed to utilize computing to serve citizens in new ways that utilize the technology's potential. For example, computing has rarely been used to enhance citizen participation in government, to inform citizens of their rights (e.g., entitlements and allowances under existing laws) and duties, and to provide new information services to citizens (Kraemer 1980).

We feel that democratic processes should be extended within public organizations wherever they might improve the responsiveness of the organization to the general public. We therefore argue that computing should be organized more democratically, so that many values and interests currently excluded by the dominant coalition in local governments will be able to affect the technology's use and impact. We recognize that "democratization" is only one value, and that it continually competes with others. Nonetheless, computing normally reinforces the values and interests of dominant organizational elites and can disadvantage many other groups with legitimate values and interests. Thus in the final section of this concluding chapter, we shall examine the desirability of democratizing strategies in three broad areas related to computing that have been examined in this book: resource politics, information politics, and service politics.

Initially, this final chapter provides a broad overview of our findings and of some of their general implications. We review the dominant, perhaps idealized, view of computing in organizations—that is, the view promoted by advocates of managerial rationalism. We present the major critical alternatives to managerial rationalism, critiques articulated by those who oppose it on normative grounds and by those who find stronger evidence for the existence of technological elitism or organizational pluralism.

We then examine the major technical, social, economic, and political-administrative constraints that seem to affect the capacity of any single interest or group to control the computer package, and summarize our analysis of actual impacts of computing in local government. In doing so, we also present our analysis supporting reinforcement politics as the most apt perspective for understanding the politics of computing in organizations.

Finally, in the last section of the chapter we discuss what can and should be done to reform the politics of computing in public organizations. We advocate policies that might lead to a more democratic administration of the computer package and that, therefore, might allow broader interests to be served by the technology. The implications of a more democratic administration of computing are considered, as are the problems that might arise.

PERSPECTIVES ON COMPUTING IN ORGANIZATIONS

The characterization of computing in organizations has been dominated by a rationalist perspective. This perspective, grounded in a classical model of administration and in the concepts of scientific management, views computing as a tool for effective management and for enhancing the efficiency of organizational operations. It implies that computer technology should serve the interests of the organization as a whole and should be firmly controlled by top managers, who alone have the necessary breadth of perspective to guide it toward those interests.

With respect to public organizations, the rationalist perspective portrays computer technology as an apolitical tool that serves "the public interest"[1] —both directly and indirectly. Computing serves the public interest directly, by providing new information processing services that, in turn, facilitate the provision of public goods and services that were impossible or less feasible without the technology, and indirectly, by improving the performance of public organizations through improvement of the quality, quantity, and manipulation of information for operations and for decisions.

Thus, by improving the efficiency and effectiveness of the more administrative activities of the public organization and by enhancing the organization's capability to provide direct services to citizens, computer technology lends itself to this rationalist characterization as a servant of the public interest. Most accounts from this perspective have not provided any empirical test as to whether or not this view is accurate; rather, they focus on questions of how to maximize the benefits from the technology. Typical topics are discussions of the "optimal design of management information systems," "the benefits of on-line computing," "the value of user involvement in design," "the payoffs of automated systems," and so on.

Some scholars observe that computer technology is often controlled by the top managers of the organization, as the managerial rationalists contend it should be. But some of these scholars question if these managers' decisions and policies are primarily oriented to serve organization-wide goals—managers, like others with professional and personal agendas, try to use computer applications to achieve their own interests and objectives, which usually will be related to, but not identical to, organization-as-a-whole interests. For example, the manager may attempt to use an automated information system to ensure that a department uses personnel to provide the services that are the manager's highest priorities; but the department head may have an alternative notion of the optimal use of personnel—in order to improve those services that reflect organizational or departmental-professional priorities. Hence some studies indicate that top managers use computing to reinforce their organizational influence over decision making vis-à-vis top elected officials and their subordinates (Kling 1978b; Dutton & Kraemer 1978b; Kraemer & Dutton 1979; Markus 1979).

A few observers suggest that top managers do indeed use computing to serve the interests of the organization as a whole, but that such organizational interests are often in conflict with broader conceptions of the public interest. Widespread citizen movements to limit the taxing and spending powers of local government are a recent example of the disjunction between the organizational maintenance and expansion objectives of local government and the resistance of the citizens to the financing of such objectives. As to computers, Sterling (1979) has suggested that an overriding interest in operational efficiency might entail neglect of time-consuming searches for errors in computerized records, resulting in inconvenience and possibly harm to citizens. And Rule (1974) contends that organizational interests in the development of large-scale data banks containing personal information create the conditions for serious abuse of the broader public interest in the use of those data.

One major alternative to the rationalist view of computing in organizations is technocratic elitism, which holds that top managers do not (and perhaps sometimes should not) control computing decisions in organizations. Some who endorse this viewpoint believe that computing is, and should be, largely controlled by experts with sophisticated technical knowledge of computer technology, because only such experts know how to utilize the tool most effectively. In this view, the computer elite may involve users in defining their information processing needs, but control of the actual development and application of the computer should be the domain of experts with formal and technical training (Fuller 1969). Other analysts take a less sanguine view of technocratic elitism and contend that when technocrats gain control of the computer package, they use this control primarily to serve their own professional and bureaucratic interests rather than the interests of the users of computer services, the organization as a whole, or the public (Danziger 1979a; Weizenbaum 1976). For example, the technocrats would use long-run computer resource planning more as a mechanism to legitimate the purchase of more advanced equipment and the expansion of computer staff than as a means to meet user needs through more rational allocation of computer resources. Raising the banner of technical competency and speaking in the language of "bits" and "nanoseconds," the experts disguise their dominant concern—the maintenance and enhancement of their own data-processing function.

Those with a perspective we have termed organizational pluralism also maintain that control of high technology is unlikely to be centralized in top management. In this view, various groups—politicians, administrators, technocrats, line professionals—have sufficient resources to influence decisions and applications of the technology within the organization. Those who celebrate such pluralistic decision making view it as a desirable process, because there is no single interest whose agenda ought to prevail. Organizational pluralism is advocated because it is assumed that the pulling and hauling among contending interests within the organization will tend to yield decisions and outcomes that merge alternative views into a composite that is a better approximation of the public interest than any particular actor's position. Thus, for example, an automated welfare case tracking system may be viewed by the mayor as a means to deal with welfare cheaters, by the department head as a means to monitor the performance of the caseworkers, and by the caseworkers as a means to reduce paperwork in handling welfare recipients. And when the technical experts of the data-processing unit involve all these groups in designing the automated system, it is assumed that the system will be a reasonable compromise of the interests and major concerns of each.

However, some of those critical of organizational pluralism argue that the distribution of "influence resources" in the organization is so unequal that the notion of wide-ranging compromises and some benefits for virtually all interested participants is totally unrealistic (Parenti 1979). And other critics, while acknowledging that it may be a relatively accurate characterization of how the decision and implementation processes operate, argue that pluralism is not likely to yield rational decisions or even to produce decisions and outcomes that are in anyone's interest. Compromises are as likely to benefit no one as they are to "satisfice" everyone. Clearly, such results would be unsatisfactory to the advocates of either managerial rationalism or technocratic elitism, since each would argue that hard decisions should be made regarding the critical purpose(s) of an automated system so that it can be designed in a precise and technically efficient manner rather than as an expedient compromise.

In our own analyses of the computer package in local government, we have found little support for the perspective of managerial rationalism. We have found some instances where the perspective of technocratic elitism or organizational pluralism aptly characterizes aspects of the decision processes regarding computing. But, on balance, we have found that our concept of reinforcement politics is best supported by the data, fieldwork, and analyses.

Briefly, reinforcement politics argues that decisions regarding high technology may be controlled by a rational-managerial elite, a technocratic elite, or a pluralistic array of participants. Decision-making power over technological resources varies from setting to setting, with the dominance of particular groups contingent on the local political system and its specific configuration of dominant values, interests, and actors. Those who control the decision process will operate to promote their own interests and the resulting decisions will serve to enhance the position of those who represent the dominant political coalition. Thus, technological decisions will *reinforce* the power and influence of those actors and groups who already exercise substantial control over the authority structure and resources of the organization. Reinforcement politics further argues that the dominant political coalition need not directly control technological decisions. Rather, those groups who do directly control the technology will attempt to anticipate the values and interests of the dominant coalition, and to serve this dominant coalition, as means to secure their cooperation and support (Dutton & Kraemer 1978b; Kling 1978b; Kraemer & Dutton 1979; Noble 1977; Straussman 1978). The evidence accumulated in this book supports the reinforcement politics view of computing in organizations. The next section summarizes the evidence.

REINFORCEMENT POLITICS AND CONTROL
OF THE COMPUTER PACKAGE

We have considered questions of power, influence, and control over the computer package in local governments. The empirical study of such issues is difficult because these concepts are difficult to define, they operate at multiple levels of analysis, and they involve extremely subtle dynamics. Analysis is further complicated by certain critical factors that constrain the extent of control over computing decisions that can be exercised by *any* organizational actors. Our study has indicated that the most significant constraints for local government computing are the complexity of the computer package itself, the environment within which local computing operates, and the political-administrative context of the local government.

Chapter 2 revealed that because of the great complexity of the computer package, no one person fully comprehends the technology. This stems from the very nature of high technology—a complex system of people, equipment, and technique. And this inherent complexity is exacerbated by the dynamism and instability of the computer package in most organizations.

A recent occurrence in a medium-sized southern city offers a characteristic example of how complexity leads to intractability and interaction among elements of the computer package. The newly elected mayor committed himself to revamping the city's financial reporting system, which was widely held to be inadequate. He appointed a trusted former business associate as director of finance. One year later, and four months after the end of the fiscal year, the automated system still could not produce data on the previous year's revenue and expenditure totals. Under pressure from the mayor and council, the finance director replaced the data-processing unit's manager. This new manager then replaced all the city's computing equipment, blaming the "out-of-date" equipment for the problems and installing a type of equipment with which he was familiar. After a further year and hundreds of thousands of dollars spent on the computer package, the automated revenue and expenditure reporting system was still judged inaccurate and unsatisfactory. Thus the mayor, despite his level of commitment, clear goal, financial resources, and apparent control over the organizational environment, was still not able to control the computer package in order to realize his goal.

Chapter 3 provided evidence that the social, economic, and political milieu of a local government also place important constraints on the latitude of local decision makers dealing with the computer package. Larger governments have greater need for automated information services, and thus greater likelihood of earlier adoption and more extensive use of computer technology. External funding support for computing encourages an increased level of use. And the level of local government computing activity in the region also seems to influence the computing decisions of individual local governments. These findings indicate that the characteristics of a government's computer package are, at least in part, contingent upon environmental forces over which local officials have little or no control. In addition, there is evidence that computer utilization is greater in local governments whose administrative systems are characterized by a stronger reform orientation, by more user involvement in computer decisions, and by more decentralization of such decisions.

The political-administrative constraints on decisions regarding the computer package were further specified in chapters 4 and 5. Local governments, like most organizations, contain a plurality of interests and values. Chapter 4 revealed the different conceptions of computing that are likely to be held by those in such different roles as top managers, elected officials, computer professionals, department heads, and large users and small users of computer services. Moreover, different conceptions of computing might be held by people within any given role. For example, computing professionals within the central computing facility have certain interests in the centralization of the computing function that are not likely to be shared by computing professionals within the user departments. Given widespread differences in personal, managerial, professional, and technical perspectives, it is not surprising that there are conflicting views of the interests and values that computing should serve, and that there is no unitary conception of the relationship between computing and the public interest. In a context of plural interests and values, any single interest, whether that of managers or of technocrats, could be served only if control of the resource were highly centralized.

But control is not highly centralized. Indeed, nearly every textbook account of control within urban government stresses the extreme fragmentation of authority. Local governments are not unitary and hierarchical, and the fragmentation of formal authority is apparent in most decision-making processes (Lineberry & Sharkansky 1978; Yates 1977). Our analysis of the computer package is fully consistent with this general observation. The data in chapter 4 indicate that the pattern of participation in computing decisions is pluralistic—no single role or interest has concentrated control over the entire computer package in most of the governments in the analysis.

Although control of the computer package seems rarely to be monopolized by a single role, such control is far from random. At a general level, computing decisions in most local governments are governed by the pulling and hauling among various participants. The groups that tend most often to have a central role are the computer elite, the top managers, and the departments that are big users of computing.

This seems to be strong evidence in support of the organizational pluralist perspective; but the ultimate control of decisions regarding computing is usually more complex than this perspective implies. Although different groups might have substantial influence, a central finding of our study is that the dominant coalition within the government tends to be served indirectly by those with the most direct decisional control. This dominant coalition is composed of those people that enjoy general control over the authority structure and the resources of the organization at a given point in time (Aiken & Bacharach 1978).

Members of the dominant coalition do not necessarily make the computing decisions, but it is clear that those who do make those decisions have the apparent interests of the dominant coalition in mind. Thus each major participant concerned with decisions about the computer package usually seeks to maintain and enhance his or her position within the organization both by guiding computing resources toward his or her own agenda and also by anticipating the interests of the dominant political coalition. In sum, the decision process is pluralistic; but, as "nonpluralists" like Bachrach and Baratz (1972) would predict, the decisions are fully congruent with the fundamental biases of those who dominate the organization as a whole.

REINFORCEMENT POLITICS AND THE IMPACTS OF COMPUTING

We have argued in this book that control of decisions on computer use does not necessarily imply control of the impacts from computing. Even when a single interest enjoys near-monopoly control over the application of a resource such as computing, the implementation process and the environment are extremely dynamic. These factors as well as the complexity of the computer package itself mean that there may be major unanticipated effects from its use. Moreover, we have argued that control over computing is best understood as the product of variable configurations of decisional control among a variety of participants more or less sensitive and responsive to the interests and values of the dominant organizational coalition. For all of these reasons, there would be little reason to expect that the actual impacts of computing would serve only a single interest.

The evidence in chapters 6, 7, and 8 suggests that computing does not, in fact, serve any single interest. Rather, the computer package in local government is a malleable technology and its use results in partial fulfillment of aspects of the personal, professional, and bureaucratic interests of various roles. For instance, the example earlier in this chapter of an automated welfare client tracking system showed that the system could serve certain interests of top managers, department heads, social workers, and welfare recipients, as well as interests of the computer elite and others. But such an automated system could be designed and applied in a manner contrary to the interests of any particular group. The department head might find it used by central managers to limit his or her discretion on personnel allocation, the social worker might find it used to monitor his or her workload, the client might find it used primarily to identify "cheating."

Given this variability, must we conclude that the effects of the computer package are random or totally unpredictable? The evidence in chapters 5, 6, and 7 suggests not—computing generally serves the interests and values of the dominant coalition within the organization. Chapter 5 indicates that when resource politics was most prevalent, and even when a significant information politics developed, computer technology most fully served top managers and central administrators. And the computer elite, big users, and an information elite of planners and analysts also have been served, since their use of automated information has tended to serve both their own agendas and those of the dominant coalition. Chapter 6 argues that automated information primarily has been used in the policy process in those forms and at those stages where those in control of the organization believed that the use and impact of such information would serve their agendas. Moreover, the data in chapter 7 document that the most common power shifts attributable to computing have benefited top managers and central administrators.

Broadly, these chapters indicate that there is a general bias in the impacts of computer technology on local government: increasingly, those with broad power and control of the organization have benefited. Many other groups and interests are served only incidentally or secondarily by the use of the technology. By serving the interests of those who control the local government, then, computing reinforces the prevailing interests and values of the organization. In this sense, it is a conservative technology and not an instrument for change or redistribution.

Given the current generally conservative orientation toward local government among the public, it may be that computing does, indeed, serve the "public interest." In chapter 8, we have shown that current applications of computer technology primarily serve the objectives of bureaucratic and social control, particularly in the areas of financial administration and public safety. And in recent years, what the public has wanted most from local government has been financial control (especially efficiency and constraint on expenditure and on revenue generation) and public safety activities (especially the control of crime and the apprehension, conviction, and incarceration of criminals). And the public also wants control in many other specific areas—over welfare cheats, in zoning, over animals, and over traffic, for example. Thus by accident or design, it happens that many computer applications in local governments do in fact serve the current central concerns of the public.

POLICIES FOR "DEMOCRATIC" COMPUTING

We have seen that many values and interests are currently excluded by the inherently conservative and elite-dominated politics of computing in organizations. It is tempting to propose a simplistic "democratic" position, and to argue that, irrespective of the nature of local governments or the current conservatism of the citizenry, computing should be organized more democratically. There certainly are compelling arguments for political democracy (McPherson 1977), participatory organizations (Bennis & Slater 1968), and the control of working conditions by workers (Hunnius, Garson, & Case 1973; O'Toole 1974). The basic difficulties with this sort of prescription arise from the dual nature of local governments.

Local governments are organizations that serve a variety of public functions, including the provision of services, the resolution of conflicts among competing interests, and the regulation of private activities. From one perspective, public agencies operate in these functions as relatively passive instruments that interject no interests or biases of their own. Whatever democracy there is will be the democracy of public mobilization and choice. This view of public agencies as passive instruments implies that the actions of public-agency staff should reflect the preferences of residents in the affected communities, or, more practically, the preferences of the "average" voter. An alternative viewpoint holds that public agencies are not simply passive social instruments staffed by robots—organizational staff have interests of their own and do not act merely as the passive agents of the legislative mandates that they implement (Rogers 1968; Selznick 1949). In this book, we have emphasized the role of such interests, particularly those of technical specialists and professional administrators.

Even if the staff of public agencies ought to have no substantive influence over public policy, they should have two kinds of influence that cannot be discounted and that have a strong bearing on computer use in public agencies. First, they often suggest guidelines or procedures to improve or simplify their work. In the case of computing, this means that they should be expected to assert their interests when they are requesting computer support as an instrument for carrying out their work, or when they are advising elected officials about the efficacy and cost of computing support. Second, like other workers, they should have some control over their own working conditions, independent of the content of their work (Hunnius, Garson & Case 1973; O'Toole 1974). These considerations imply that the staff of public agencies should have some role in the politics of computing.

However, there are normative limits to staff influence that might not apply to private enterprises. Public personnel should be accountable to broader publics for what they choose to do, if not for the specifics of how they choose to do it. In American local governments, the paths of accountability run upward through an administrative hierarchy from the lowest-level staff to elected officials who formally represent the community. Even if local governments were less "bureaucratized," their staff would and should still be accountable to top elected officials for the procedures they follow, the policies they implement, and the services they provide.

Democracy versus Efficiency

Analysts of democratization fall into two schools, with two apparently contradictory arguments. "Radical democrats" argue that any sphere of social life should be fully democratized, unless there are compelling reasons to the contrary, such as inefficiencies so substantial that effective public purpose is lost (Bennis & Slater 1968). A radical democrat would argue that decisions about computer usage ought to allow fair and equal participation by all interested parties and ought not to be dominated by a few privileged parties, and would justify the argument on the grounds of the moral and political value of participation (McDermott 1969; McPherson 1977). At minimum, this would imply that all organizational subunits with an interest in computing should participate in an open decision process dealing with the allocation and application of the technology.

In contrast to the "radical democrats," others argue that allocational and organizational efficiency should be the basic criteria for appropriate organization, and that democratization is either a secondary value, or one that should be treated in the "broader" social system (Auerbach 1979). For example, we indicate in chapter 4 that "big users" (e.g., police and finance) often dominate computing resource decisions in local governments and that "small" users (e.g., public works, fire services, planning) have little influence. This may simply be viewed as an "efficient" arrangement because those groups that make most use of computing resources can influence policies so that computing arrangements (e.g., modes of computing selected, pricing schemes) serve them best. Moreover, because the most knowledgeable computer specialists in local governments are usually found on the staffs of the computer center and larger computer-using departments (and in certain analytical departments such as policy analysis bureaus), the data-processing administrators can gather relatively informed suggestions and spend less time explaining their options and choices if they develop a coalition with "big users."

During recent decades, much has been written about private citizens' feelings of confusion and powerlessness in the face of the actions of modern bureaucracies. Many of the same arguments can be applied to social life within public agencies. "Participatory bureaucracy" denotes those strategies meant to enable the staff of public agencies to have voice in decisions that affect them and to understand the bases for relatively complex actions, such as those that involve computer use.

There is one important qualification of the democratization argument that should be borne in mind when developing normative strategies for public organizations. In chapter 7 we indicated that the bases of power in local governments vary with size. In particular, chief executives are likely to have substantially more control over government operations in smaller than in larger jurisdictions. In the largest cities, chief executives and elected officials might have so little power that they face an effectively "ungovernable" bureaucracy (Yates 1977).[2] We believe that local governments, ultimately, should serve as instruments of broad public policies and as providers of public goods and services such as policing, parks, sewers, roads, and fire fighting. Thus, the maintenance of management coherence by means of a strong administrative authority is of critical importance in urban governments. When analysts such as Yates suggest that (large) cities are "ungovernable," they mean that the many demands of individuals and interest groups within urban jurisdictions cannot be met simultaneously, or even sequentially, by public agencies or politicians. Cities have become "ungovernable" because the city's "weak control system" cannot respond to the difficult and apparently legitimate demands made upon it. Thus, Yates (1977:174) argues that "good management and good democracy must go hand in hand in urban service delivery."

"Democratic" organization and "efficient" organization are sometimes complementary and sometimes competing values in organizations. We are interested in extending democratic processes within organizations wherever they might improve the responsiveness of the organizations to the general public.[3] Clearly, "democratization" is not an absolute value, and our democratic bias is not so unqualified that we believe that urban administrations should be democratized in every conceivable way. But, if computing normally reinforces the values and interests of dominant organizational elites, it can also undermine the values and interests of certain groups who are excluded from the dominant elite.

In the case of computing, claims about participatory democracy and efficiency are both salient, and neither value can be casually dismissed. The technology is expensive and complex; it is also better understood by some than by others. Strategies that emphasize efficiency can save thousands or millions of dollars in operating costs and months or years of time. But strategies that deemphasize the value of participation in computing decisions can leave those who are affected feeling victimized by actions that they may not comprehend or that serve them badly.

Thus it is appropriate to ask how and when the democratization of computing might improve the responsiveness of local governments to wider legitimate public interests without reducing the capacity of executives to manage the government. In these concluding sections, we will examine the democratization of computing in three areas: resource politics, information politics, and service politics. As will be seen, some of our recommended policies for democratization do not relate to computing specifically, but to the environment within which computing and computerized information is used. The reason is simple. Reforms of computing without corresponding reforms of public organizations will not achieve the desired effect of greater democratization; they will be ineffectual at best, and at worst, they might further contribute to reinforcement politics.

Resource Politics

In the ways in which different groups within the government gain access to computing resources, conflicts between organizational efficiency and participatory bureaucracy are most remote from the public and also perhaps least troublesome. In chapters 4 and 5 we argued that computing resources are available in some measure to most departments that seek them, but that "big users" such as finance departments dominate computing use in many American local governments. Under current arrangements, some groups that should fare well, (e.g., planners) often have considerable problems gaining access to computing resources. Resource politics would be more "democratic" if all groups with computing needs were able to: 1) develop expertise in learning about how to match computer technology to their needs; 2) garner a "fair share" of computing resources; and 3) have a significant voice in major decisions about policies for adopting, developing, and using computing.

The key to achieving these objectives seems to be radical decentralization—of computing expertise and of computing arrangements. Local governments vary considerably in the extent to which computing expertise is distributed among the departments. Such expertise entails more than the capability to program a digital computer—it entails an understanding of the skillful application of computing to the activities of an organization. Moreover, it requires a keen understanding of the various components of the computing package and of the economics of computing use. Expertise in the use and management of computing is rare in local governments, even when programing skill is abundant. Yet it is essential for the staff of an organizational unit that must understand whether it should consider computer use in its operations, decide the tasks for which computerization would be appropriate, specify the payoffs it can expect from computing, and anticipate the difficulties its use will entail. This kind of computing expertise should be widely distributed.

The distribution of computing expertise to achieve democratization requires much more than providing an occasional orientation and training course for the user department staff or sending them to classes and schools, although such activities might be useful. It also requires recruiting into the departments computer and information systems specialists who know both the technology and its application to specific functional areas of government, and whose orientation is toward departmental needs and how the technology can serve those needs. Thus, these people will not be systems analysts and programmers per se, but a new class of personnel such as system accountants, police computer specialists, management systems analysts, and planning computer specialists.

There are, of course, other strategies for decentralizing access to computing resources. Assignment of programmers and analysts to the user departments is likely to enable the staff of those departments to develop computer applications that better meet their needs. Such assignment can occur several ways. First, programmers and analysts can be hired directly by the user departments. Second, they can be hired by the data-processing department but assigned to work physically in the user departments. Third, they can be hired by the data-processing department and work out of that department but be responsible for working with specific user departments.

Each of these arrangements involves differing degrees of decentralization and thus potentially differing degrees of democratization. But, it is also possible that decentralizing analysts and programmers could, under certain circumstances, lead to further reinforcement of the dominant coalition rather than to greater democratization. That is, this decentralization strategy could be used primarily to reinforce (or could have an actual tendency to reinforce, whether intended or not) the access of current major beneficiaries to computing resources rather than to redistribute and equalize access. While this power-reinforcing use of the decentralization strategy is less likely to occur in periods of expansion of the computer package, it is quite likely to occur in periods of cutback. The most effective way to combat this tendency would be to adopt a relatively simple allocation rule: namely, to cut the larger departments proportionately more than the smaller departments when cutting back on computing staff resources, and to allocate a proportionately greater share of computing resources to the smaller departments when expanding. This would gradually reallocate departmental access to computing staff resources toward a more equitable overall distribution.

As computer expertise and staff become more widely distributed in the government (or perhaps even in conjunction with such a strategy) the decentralization of computing equipment can be another effective strategy for democratization. More than ever before, the decentralization of computing equipment to many user departments is both a technical and practical possibility available to a wide range of governments. In the past, it was only the large local governments that could do this—equipment was too expensive to let each department have its own major hardware, and the technology for linking decentralized facilities was too fragile and limited in performance. The advent of minicomputers, microcomputers, and distributed computing networks has changed the situation dramatically, because it makes considerable computing power and capabilities available at costs that are within the realm of fiscal feasibility for individual departments, even in small cities.

The decentralization of computing equipment does not, in itself, democratize computing. But potentially, it makes greater democratization possible because increased local control usually evolves from local ownership. When combined with the distribution of computer expertise and staff to the departments, the distribution of computing equipment can have a powerful democratizing effect. Technological decentralization is not free from risk—it can lead to computing chaos rather than to computing democratization. But effective coordination and control (related to standardization of computer equipment, software, applications development procedures, and documentation standards), can prevent such outcomes.

Finally, democratization of many computing decisions can be achieved through the creation of a policy board that sets priorities for current and new developments and that provides a voice for a variety of organizational interests. Although such boards could be manipulated by the computer specialists, they can provide another avenue for wider participation in computing decisions. Policy boards with one representative for each department would be especially useful in giving smaller departments greater equality with larger departments in the allocation and application of the computer package.

Our arguments for such decentralization of computer expertise in local governments are much the same as those that we would make for decentralizing most kinds of technical expertise in democratic communities: it is proper for the participants to understand the technical and social character of decisions in which they are implicated. As we have indicated earlier, the staffs of organizational units with inadequate computing expertise will tend to err in their adoption and use of computer resources or to lose out in policy decisions about computer use to other units with greater expertise. We assume that access to expertise will, other things being equal, afford them greater technical competency and provide them with greater voice in important decisions.

More broadly, service departments have the closest contact with various publics and therefore have the greatest understanding of their clients' needs. And they also have the greatest motivation to be responsive to these needs since at least their professional values tend to be closely aligned with serving the interests of their clients. Therefore, it seems reasonable that decentralizing computing expertise within the government could positively influence the quality of services that local governments provide to the public, and their responsiveness to citizen demands. At any rate, given the plurality of interests in urban communities, it seems that centralizing computer expertise in a skill bureaucracy would be unlikely to enhance citizen interests.

Information Politics

In chapters 5, 6, and 7 we analyzed the role of computerized information systems in the information politics of local governments. Our primary focus was upon the uses of automated data systems in policy making. However, automated data systems also play an important role in enhancing the control of managers over operations within their administrative domains. We have discussed such managerial-administrative control applications of computing in chapters 7 and 8. Since policy making and administrative control have markedly different political dynamics, and since the notion of democratization has different meanings for each, we consider them separately here.

MANAGERIAL CONTROL

Control systems are usually initiated by or for managers to help them direct their organizational resources or the activities of their subordinates. These systems tend to parallel existing lines of actual authority and they usually measure only a few aspects of organizational behavior or activity. It is reasonable to assume that computer-based information systems can dramatically increase the control of higher level managers over their subordinates. In particular, automated control systems are seen to provide managers with fine-grained, timely, and accurate information about activities within their administrative domains.

Whether or not they are automated, such control systems might provide administrators with information about the resources at their disposal (e.g., budget) and with indices of the performance of their subordinates. It is difficult to quarrel with the intention of these control systems. Program administrators need some way to know what resources they have at their disposal, how they are being used, and what their subordinates are accomplishing. Theorists differ in suggesting how managers should control (e.g., by resources, activities, or outcomes), but there is agreement that they should have some means to learn about the activities for which they are held accountable by elected officials and the public.

But the efficacy of managerial control systems, whether automated or manual, varies considerably (Kling & Scacchi 1979; Kling 1980). Two considerations relevant to democratization are especially pertinent. First, the most questionable automated control systems are those that managers use to evaluate the performance of their subordinates. Existing automated performance monitoring systems tend to focus on the most quantifiable aspects of performance, although these are not necessarily the most important aspects. And those with lower performance levels tend to suffer (e.g., be passed over for promotion), independent of the quality of their overall job performance.

Managers vary in the extent to which they are punitive and "Stakhanovite" in their approach to performance monitoring and the extent to which they share data about resources and performance with their subordinates. Generally, we favor more open and less punitive approaches to management, and there is evidence that such approaches are effective (Lawler & Rhode 1976). But most current automated applications for management control tend to be biased against such approaches.

In addition to open and nonpunitive management, we favor a government-wide information policy that provides for "city" rather than "departmental" ownership and control of data. Related to implementation of such a policy is the need for a city-wide data access control board, which would define the differing classes of confidentiality to be assigned to data collected by the departments and, correspondingly, define the criteria and rules for access to data (Stallings 1972). We favor city rather than departmental ownership and control of data because such a policy is likely to promote easier access to data and greater sharing of data among departments and agencies within the government, among levels in the politico-managerial hierarchy, and between the government and citizens. While upward hierarchical flows of information are important to legitimate managerial control, the best protection against misuse of information for control and the most effective utilization of information as a government resource is likely to occur when there is relatively free flow of information up, down, and across hierarchical levels within the government, and between the government and its citizens. And, as we have noted in chapter 6, automated information systems are especially well suited to facilitate such information accessibility.

POLICY MAKING

Most policy analysis in local governments emphasizes centralized expertise. Where an analytical approach is undertaken, it is most common for one analysis exploring a few alternatives to be carried out by a single organizational unit. As we indicated in chapter 6, such centralized analyses lead to reinforcement politics—powerful groups are able to dominate and exploit automated data analyses to their own best advantage. While reinforcement politics might easily be construed as a "conservative" politics, it actually means that already powerful groups, whatever their ideological orientation, will be able to exploit automated data during the policy process to accumulate further advantage. For example, in Eugene, Oregon, when the city council majority was cautious about new residential development, computerized models congruent with a slow growth agenda were significant in formulating policy. In contrast, in Orange

County, California, when the majority of the powerful board of supervisors was in favor of new residential and commercial development, county planners who presented analyses suggesting slow growth alternatives found that these analyses were coolly received and often quietly buried. Although the automated data brought to bear were not necessarily compelling in either case, the examples illustrate the reinforcing role of the use of computerized information in the policy-making process.

The normative problem with computer use in policy-making characterized by reinforcement politics is that more powerful groups are able to mobilize automated data analyses to gain disproportionate advantage over weaker groups. Certain structural reforms may be helpful to democratize computer-based policy analysis in local governments. We have already suggested that local governments adopt a policy of "governmental" rather than "departmental" ownership and control of data and data access. We would extend that ownership policy to include not only the data upon which analyses are based but also the computer programs and models that utilize the data, and the resultant analyses themselves. Use of the computer package should encourage the free flow of data, programs, models, and analyses.

Allowing data, computer programs, and the results of automated analyses to be widely and easily accessible to legitimate groups inside and outside the bureaucracies is clearly one important means to allow a wider variety of voices to be heard during policy formation and implementation. But this still may not be enough to give any real influence to those groups that are now powerless. As Marris and Rein (1973) indicate, simply providing communication channels to relatively disenfranchised groups may be of little consequence. When policy formation and analyses are "opened up," established groups can wait until they see the proposals that develop. If their interests are threatened, they can simply ignore the analyses provided or they can mobilize their considerable resources to lobby against the proposals.

However, relatively powerless groups might need arrangements through which their arguments can have visibility and potency. In social services, some argue that the courts provide such an arena. In land-use planning, environmental impact reports that are backed up by legal sanctions are one possible resource. In policy analysis, new structures may be needed that are explicitly devoted to countermodeling, peer evaluation of models and data analysis, and advocacy modeling for unrepresented or underrepresented interests. The extraordinary processing capabilities of computers could facilitate this distribution of information, but as in the earlier cases, such a distribution requires the support or acquiescence of those who currently control the computer package.

Thus much more than accessibility to policy analyses is required for genuine democratization of such analyses. The key point is that in reality policy analyses are partisan, rather than purely scientific. Policy analyses must be made "more scientific," not simply by adopting quantitative methods, but also by employing the social process of science, which entails scrutiny of data, programs, and models by many people with different perspectives, advocacy of diverse and competing ideas, and adversary analyses in open forums.

These methods are risky for managers and policy makers, and even for analysts. As chapter 6 noted, such processes can substantially increase the uncertainty of participants, can increase conflict, and tend to reduce the autonomy of those who are already dominant in the policy process. These political realities reveal the enormous obstacles to implementation of such a strategy of adversarial information and analyses. Yet such strategies are consistent with the social movements characterized by "the new public administration," "advocacy planning," and "public interest advocacy" in the public service professions. Thus, at least some professional analysts, managers, and policy makers can be expected to have a direct interest in implementing such methods, as part of a general strategy of reforming public organizations.

Service Politics

In general, our analyses have shown that automated applications are not now widely used to improve the quantity and quality of direct services from local government to the public. Yet in chapter 8 we concluded that the distribution of automated support for local government services reflects the current priorities of both powerful elites and the middle class in American society. For example, the emphasis on automated applications for police services mirrors recent concerns for "law and order," and the limited computer use in the wider distribution of social services reflects the limited support for social welfare services in many communities.[4]

We do not believe that the politics of computing is a critical determinant of the distribution of public goods and services in a community. The politics surrounding the application of computing follows rather than leads the politics surrounding service provision in a community. If a particular government service enjoys a large share of the community's or the government's support and resources, then it will also tend to enjoy a proportionately larger share of computing support and resources—the service politics of computing fundamentally conforms to the dominant values and power in the broader community. Furthermore, the reinforcement politics perspective suggests that computing is not likely to serve a broader array of interests unless power and influence become more broadly distributed. In the area of service politics, far more than in computing resource politics or information politics, broad political reforms must precede any meaningful computing reforms in American local governments.

The Prospects for Reform in Computing

At no time in the history of computing in American local governments has there been more need or opportunity for reform. The need is illustrated by our analyses in this book, by the pervasive problems which often accompany the use of computers in many local governments, by the deep undercurrent of dissatisfaction with many aspects of computing among departmental users, and by the shortcomings and even failures that characterize a substantial number of more sophisticated applications of computers in local governments.

There is widespread opportunity for reform. Medium- and larger-sized cities and counties are embarking upon a "second generation" of computing. Many smaller governments are now adopting the technology, thereby entering a "first generation." The second generation computer users are characterized increasingly by movements toward: 1) the redesign of existing stand-alone computer applications into more integrated systems; 2) the integration of departmental users with the technology, and the reintegration of departmental processes through wider deployment of on-line, real-time capabilities in the new redesigned applications; 3) the development of more management- and policy-oriented applications through using the data in the automated systems of the government and through the introduction of specific applications geared towards specific management concerns (e.g., facility location, manpower allocation) and policy issues (e.g., fiscal impact analysis, land-use and transportation planning analysis); and potentially, 4) the development of citizen-oriented applications of the technology. The smaller, first generation users stand to gain not only from the technical experiences of those who have developed and routinized specific applications, but also from the accumulation of knowledge about the politics and management of computing.

There is no question about whether computing change will take place during the 1980s. It is already occurring in most local governments and in protean forms. The issue is whether and how computing "reform" will take place. In the concluding sections of this chapter, we have made a case for certain changes. If fully implemented, these changes in computing resource politics, information politics, and service politics would be of such magnitude that the concept of reform would be too modest. However, in the world of realpolitik, these kinds of fundamental reforms are unlikely. Change is likely to be incremental, involving many small changes continuously made as local governments develop new understandings of how to use the technology more effectively.

Yet the growing organizational and technological pressures for decentralizing the computer package create the conditions for changes in the directions we have advocated. Cumulatively, these changes could constitute a "reform" in the computer package—a redistribution both of access to computing and of the benefits of the computer's application in local governments. Moreover, since such computing reforms are often instituted as part of broader administrative reforms, such as improved financial management or greater services integration, it is imperative that changes in computing be designed with knowledge and sensitivity regarding how computing is shaped by these broader reforms and, concomitantly, how computing reforms interact with and reinforce or diminish the attempted reform of government services.

A central purpose of this book has been to illuminate the political environment within which computers are used and to indicate the implications of computer use in such a setting. It is clear that the tools now exist to provide better understanding and implementation of the computer package. But we realize that ultimately, whether a redistribution of computing access and benefits is achieved depends upon the will and motivations of policy makers, managers, analysts, and computer specialists both in local governments and in the state and federal agencies that attempt to shape local computing developments.

APPENDIX: URBIS RESEARCH METHODOLOGY

The URBIS research methodology has been designed to study the subject of computing in organizations. The two major phases of the research involved a census survey of all the larger city and county governments in the United States and a more narrowly focused field analysis of 42 city governments. In addition, extensive case studies were conducted in various cities and counties to explore and elaborate the research issues and research design. This appendix briefly characterizes the research strategy of the URBIS Project. Fuller elaboration can be found in Hackathorn (1975), Kraemer et al. (1976), Kraemer, Dutton, and Northrop (1981), and Kraemer and Schetter (1979).

PHASE I: CENSUS SURVEY

The primary intent of the Census Survey was to provide base-line data on computing arrangements and on the policies relating to the computer package in American local governments. This survey provided a data base from which to analyze the characteristic patterns of use and diffusion of current computer technology and also to select appropriate sites for more extensive study in the later phase of the research.

A three-part survey of cities and counties was designed. Each part entailed a separate mail questionnaire, with telephone follow-up. One gathered information on the personal views of the government's chief executive toward computer technology in local government. The second collected extensive information from each computer installation serving the government, measuring such characteristics of the computer package as types of equipment, levels and types of personnel and budget, and the kinds of policies governing the use of the computer package. The third questionnaire, which also was completed by each computer installation, was an inventory of the current and near-future automated applications provided to the local government by that installation.

The criterion for including local governments in the census survey was population size (1970). The three surveys were sent in early 1975 to all cities with greater than 50,000 population and all counties with greater than 100,000 population—403 municipalities and 310 counties in all. The chief executive questionnaire was returned by 82 percent of the cities and 77 percent of the counties. The computer installation questionnaires were returned by 81 percent of the cities and 67 percent of the counties using computers (Hackathorn 1975). Information derived from this data base is especially evident in chapters 2 and 3.

PHASE II: FIELD STUDIES

The central purpose of the second major phase of the project was to perform an empirical evaluation of the impacts of automated information systems on local governments and to specify the effects of alternative management policies in an attempt to identify those policies that improve the performance of computer technology. The attempt to identify the effects of alternative policy mixes required the development of a somewhat unconventional probability sampling method for selection of Phase II sites. The sampling design was most critical for the analyses in the companion book, *The Management of Information Systems* (Kraemer, Dutton, & Northrop 1981), and has had no major effect upon the analyses or conclusions in the present book. However, the design did determine the cities from which some of the data and insights in this book have been derived. Consequently, it seems appropriate to explain the sampling strategy briefly, as well as to explicate the research strategy in the field.

Sampling Design

For Phase II, we needed a sample that was small enough to allow intensive field research in each site and large enough to enable us to make generalizations. We decided to study only municipal governments so that the organizational units would be comparable. Our interest in alternative computing policy configurations, many of which were relatively rare, meant that we could not use conventional probability sampling, as it would not provide a sample of sites with extreme policy mixes from which the optimal computer policies for America's "future cities" could be identified (Kraemer et al. 1976).[1]

Our solution was a variation of a disproportionate stratified sampling technique. Six key computer package characteristics were identified: 1) total number of automated applications; 2) degree of centralization of the package; 3) charging policy for computing services; 4) sophistication of hardware; 5) level of integration of data in the system; 6) extent of user involvement in application adoption, design, evaluation, and programing. Each of the six variables was dichotomized on the basis of Phase I data for city governments, with all scores below the third quartile treated as low scores and all scores above the third quartile as high.[2] This produced a partitioned sample with $2^6(64)$ strata.

All cities were located in their proper stratum on the basis of actual Phase I scores, or estimated scores for cases where there was no data for the variable. A balanced set of 40 strata was then randomly selected, ensuring 20 cities on each side of each policy (with two additional strata added to compensate for city refusals and missing data). Where a stratum had no cities within it, the city with the closest variable scores was employed. Finally, a specific city was selected randomly from each strata. These 42 cities are listed in table A.1.

Our research design meant that the field sites would not be fully "representative" of the computer package in all cities in Phase I. In general, Phase II cities are, relative to Phase I cities, more populated, more highly automated, and more sophisticated, decentralized, and integrated in their computing. They involve users more with the computer package, and they charge more often for computer use (see Kraemer, Dutton, & Northrop 1981: table 2.3). While the municipal governments that we studied in Phase II were somewhat more "developed" with regard to computing than were other municipalities in 1975, there were many instances in Phase II, as well as in other parts of our research, where we did our empirical research in governmental settings with more typical computing. And, with the continued expansion and evolution of the computer package in most governments, "high" development of 1975 would be more "typical" today.

Information-Processing Tasks

People tend to speak generally about the impacts of computers and computer-based information systems. However, we felt that an assessment

Table A.1   Cities Visited in Phase II Study

City	Population	City	Population
Albany, N.Y.	115,876	Milwaukee, Wisc.	717,124
Atlanta, Ga.	497,024	Montgomery, Ala.	183,471
Baltimore, Md.	905,759	New Orleans, La.	593,471
Brockton, Mass.	89,040	New Rochelle, N.Y.	75,385
Burbank, Calif.	88,580	Newton, Mass.	91,073
Chesapeake, Va.	89,580	Oshkosh, Wisc.	53,155
Cleveland, Ohio	751,046	Paterson, N.J.	144,830
Costa Mesa, Calif.	72,729	Philadelphia, Pa.	1,948,609
Evansville, Ind.	138,690	Portsmouth, Va.	110,963
Fort Lauderdale, Fla.	139,543	Quincy, Mass.	87,966
Florissant, Mo.	66,006	Riverside, Calif.	139,269
Grand Rapids, Mich.	197,534	Sacramento, Calif.	254,362
Hampton, Va.	120,779	San Francisco, Calif.	715,674
Kansas City, Mo.	507,242	San Jose, Calif.	446,504
Lancaster, Pa.	57,589	Seattle, Wash.	530,890
Las Vegas, Nev.	125,641	Spokane, Wash.	170,516
Lincoln, Neb.	149,518	St. Louis, Mo.	622,236
Little Rock, Ark.	132,482	Stockton, Calif.	107,459
Long Beach, Calif.	358,673	Tampa, Fla.	277,736
Louisville, Ky.	361,453	Tulsa, Okla.	331,800
Miami Beach, Fla.	86,974	Warren, Mich.	179,234

NOTE: 1970 Census populations.

should focus on the specific tasks computers perform. For example, statements that computers "save time" are more easily and more objectively assessed by studying specific computerized tasks. Do computers save time in processing traffic tickets, balancing the city's expenditure and revenue figures, or searching for a want or warrant on a criminal suspect? For this reason, primarily, Phase II used the information-processing task as a focal analytic unit for selecting respondents, gathering data, and assessing policy outcomes.

"Information-processing task" is a term used to signify an activity which has a specific objective, explicitly involves information-processing, and *could* be automated (Kraemer et al. 1976). For example, most cities regularly issue a payroll. This involves translating records of hours worked, pay rates, and payroll deductions into a payroll check. Thus "payroll processing" can be designated an "information-processing task" (IPT). Similarly, the searching of a file of utility customers for unpaid bills is an IPT that might be called "utility customer inquiry."

The IPT is an attractive unit of analysis, because it permits more objective and quantifiable observations of computer impacts for particular types of activities. However, there are more than 300 such IPTs that can be automated (see chapter 8), covering the full range of services provided by most city governments (although the IPTs do cluster in functional areas). Therefore, in order to be able to generalize beyond any specific IPT, and also to investigate them in a systematic fashion, it was necessary to focus on a small sample of IPTs.

IPTs were sampled on the basis of two criteria. First, we wished to generalize beyond the specific type of activity which a particular IPT involves, and therefore we sampled IPTs from each of six generic types: record-keeping, calculating/printing, record-searching, record-restructuring, sophisticated analytics, and process control (see Danziger 1977). Second, since we could investigate only a few IPTs, we wanted to generalize beyond any single functional area of government services. Hence, we chose seven IPTs within four functional areas: police, courts, finance, and planning and management. Table A.2 indicates the general characteristics of each IPT type and the specific IPT(s) studied.

Thus, by focusing on seven specific IPTs within six generic types of tasks and four functional areas, we increased our capacity to generalize beyond any particular IPT or functional area and also to collect objective indicators of policy outcomes.

Data Collection

Each city selected for Phase II was visited by one to three of six investigators, including the authors. We spent an average of three person-weeks in each of at least eight sites as part of the fieldwork. This field research gathered three kinds of systematic data, as well as extensive "informal" information.

First, 50 to 100 self-administered questionnaires were completed by the users of computer services in each site. Respondents were selected on the basis of their roles in city government and their relationships to the seven IPTs. Table A.3 shows each kind of respondent, the number of questionnaires distributed to respondents of each role, and the percentage of returned questionnaires. We obtained a high response rate for most roles, the average being 82 percent, due to investigators' collecting most questionnaires while in the city and to thorough follow-up by mail and phone. These lengthy questionnaires measured users' perceptions of the

Table A.2   Types of Information-Processing Tasks and Associated Applications

Type	Characterization	Applications Chosen
1. Record-keeping	Activities that primarily involve the *entry, updating and storage of data*, with a secondary need for access; the computer facilitates manageable storage and easy updating for nearly unlimited amounts of information.	Traffic Ticket Processing
2. Calculating/printing	Activities that primarily involve *sorting, calculating and printing of stored data* to produce specific operational outputs; utilizes the computer's capabilities as a high-speed data processor.	Budget Control (reporting)
3. Record-searching	Activities where *access to and search of data files* is of primary importance; by defining parameters, relevant cases can be retrieved from a file with speed and comprehensiveness; on-line capability of computer is particularly useful.	Detective Investigative Support Patrol Officer Support
4. Record-restructuring	Activities that involve *reorganization, reaggregation and/or analysis of data;* the computer is used to link data from diverse sources or to summarize large volumes of data as management and planning information.	Policy Analysis
5. Sophisticated analytics	Activities that utilize *sophisticated visual, mathematical, simulation or other analytical methods to examine data;* the special capabilities of computers make possible the manipulation of data about complex, interdependent phenomena.	Patrol Manpower Allocation
6. Process control	Activities that approximate a cybernetic system; *data about the state of a system is continually monitored and fed back to a human or automatic controller* which steers the system towards a performance standard; the computer's capabilities for real-time monitoring and direction of activities are utilized.	Budget Control (monitoring)

Table A.3 **Survey Respondents and Response Rates**

Kind of Respondent	Number of Questionnaires Distributed	Number Returned	Response Rate
Mayor & mayor's staff	79	58	73%
Council & council staff	266	117	44
Manager (chief appointed official) and staff	97	81	84
Urban data bank custodians[a]	106	93	88
User department and division heads	544	494	91
User department administrative assistants	161	120	75
User department accounts	96	81	84
Budget reporting and monitoring heads	75	65	87
Budget analysts	83	70	84
Accountants	87	77	89
Traffic ticket directors	42	35	83
Traffic ticket supervisors	70	55	79
Traffic ticket clerks	175	149	85
Police manpower allocation supervisor	40	40	100
Police manpower allocation analysts	57	48	84
Police records division clerks	67	62	93
Police EDP specialists	6	6	100
Detective supervisors	90	81	90
Detectives	533	435	82
Patrol officers	548	468	85
ALL RESPONDENTS	3,222	2,636	82%

[a] Includes planning staff and specially identified data bank custodians.

impacts, problems, and benefits associated with computing. The analysis of these questionnaires is a key data source throughout this study because it provides comparative assessments of perceived computer impacts within relatively well-defined roles in each city.

Second, about 40 personal interviews were conducted with elected officials and municipal personnel involved with the seven IPTs studied in each city. These interviews were semistructured. That is, we used probing questions to multiple respondents, department records, and our own judgment, all within the structure of a general investigative approach in order to code each city on the basis of a set of well-defined issues regarding the particular IPT. For example, in order to determine who were major and minor participants in decisions over whether to adopt computer applications to support detective investigation activities, an investigator might speak with the police chief, several police captains, lieutenants, and detectives, those computer specialists dealing with the relevant automated applications, and the city executive's staff; and also might search police department and data-processing unit documents. We refer to this strategy as "structured field coding" to indicate its central feature: coding cities on each research question in a structured way, and coding by considering all relevant information while in the field rather than by combining various sources of data long after the investigator had visited the city.

The third source of systematic data came from one additional questionnaire that was completed by the data-processing manager(s) and staff of each computer installation in each city visited. These installations included independent computing departments, subunits of the finance department, police units, utility and planning department installations, joint city and county installations, and so forth.[3]

Finally, a source of relatively systematic data was the lengthy case-study reports which were written up by the field researcher after each site visit. These detailed case reports followed a specific format to increase their comparability, and they form the basis for many of the discussions in the book.

Respondent Selection

The methods used for respondent selection were specifically tailored to each information-processing task. The general strategy was to identify those roles most important to each information-processing task and to sample among people within those roles. Certain roles, such as mayor, manager, and head of the budget-reporting unit, defined specific respondents. In these cases, each specific respondent was contacted. Other roles, such as council member, detective, or traffic ticket clerk, defined larger groups of potential respondents. In these cases, we attempted to approximate a random sample of these respondents at each site.

"EXPLORATORY" CASE STUDIES

Throughout the research project, additional city and county governments were subjected to detailed field study. These case studies served different purposes at different stages of the research. Before development of the Phase I questionnaires, we used them to ensure that the orientations and assumptions of the research were realistic. Similarly, the development of Phase II instruments was clarified by creating and testing them in field settings comparable to those to be selected in Phase II. Moreover, each of the authors did complementary field research in conjunction with his own particular interests regarding the role and impacts of the computer package in local governments.

In total, more than fifty additional local governments were field research sites at one time or another during the URBIS research. Some of the sites were selected within the context of a comparative case study project during 1975, other sites were studied because of particularly interesting configurations of automated applications or computer policies, and still others were chosen because they were especially useful sites in which to develop and refine research instruments. The written case reports, transcribed interviews with city and county government personnel, and other written documents from these exploratory case studies provide further grounding for the discussions and analyses in this book.

MULTIPLE MEASURES, MULTIPLE APPROACHES

A research project as extensive as the URBIS Project provides many types of data and facilitates the consideration of the research issues from many perspectives. Since most empirical measures are subject to one or another form of bias, it is usually desirable to employ "multiple operationism"—the use of alternative measures that attempt to tap the same phenomenon (Webb et al. 1966). In analyzing the computer package in larger American local governments, we have used numerous exploratory case studies, an extensive, multipart survey instrument in virtually the entire population of cities and counties, and intensive field research in a relatively large number of sites where structured case coding, discursive case reports, and a widely distributed survey instrument were used.

In addition, we have specified several theoretical approaches that appear to provide alternative explanations of how a high technology will interact with an organization. The aim has been to employ each approach as a different and, potentially, valuable orientation that might enhance our understanding about computer technology in public organizations. In *Computers and Politics*, we have attempted to fuse these multiple measures and multiple approaches into a general and comprehensible assessment of the role of the computer package in contemporary American local governments.

NOTES

1. Computers and Politics

1. Recent exceptions include a review of research on computer use in the public sector by Kraemer and King (1977), and a systematic evaluation of the effects of computers in local government by Kraemer, Dutton, and Northrop (1981).

2. A similar set of concepts is found in Winner (1976:15), who uses "the term organization to signify all varieties of technical (rational-productive) social arrangements" such as factories, workshops, bureaucracies, research and development teams, and the like. He uses the term *network* to mark "those large-scale systems which combine men and apparatus linked across great distances."

3. Unrecognized consequences are also sometimes referred to as "latent effects." Unintended consequences are often referred to as "spillover effects" or "side-effects."

4. For Nelson and Winter (1973), the selection environment can include factors that are part of what we term the external and the internal environments. Here, we apply this concept only to aspects of the external environment.

5. Much of the research on technological innovation in public organizations tends to ignore the political determinants of innovation. The apolitical treatment of technological innovation is related to a tendency in Western cultures to view technologies as neutral (if not benign) innovations which have no redistributive effects of political consequence.

6. The systems-analysis literature usually distinguishes outputs from impacts or outcomes, which are the actual effects of the outputs (Easton 1965). In this study, we are interested in the outputs, and particularly in the impacts, of using the computer package.

2. The Computer Package: Dynamic Complexity

1. Brewer (1974) provides an excellent discussion of the complexity issue, although from a perspective different from that of this book.

2. Local governments, as well as other organizations, often purchase package programs and computer-based models that are often incomprehensible to the adopting organization because of proprietary protection of the programs, their size and complexity, and the skills of local staff. An example is provided by Dutton & Kraemer (1980).

3. During our fieldwork it was usually necessary to interview a sizable number of computer specialists and departmental personnel before we were confident that we had a reasonably comprehensive account of operational computer applications.

4. Unfortunately, this efficiency explanation is confounded by other issues. More sophisticated computing systems require additional overhead—storage space to store complex operating systems. Acquisition of a more flexible operating system will usually require a new system that takes more absolute resources than the system it is replacing. In addition, computer vendors capitalize on the market for more sophisticated systems by tying the acquisition of more sophisticated operating systems to larger machines (Kling & Gerson 1977). Thus, upgrading systems may cost more than the savings realized by greater efficiency in information processing.

5. This finding might result from the underreporting of user-department computing personnel in larger cities where departmental operations are less visible because of their greater scale and economy.

6. Chapter 5 includes a broader discussion of the implications of these service provision choices.

7. Since our 1975 and 1976 surveys and field research, each of the authors has maintained touch with trends in a sizable number of the cities that were studied. These less formal data clearly support the slower-than-expected rates of expansion in most local governments.

3. The Computing Milieu

1. The concept of a "milieu" for a technological innovation is emphasized in Feller and Menzel (1977).

2. This section is adapted from Danziger and Dutton (1977a; 1977b). The set of independent (milieu) variables whose statistical associations with indicators of computer use are analyzed is treated in greater detail in Danziger and Dutton (1977a).

3. Useful reviews of parts of this literature are Fenton and Chamberlayne (1969) and Fried (1976).

4. This summary measure is an index that sums the standardized scores (for cities and counties separately) of each of five components. Four of these are the dependent variables discussed in this paragraph: (1) the speed of adoption of computing, measured as the number of years prior to 1975 that the government has used computing; (2) the total number of computer applications (from a list of 258) currently operational in the government; (3) the total expenditure of all government computing installations as a percentage of total governmental expenditures in 1975; and (4) the total expenditure of all government computing installations divided by total population. The fifth component is a computing sophistication index, ranging from 0 to 4, based on the number of the four different types of "information-processing tasks" within which the government has at least two operational automated applications (see Appendix). For the five components of the index, Cronbach's alpha is 0.77 for cities and 0.79 for counties, levels that support the coherence of the index. For detailed discussion of this index as well as extended analyses of its linkages with milieu characteristics, see Danziger and Dutton (1977b).

5. The hypotheses in the following paragraphs are based on research on the determinants of technological innovation in general, and computer innovation in particular, in public organizations. See Bingham (1978a); Danziger and Dutton (1977a; 1977b); Feller and Menzel (1977); Perry and Danziger (1980); Perry and Kraemer (1979); Yin et al. (1976). For a more generalized summary, see, for example, Row and Boise (1974) and Yin et al. (1979).

6. The classic delineation of these two orientations is in Banfield and Wilson (1965).

7. There are quite contradictory findings in studies of the effects of the distribution of decisional control over innovation. While some studies suggest that decentralization fosters innovation (for example, Thompson 1965), the survey of research by Yin et al. (1976:85–91) supports the opposite position.

8. There is a general problem in using cross-sectional measures of independent variables to explain phenomena that are the product of decisions that have evolved over time. Broadly, it is reasonable to assume that for most local governments, the values on the independent variables (particularly the differences between governments) have been relatively stable over time. Nonetheless, this is one threat to the validity of the analyses for the dependent variables in this section. It is a particular problem for the measure of the speed of adoption of computing, since

3. THE COMPUTING MILIEU

this decision was taken, on average, about nine years prior to the point of measurement of most of the independent variables.

9. In table 3.2, and throughout the book, we shall present levels of statistical significance with statistical analyses. There is controversy concerning whether tests of statistical significance are superfluous when the sample size approaches the population, as is the case for our Phase 1 data from cities and counties (see Winch & Campbell 1969). We report levels of significance in order to aid in the interpretation of correlation and regression coefficients and to place added emphasis on those statistical associations that are quite substantial, given sample size and possible measurement error. Whether the relationships are "significant" or "important" in a substantive sense is, of course, a subjective assessment.

10. While none of the relationships contrary to the hypotheses in table 3.1 is dramatic, it does seem that a reasonable number of the associations between the percentage of the budget allocated to computing and certain milieu variables (e.g., city population growth rate, county per capita income, county chief administrative officer) are contrary to expectations. To the extent the variable measuring pluralism of control over computing decisions displays notable associations, these data support the "minority" position that greater pluralism, rather than greater centralization of decisional control, tends to stimulate the level of innovation.

11. Regression and path analysis, like correlation techniques, measure linear patterns of association. To the extent that the relationships are nonlinear, these data are likely to underestimate the impact of the milieu variables upon the level of computer use. Perry and Kraemer (1979) and Perry and Danziger (1980) provide suggestive evidence that some of these relationships with computing innovations might be nonlinear.

12. The path analyses are derived on the basis of the conceptual model characterized in figure 1.2 and further developed in this chapter. For economy and clarity of expression, we occasionally deviate from strict statistical terminology and discuss the various relationships in *causal* terms. It is important to note that our "one point in time" correlational design does not strictly permit such causal interpretations. Although we can rule out (disconfirm) some plausible alternative hypotheses by using an array of multivariate techniques, we cannot assert that the findings of our study *confirm* a specific set of causal statements. However, when we have theoretical or empirical evidence to suggest causal relationships among our variables, we use causal language. While many of our observations are restricted to only one point in time and some to only 42 cities, the Phase 2 research design maximizes our ability to discern any policy-outcome relationships under these restrictions (see Appendix).

13. All case-study discussions in this section are based on fieldwork in 1975–1976, and we assume that substantial differences may exist between the computing and political conditions reported and some current situations.

14. The importation of computing does have some advantages. It can be a means to develop the computer package with relative efficiency. The contract for service from the outside company can be based on fixed prices, thus stabilizing fiscal planning for computing services. More skilled staff can be utilized because the contractor can operate outside of civil service requirements on salary levels and advancement criteria. And flexibility in staff can be ensured, since it is possible to alter the mix of staff size and staff skills necessary for current developments and operations as the occasion demands.

The underlying risk from the importation of computing is that of dependency—if an outside contractor has direct control over aspects of the computing package, the contracting government or organization may become highly dependent on that contractor. This is particularly troublesome where the FM owns the hardware; but it is also a problem if the skilled technical staff are not continuing members of the government. Kraemer (1977) has shown the liabilities of transfering in technology without slowly and solidly building in-house skills regarding that technology. New Orleans' use of a systems-development approach seems to offer a partial solution to the problem of dependency. Although there are still risks that the local staff will be insufficiently involved with the new systems or will fail to absorb the necessary skills, this approach does seem to offer the best possibilities for using outsiders to upgrade the computer package within the organization.

4. The Participants in Computing Decisions

1. Distinctions between direct and indirect influence are discussed by Dahl (1961). In general, an actor's influence is indirect when a second actor alters behavior or action in order to anticipate and preclude the actions that the first actor would take in order to achieve an objective. Although the existence of indirect influence must usually be inferred rather than measured empirically, we do specify instances where a strong case can be made for the indirect influence of a participant. Since virtually all participants have some indirect influence, we focus only on cases where such influence has major impact on decisions regarding the computer package.

2. This measure tends to underestimate the role of big users on policy boards. Most local governments do not have such boards. However, this chapter will reveal that such boards are more common in governments with more extensive computer packages, and big users tend to be active participants on these boards.

3. These governments are those in which the number of areas automated (e.g., police, fire, public works, etc.) is greater than the mean number of areas automated in all local governments (11), and those in which the total number of automated applications is greater than the mean number of applications in all local governments (30).

5. The Bureaucratic Politics of Computing

1. An earlier version of this chapter is Kraemer (1980).

2. Only the larger governments have developed sufficiently to permit historical analysis. But it appears that smaller governments are following similar patterns of development (Kraemer, Danziger & King 1978); although they are in the early stages of development, they are expected to pass through these same stages.

3. These stages conform to Lowi's (1964, 1971, 1972a, 1978) characterization of "development eras" in the history of the United States. Basic to the analysis is the notion that "a political relationship is determined by the type of policy at stake, so that for every major type of policy there is likely to be a distinctive type of political relationship" (Lowi 1968: 688). Four types of policy are related to various stages: constitutive, distributive, regulatory, and redistributive. Briefly, constitutive policy is concerned with setting up a system, distributive policy with husbanding a system, regulatory policy with regulating the system, and redistributive policy with manipulating the existing system to achieve greater equity.

4. Cities located computing in finance (or the controller's office) more often than counties, although this was the dominant location in both. Other initial locations for the computer were revenue and finance-related departments, such as the utility and tax departments. Counties led the way in setting up computing as an independent department.

5. A 1975 survey of local governments indicates that most computers continue to be located in the finance department. However, this dominance appears to be diminishing. Cities are turning to creation of independent computing departments serving all municipal departments, and to creation of computing installations in other departments (police, public works, administrative services). This pattern is even more pronounced in counties. Over the last ten

years, independent computing departments, and computers located in other departments, appear to have gained at the expense of the finance/controller department. Indeed, independent computer installations are now the dominant form within counties. See Kraemer, Dutton, and Matthews (1975) and Matthews, Dutton, and Kraemer (1976).

6. The finance function has been automated by more cities and counties than any other function. It also has a proportionately greater number of automated applications, on the average, than any other function (Danziger 1978a; Kraemer, Danziger, & King 1978).

7. In counties, however, the dominance by finance was less than in cities, and control over the computer resource began to shift toward an independent computer department. For example, in 1965, only 40 percent of county computer installations were located in finance, as opposed to 70 percent of city computer installations.

8. In the past, most programs had involved simple routines, each implemented independently. Now users were demanding that all of these routines be linked, and provided in a single system. These demands severely taxed even the most competent computing staff.

9. In the smaller local governments, the advent of the minicomputer marked the beginning of the "introduction and conquest" stage, although this was affected by the fact that computing in general had reached the redistributive stage.

10. There are four general methods of acquiring data-processing services. First, and most common, the government can operate its own in-house installation (chapter 2). Clearly, this method allows the government to make most, or all, of the critical decisions about the nature and extent of its provision of data-processing services. However, it also obligates the government to create and maintain a relatively complex and costly computer package, including hardware, software, and skilled staff.

Second, the government can contract for computing services from an installation owned by another local government, or it can be a partner in a public regional installation, where ownership and control are shared by all participants.

Third, the government can contract for computing services from a private service bureau. Typically, the service bureau and the local government negotiate an arrangement that specifies the kinds of services that will be provided for a given price. These services might range from merely processing the government's data to developing and maintaining all of the government's application programs. While some use of private service bureaus is made by local governments of all sizes, the smallest governments rely upon them most. Autonomy and self-control over computing services seem less attractive, relative to the requirements and costs of a sophisticated technology, for the smaller governments.

Fourth, the government can contract with a "facilities management" (FM) organization to provide and manage the entire computing operation. Chapter 3 briefly describes this arrangement. Normally, the government owns the hardware, as well as all systems and programs developed and implemented under the contract. The software development agenda, as well as the operations requirements and the total cost, are determined by a negotiated contract between the FM organization and the government. Usually, the computer management and skilled personnel are employees of the service agency. Some local governments have found FM an attractive alternative because top quality management and personnel can be employed without the hiring, salary, or retention constraints of civil service systems; a competitive private market system can (it is believed) provide specialized services more economically than a noncompetitive government agency; and the development program and cost of computing operations are fixed for a multiyear period, so that the FM organization is obliged to fulfill its commitments to the government's satisfaction.

11. For example, Orange County, California, Grand Rapids, Michigan, and Cleveland, Ohio have implemented facilities management. As chapter 3 indicated, New Orleans, Louisiana has implemented a modified version of FM called "systems management"; and San Diego, California has established a nonprofit corporation for its data services.

12. For example, the fiscal problems of Cleveland are compounded by its contract arrangements for the provision of data processing. Under an FM contract, Computer Sciences Corporation (CSC) provided computer services to the City of Cleveland. However, CSC filed suit to recover about $1.4 million in unpaid bills, and notified the city that its FM contract would be terminated in August, 1979. According to a *Computerworld* interview,

> If CSC discontinues Cleveland's DP operations, according to a reliable source, it would have a "considerable and even a disastrous impact" on the city. "Obviously [CSC] prints and distributes and receives all utility bills" to generate city revenues, "and maintains all payroll and personnel and financial systems."
>
> Particularly vulnerable to a DP shutdown is the city's police force which uses the mainframes to support a real-time information system that indicates wanted criminals and outstanding warrants, the source explained.
>
> Meanwhile, since Cleveland defaulted on approximately $15 billion in municipal notes last year, a number of CSC's FM employees have resigned from the city's computer center. In fact, the DP staff has dwindled from 110 employees to about 65, and more resignations are expected. (Scannel 1979)

13. This is not to say that the computer per se might not have an independent effect. But that effect is likely to be small in comparison to the effect of the political context, and very difficult to disentangle from it. Clearly, computing doesn't cause power shifts, but it does contribute to them along with other organizational factors.

7. The Automation of Bias

1. The following is a major revision and extension of Kraemer and Dutton (1979).
2. The power-shifts hypothesis has attained credibility by virtue of multiple predictions (Crecine & Brunner 1973; Downs 1967; Kraemer & King 1976; Leavitt & Whisler 1958; Oettinger 1971; Whisler 1967, 1970) and empirical research (Dutton & Kraemer 1978b; Laudon 1974).
3. Chapter 3 has shown that those who control technology within public organizations influence the adoption, development, and orientation of the technology (Danziger & Dutton 1977b; Dutton & Kraemer 1978b).
4. In most strong mayor cities, these officials tend to be the director of finance or the director of management and budget. These officials tend to have professional management backgrounds and tend to be given chief administrative responsibility by the mayor. These officials should be distinguished from another group of operating department heads whose management role is much more limited, and from the mayor's political advisors who often fill one or two department head positions but serve little or no management role.
5. While both Danziger (1979a) and Downs (1967) broadly suggest that technically educated officials are more likely to control high technology, they do not specifically deal with the planner analysts upon whom we focus.
6. For example, the use of computing to send utility bills has no obvious power implications for relations among managers, planners, and elected officials. However, it has very subtle implications for the relative control relationships between government and the general public.
7. For a more complete description of the uses and operational impacts of such systems, see Kraemer, Dutton, & Northrop (1980).

8. For example, surveys have been used to determine which projects the public would support by voting for the issuance of bonds.

9. Some data in these tables are similar to those in table 6.3. However, additional role-types are included, quite different analytic issues are addressed, and the data are organized differently.

10. These data are based on open-ended responses in which public officials *mentioned* the use of data banks in ways conforming to our categories of administrative reporting, planning analysis, and political uses. Planners mentioned administrative uses in 90 percent of the cities, planning uses in 90 percent, and political uses in 22 percent. Managers mentioned administrative uses in 63 percent, planning uses in 47 percent, and political uses in 23 percent. Elected officials mentioned administrative uses in 40 percent, planning uses in 54 percent, and political uses in 47 percent.

11. This study of FIBS is drawn from Dutton and Kraemer (1979a, 1980).

12. A management science approach to the fiscal crisis has been the allocation of scarce resources with the help of management-science techniques such as mathematical programing and simulations (Drake, Keeney, & Morse 1972; Morse & Bacon 1967). While such techniques cannot solve urban fiscal problems, they might make a contribution by suggesting more efficient resource allocations. Furthermore, these techniques are politically attractive in two respects. One, they promise to improve the quality of management decisions in the performance of day-to-day operations, thus offering decision makers the capacity to provide more services for the same or fewer resources. Two, they appear *at first glance* to benefit many political interests and to harm very few. But management-science techniques are also appealing on less political grounds. They are perceived by many people as "hard" social science. They have also had a successful track record in some business operations with reputations for efficiency and effectiveness seldom attributed to government operations.

8. Computing and Urban Services

1. We have excluded considerations from the perspectives of technological elitism and organizational pluralism from this chapter, as we consider them less relevant to the examination of the relationship between computing and citizens than are managerial rationalism and reinforcement politics. Moreover, our data do not support an adequate test of these perspectives.

2. Scholars who are particularly interested in social control (Rule 1974) emphasize the nature, construction, and enforcement of social rules; they do not pay much attention to the nature and quality of services that government agencies provide to their publics. In contrast, organizational scholars have developed theories of organizational behavior that emphasize both administrative exchanges and social control (Blau 1955; Friedson 1970; Lawler & Rhode 1976). Much of the literature on "management information systems" includes accounts of managerial control—such systems are often described in terms of their potential for enhancing the control of managers (Dutton & Kraemer 1978; Whisler 1967). In contrast, most advocates of "urban information systems" tend to emphasize service delivery and systematically to neglect social control (Evans & Knisely 1970; Nanus 1972; Sackman & Boehm 1972). They share their "apolitical" emphases with other analysts who study strategies for urban management (Larson 1978; Morse & Bacon 1967). The role of computing in facilitating the control of citizens by local governments has been largely neglected, despite some promising theoretical work and important exploratory case studies (Downs 1967; Kling 1978; Laudon 1974).

3. Of course, the actual level of control that public agencies exert over the public varies

considerably. The police in Costa Mesa may give more traffic citations than the police in Minochee. And the police in Wakago may operate a speed trap. In any of these places, a member of the local city council driving an Oldsmobile Cutlass may receive fewer citations than a leather-jacketed teenager driving a chopped hog, despite comparable driving. Still, one may make distinctions among agencies; clearly, greater social control is *typically* exercised by the policemen who monitor traffic than by the garbagemen who pick up the weekly trash.

4. In general, many applications that are classified as administrative support could be used to accomplish considerable bureaucratic control, but they usually are not. Our characterization of administrative applications by the extent to which they support bureaucratic control may underestimate that extent.

In addition, the extent to which applications that support public services also support increased social control is probably underestimated. For example, we classified automated welfare information and referral systems as low social control even though welfare caseworkers using such systems might attempt to alter the social lives of their clients (Handler 1973).

Last, some computer applications serve multiple ends. Welfare information and referral supports both clients who are trying to gain some assistance with a minimum of inconvenience, and administrators who want systematic data on the clientele they are serving (Kling 1978a). The dispatch of police cars serves administrators who wish to utilize efficiently the limited number of vehicles under their command; it also serves a broader agenda of social control, since most police dispatches are calls to help ameliorate disturbances and to stop or report crimes. In these few cases, each application was counted in each of the appropriate categories.

5. These data should not be taken without qualification. We were quite conservative in coding applications as increasing control over services or administration. For example, payroll programs are sometimes run for urban managers who wish to examine and control patterns of overtime, sick leave, and accrued vacation. But since such uses are atypical, applications such as payroll were not coded as supporting bureaucratic control. On the other hand, we were quite liberal in coding applications as supporting citizen service. For example, welfare information and referral systems were listed as increasing public service, although the empirical evidence indicates that they sometimes support administrators at least as much as they do welfare applicants (Kling 1978a). Thus the data underestimate social control.

6. The inventory in table 8.7 was constructed from applications included in prior surveys of computer use, from applications known to exist in at least some governments, and from packaged applications being promoted by government or private agencies. While the inventory was not a specification of *all* possible uses, it was a specification of *known* possible uses in 1975.

7. The first uses of computing in local governments evolved from earlier uses of unit-record equipment, mainly in accounting. The first applications to be automated—payroll, billing, accounts payable, etc.—were simple translations of the kinds of data processing that occurred with the more primitive card-sorting and card-punching equipment. Because the first uses of computing were for accounting and financial applications, control over the computer and its subsequent use was frequently given to the finance department. For example, in 1965 approximately 70 percent of the cities and 40 percent of the counties located their computing shops in the finance departments. As late as 1975, 50 percent of the cities and 18 percent of the counties had their computing shops centralized in the finance departments. As might be expected, finance naturally gave first priority to its own uses. Consequently, it is not surprising to find that in 1975 approximately 90 percent of the larger U.S. local governments devoted one-fourth of their computer applications to finance. For them, computing is still "finance computing."

8. It is important to note that this discussion is about general-purpose local governments; namely, cities and counties. It specifically excludes schools and special districts, in which many of the activities are more service-oriented.

9. Policy, Politics, and Computers

1. How can one define "the public interest"? The concept implies that there is only one goal or set of goals that is shared by virtually the entire population served by the government. But the attempt to define or measure this concept leads quickly to the conclusions that the interest of "the public" varies from issue to issue and, more importantly, that even within a single issue there is usually substantial divergence in the definition of interests. Despite commonly shared basic goals of system maintenance and social order, and a generalized preference for efficiency, honesty, and fair treatment from public agencies, the citizens are not of one mind when these principles are converted into public policies and actions. Even in "homogeneous" communities, there is wide disagreement on such public issues as the appropriate levels of expenditure and taxation on many public goods and services, development of local resources, the proper functioning of the public safety and criminal justice system, and the government's activities in social welfare. Thus we shall use the concept of "the public interest" more in the sense of an idealized notion than as a set of citizen preferences with clear empirical referents.

2. Yates (1977) writes about municipal government, and does not distinguish smaller from larger jurisdictions. But his data are drawn primarily from New York City and New Haven, Connecticut, one a massive metropolis which encompasses over 1400 independent jurisdictions, and the other a smaller but still relatively large city. The qualifications about size are our own.

3. Some modern-management theorists argue that participatory organizations are most efficient under certain conditions, particularly when the staff must cope with extreme uncertainty regarding either the external environment or the technologies used to accomplish necessary work. They argue that, conversely, traditionally "bureaucratic" forms of organization with top-down flow of command, extensive formal procedures, and sharp divisions of labor tend to be most efficient when the external environment or organizational methods are highly predictable (Lawrence and Lorsch 1967). Public agencies span these extremes, with agencies like planning departments tending to face uncertain environments, and other agencies such as offices for collecting taxes and recording vital statistics tending to operate in relatively stable contexts. But for us, the crucial question is not "When does participation encourage efficiency," but rather, "Under what conditions does participatory organization make sense, even if it entails some losses in efficiency?"

4. Ironically, recent popular movements to restrict government spending and reduce public services (e.g., California's Proposition 13) share some of the values of radical critics regarding "big government" and those applications of computing that feed the "appetites" of bureaucratic organization (Moshowitz 1976).

Appendix: URBIS Research Methodology

1. Two conventional approaches for addressing such issues were not appropriate. The most common approach is an experimental design in which conditions are controlled such that only the policy variables are manipulated in order to examine how they affect the policy outcome variables (Campbell 1969; Campbell & Stanley 1963; Suchman 1967). In such an approach, the experimenter has control (preferably by random assignment) of the policy variables.

However, the natural settings of the governments do not allow for such control, and it was not feasible to await the occurrence of natural experimental conditions.

The second conventional approach is to sample cities randomly, statistically controlling for other policies and city characteristics in order to determine the impact of a given policy on a given impact variable (Kerlinger 1967; Leege & Francis 1974). Such a design would be useful if the sample were quite large, if the policies of interest were adequately represented in a random sample, and if the effects of each policy were easily distinguishable. However, we were limited by resources to sampling about 40 cities in depth. Moreover, many policies of interest are rare and therefore would be underrepresented in a random sample, and we expected policy outcomes to be quite difficult to discern, given the large number of other variables (noise) affecting the same outcomes. Consequently, the random sample approach did not seem an adequate method to answer our research questions.

2. The choice of the third quartile as the cutting point was based on the distribution of cities on each (policy) stratification variable such dichotomization tended to group cities on each index into those with common policies and those with relatively rare policy extremes—those that were highly automated, decentralized, integrated, sophisticated, involving users, and charging for services.

3. Private service bureaus that sometimes provide computing services (e.g., banks, universities) were not surveyed.

REFERENCES

ACM (Association for Computing Machinery). 1973. Computers in the service of citizens. *Proceedings of the ACM National Conference* (Atlanta, Ga.). New York: ACM Press.

Aiken, M. and S. Bacharach. 1978. Politics, the urban system, and organizational structure. In Lucien Karpik, ed., *Organizations and Environment*, pp. 199–252. London: Sage.

Allison, G. 1971. *The Essence of Decision*. Boston: Little, Brown.

Anderson, R. E. 1971. Computerization: Panacea or part of the problem. *Public Management* 53(10):20–21.

Auerbach, I. 1979. Computing in China, 1979—An update. *Computer* 12(11):52–60.

Bachrach, P. and M. Baratz. 1963. Decisions and nondecisions: An analytical framework. *American Political Science Review* 57(4):632–42.

—— 1972. *Power and Poverty*. New York: Oxford University Press.

Banfield, E. 1961. *Political Influence: A New Theory of Urban Politics*. New York: Free Press.

Banfield, E. and J. Q. Wilson. 1965. *City Politics*. Cambridge: Harvard University Press.

Bell, D. 1958. *The End of Ideology*. New York: Free Press.

—— 1973. *The Coming of Post-Industrial Society*. New York: Basic Books.

Bennis, W. and P. Slater. 1968. *The Temporary Society*. New York: Harper & Row.

Benveniste, G. 1977. *The Politics of Expertise*. 2d ed. San Francisco: Boyd & Fraser.

Bingham, R. 1976. *Technological Innovation*. Lexington, Mass.: Lexington Books.

—— 1978a. *The Adoption of Innovation by Local Governments*. Lexington, Mass.: Lexington Books.

—— 1978b. Professional associations as intermediaries in transferring technology to cities. Milwaukee: University of Wisconsin, Dep't of Political Science.

Blau, P. M. 1955. *The Dynamics of Bureaucracy*. Chicago: University of Chicago Press.

Blum, E. H. 1972. Municipal services. In H. Sackman and B. W. Boehm, eds., *Planning Community Information Utilities*, pp. 45–68. Montvale, N.J.: AFIPS Press.

Boguslaw, R. 1965. *The New Utopians*. Englewood Cliffs, N.J.: Prentice-Hall.

Bostrom, R. P. and J. S. Heinen. MIS problems and failures: A socio-technical perspective. Part 1: The causes. *MIS Quarterly* 1(3):17–32.

Brewer, G. D. 1974. *Politicians, Bureaucrats, and Consultants.* New York: Basic Books.

Brooks, H. and R. Bowers. 1972. Technology: Processes of assessment and choice. In A. Teich, ed., *Technology and Man's Future*, pp. 219–33. New York: St. Martin's.

Campbell, D. T. 1969. Reforms as experiments. *American Psychologist* 24(4):409–29.

Campbell, D. T. and J. C. Stanley. 1963. *Experimental and Quasi-Experimental Designs for Research.* Chicago: Rand McNally.

Caplan, N., A. Morrison, and R. Stambaugh. 1975. *The Use of Social Science Knowledge in Policy Decisions at the National Level.* Ann Arbor, Mich.: Institute for Social Research.

Chartrand, R. L. 1971. *Systems Technology Applied to Social and Community Problems.* New York: Spartan Books.

Child, J. 1972. Organizational structure, environment, and performance: The role of strategic choice. *Sociology* 6:1–22.

Colton, K. W. 1972. Police and computers: Use, acceptance, and impact of automation. In *The Municipal Year Book 1972*, pp. 119–36. Washington, D.C.: International City Management Association.

—— 1975. Computers and the police: Police departments and the new information technology. In *The Municipal Year Book 1975*, pp. 214–32. Washington, D.C.: International City Management Association.

Colton, K. W., ed. 1978. *Police Computer Technology.* Lexington, Mass.: Lexington Books.

Computerworld. 1979. IBM 370/158's sell at auction for $1 million. *Computerworld* (July 30), p. 1.

Crecine, J. P. 1968. *Governmental Problem-Solving: A Computer Simulation of Municipal Budgeting.* Chicago: Rand McNally.

Crecine, J. P. and R. D. Brunner. 1972. Government and politics: A fragmented society. In *The Conference Board, Information Technology*, pp. 149–81. New York: The Conference Board.

Crozier, M. 1964. *The Bureaucratic Phenomenon.* Chicago: University of Chicago Press.

Cyert, R., and J. G. March. 1963. *A Behavioral Theory of the Firm.* Englewood Cliffs, N.J.: Prentice-Hall.

Dahl, R. A. 1961. *Who Governs?* New Haven: Yale University Press.

Danziger, J. N. 1975. Evaluating computers: More sophisticated EDP. *Nation's Cities* 13(10):31–32.

—— 1977a. Computers and the frustrated chief executive. *MIS Quarterly* 1(2):43–53.

—— 1977b. Computers, local governments, and the litany to EDP. *Public Administration Review* 37(1):28–37.

—— 1978a. Computer technology and the urban fiscal crisis. *Urban Systems* 2(3):105–19.

—— 1978b. *Making Budgets: Public Resource Allocation.* Beverly Hills, Calif.: Sage.

—— 1979a. The "skill bureaucracy" and intraorganizational control: The case of the data-processing unit. *Sociology of Work and Occupations* 6(2):204–26.

—— 1979b. The use of automated information in local government: A critical assessment. *American Behavioral Scientist* 22(3):363–92.

—— 1979c. Technology and productivity: A contingency analysis of computers in local government. *Administration and Society* 11(2):144–71.

Danziger, J. N. and W. H. Dutton. 1977a. Computers as an innnovation in American local governments. *Communications of the ACM* 20(12):945–56.

—— 1977b. Technological innovation in local government: The case of computers. *Policy and Politics* 6(1):27–49.

Danziger, J. N., K. L. Kraemer, and J. L. King. 1978. An assessment of computer technology in American local governments. *Urban Systems* 3(1):21–37.

Dial, O. E., K. L. Kraemer, W. H. Mitchell, and M. Weiner. 1970. *State-of-the-Art of Municipal Information Systems in 1970.* Washington, D.C.: Department of Housing and Urban Development.

Dickson, D. 1974. *The Politics of Alternative Technology.* New York: Universe Books.

Downs, A. 1967. A realistic look at the payoffs from urban data systems. *Public Administration Review* 27(3):204–10.

Drake, A. W., R. L. Keeney, and P. Morse, eds. 1972. *Analysis of Public Systems.* Cambridge, Mass.: MIT Press.

Durkheim, E. 1947. *Division of Labor in Society.* New York: Free Press.

Dutton, W. H., J. N. Danziger, and K. L. Kraemer. 1980. Did the policy fail? In H. Ingram and D. Mann, eds., *Why Policies Succeed or Fail*, pp. 163–84. Beverly Hills, Calif.: Sage.

Dutton, W. H. and K. L. Kraemer. 1977. Technology and urban management: The power payoffs of computing. *Administration and Society* 9(3):304–40. *Administration and Society* 9(3):304–40.

—— 1978a. Management utilization of computers in American local governments. *Communications of the ACM* 21(3):206–18.

—— 1978b. Determinants of support for computerized information systems. *Midwest Review of Public Administration* 12(1):19–40.

—— 1979a. The automation of bias: Computer models and local government budgeting. *Information Privacy* 1:303–11.

—— 1979b. Urban technology, executive support, and computing. *The Urban Interest* 1(2):35–42.

—— 1980. Automating bias. *Society* 17:36–41.

Dutton, W. H. and S. Pearson. 1975. Executives cite common data system problems. *Nation's Cities* 13(10):28–30.

Easton, D. 1965. *A Systems Analysis of Political Life.* New York: Wiley.

Edelman, M. 1964. *The Symbolic Uses of Politics.* Chicago: University of Chicago Press.

Ellul, J. 1964. *The Technological Society.* J. Wilkinson, trans. New York: Knopf, Vintage edition.

Evans, J. W. and R. A. Knisely. 1970. Integrated municipal information systems: Some potential impacts. Washington, D.C.: U.S. Department of Housing and Urban Development.

Feller, I., M. R. King, D. C. Menzel, R. O'Connor, P. A. Wissel, and T. Ingersoll. 1979. Information in state legislatures. *American Behavioral Scientist* 22(3):417–36.

Feller, I. and D. Menzel. 1976. *Diffusion of Innovations in Municipal Governments.* University Park, Pa.: Center for the Study of Science Policy, Pennsylvania State University.

—— 1977. Diffusion milieux as a focus of research on innovations in the public sector. *Policy Science* 8(1):49–68.

Fenton, J. and D. Chamberlayne. 1969. The Literature dealing with the relationships between political processes, socio-economic conditions, and public policies in the American states. *Polity* 1:388–404.

Ferkiss, B. C. 1969. *Technological Man: The Myth and the Reality.* New York: Braziller.

Fried, R. C. 1976. Comparative urban policy and performance. In F. Greenstein and N. Polsby, eds., *The Handbook of Political Science*, 6:305–380. Reading, Mass.: Addison-Wesley.

Friedson, E. 1970. *Professional Dominance.* New York: Atherton.

Fuller, R. B. 1969. *Utopia or Oblivion.* New York: Bantam.

—— 1970. *Operating Manual for Spaceship Earth.* New York: Pocket Books.

Galbraith, J. K. 1967. *The New Industrial State.* New York: Signet.

Ghere, R. K. 1977. Municipal data-processing systems and shifting organizational power. Rock Hill, S.C.: Winthrop College, Department of Political Science. Manuscript.

Gottlieb, C. C. and A. Borodin. 1973. *Social Issues in Computing.* San Francisco: Academic Press.

Greenberger, N., M. A. Crenson, and B. L. Crissey. 1976. *Models in the Policy Process.* New York: Russell Sage.

Hackathorn, L. 1975. The URBIS census survey. Irvine, Calif.: Public Policy Research Organization, University of California.

Hale, G. E. and S. R. Douglass. 1977. The politics of budget execution. *Administration and Society* 9(3):367–78.

Handler, J. 1972. *The Coercive Social Worker.* Chicago: Rand McNally.

Hearle, E. F. R. and R. J. Mason. 1963. *A Data-Processing System for State and Local Governments.* Englewood Cliffs, N.J.: Prentice-Hall.

Hedberg, B. and E. Mumford. 1975. The design of computer systems. In E. Mumford and H. Sackman, eds. *Human Choice and Computers*, pp. 76–91. New York: Elsevier.

Hoffman, E. P. 1973. Soviet metapolicy: Information processing in the Soviet Union. *Administration and Society* 5:200–232.

—— 1977. Technology, values, and political power in the Soviet Union. In F. Fleron, Jr., ed., *Technology and Communist Culture*, pp. 397–436. New York: Holt, Rinehart and Winston.

Hunnius, G., G. D. Garson, and J. Case, eds. 1973. *Worker's Control: A Reader on Labor and Social Change*. New York: Random House.

Illich, I. 1974. *Tools for Conviviality*. New York: Harper & Row.

International Task Force on Information Systems. 1968. *The Dynamics of Information Flow*. Washington, D.C.: The Task Force.

Isaacs, H. H. 1968. Computer systems technology: Progress, projections, problems. *Public Administration Review* 28(6):488–94.

Karpik, L., ed. 1978. *Organizations and Environment*. Beverly Hills, Calif.: Sage.

Kerlinger, F. N. 1967. *Foundations of Behavioral Research*. New York: Holt, Rinehart and Winston.

Kling, R. 1974. Computers and social power. *Computers and Society* 5(3):6–11.

—— 1977. The organizational context of user-centered software designs. *MIS Quarterly* 1(4):41–52.

—— 1978a. Automated welfare client tracking and service integration. *Communications of the ACM* 21(6)484–93.

—— 1978b. Information systems in policymaking. *Telecommunications Policy* 2:22–32.

—— 1978c. Information systems as social resources in policymaking. *Proceedings of the ACM National Conference* (December), pp. 664–74.

—— 1978d. The impacts of computing on the work of managers, data analysts, and clerks. Irvine, Calif.: Public Policy Research Organization, University of California.

—— 1980. Social analyses of computing: Theoretical perspectives in recent empirical research. *Computing Surveys* 12(1):61–110.

Kling, R. and E. M., Gerson. 1977. The social dynamics of technical innovation in computing world. *Symbolic Interaction* 1(1):132–46.

—— 1978. Patterns of segmentation and intersection in the computing world. *Symbolic Interaction* 1(2):24–43.

Kling, R. and W. Scacchi. 1979. Recurrent dilemmas of computer use in complex organizations. *National Conference Proceedings* 48:107–15. Montvale, N.J.: AFIPS Press.

—— 1980. Computing as social action: The social dynamics of computing in complex organizations. *Advances in Computers*, vol. 19, pp. 250–327. New York: Academic Press.

—— 1981. The web of computing. *Advances in Computers*, vol. 20. New York: Academic Press.

Kling, R., W. Scacchi, and P. Crabtree. 1978. The social dynamics of instrumental computer use. *SIGSOC Bulletin* 10(1):9–21.

Knorr, K. D. 1977. Policy-maker's use of social science knowledge. In C. Weiss, ed., *Using Social Research in Public Policy Making*, pp. 165–82. Lexington, Mass.: Lexington Books.

Kraemer, K. L. 1969. The evolution of information systems for urban administration. *Public Administration Review* 29(4):389–402.

—— 1971. USAC: An evolving intergovernmental mechanism for urban information systems. *Public Administration Review* 31(5):543–51.

Kraemer, K. L. 1977. Local government information systems and technology transfer. *Public Administration Review* 37(4):368–82.

——1980a. Computers, information, and power in local governments. In A. Moshowitz, ed., *Human Choice and Computers*, 2:213–35. Amsterdam: North Holland.

—— 1980b. Citizen impacts from information technology in public administrations. Irvine, Calif.: Public Policy Research Organization, University of California.

—— forthcoming. Use of applied systems analysis in urban policy-making. In IIASA (International Institute for Applied Systems Analysis), *Handbook of Applied Systems Analysis*. Vol. 2. New York: Wiley.

Kraemer, K. L., J. N. Danziger, and W. H. Dutton. 1978. Automated information systems and urban decision-making. *Urban Systems* 3(4):429–52.

Kraemer, K. L., J. N. Danziger, W. H. Dutton, A. Mood, and R. Kling. 1976. A future cities research design for policy analysis. *Socio-Economic Planning Sciences* 10(5):199–211.

Kraemer, K. L., J. N. Danziger, W. H. Dutton, and S. Pearson. 1975. Chief executives, local government, and computers. *Nation's Cities* 13(10):18–40.

Kraemer, K. L., J. N. Danziger, and J. L. King. 1978. Local government and information technology in the United States. In *Local Government and Information Technology*, pp. 186–237. Paris: OECD.

Kraemer, K. L. and W. H. Dutton. 1979. The interests served by technological reform. *Administration and Society* 11(1):80–106.

Kraemer, K. L., W. H. Dutton, and J. Matthews. 1975. Municipal computers. *Urban Data Service Reports* 7(11):1–15.

Kraemer, K. L., W. H. Dutton, and A. Northrop. 1980. Management control, the automated budget, and information handling. *Information Privacy* 2(1):7–16.

—— 1981. *Management of Information Systems*. New York: Columbia University Press.

Kraemer, K. L. and G. Howe. 1968. Automated data processing in municipal government. In *The Municipal Year Book 1968*, pp. 280–303. Washington, D.C.: International City Managers' Association.

Kraemer, K. L. and J. L. King. 1976. *Computers, Power, and Urban Management*. Professional Papers in Administration and Policy Studies, 3. Beverly Hills, Calif.: Sage.

—— 1978a. Laissez-innover: A critique of federal involvement in development of state and local information systems. *The Bureaucrat* 7(3):23–31.

—— 1978b. Requiem for USAC. *Policy Analysis* 5(3):313–49.

——1979. Assessing the interaction between computing policies and problems. Irvine, Calif.: Public Policy Research Organization, University of California.

Kraemer, K. L. and J. L. King, eds. 1977. *Computers in Local Government: A Review of the Research*. New York: Holt, Rinehart and Winston.

Kraemer, K. L., W. H. Mitchell, M. Weiner, and O. E. Dial. 1974. *Integrated Municipal Information Systems*. New York: Holt, Rinehart and Winston.

Kraemer, K. L. and J. Perry. 1979. The federal push to bring technology to local governments. *Public Administration Review* 39(3):260–69.

Kraemer, K. L. and D. Schetter. 1979. The URBIS project: Administrative summary. Irvine, Calif.: Public Policy Research Organization, University of California.

Lambright, W. H. 1976. *Governing Science and Technology*. New York: Oxford University Press.

Larson, R. C. 1978. *Public Deployment*. Lexington, Mass.: Lexington Books.

Latham, E. 1952. *The Group Basis of Politics*. Ithaca, N.Y.: Cornell University Press.

Laudon, K. C. 1974. *Computers and Bureaucratic Reform: The Political Functions of Urban Information Systems*. New York: Wiley.

—— 1980. Information technology and participation in the political process. In A. Moshowitz, ed., *Human Choice and Computers*, 2:167-191. Amsterdam: North Holland.

Lawler, E. E. and J. G. Rhode. 1976. *Information and Control in Organizations*. Pacific Palisades, Calif.: Goodyear.

Lawrence, P. and J. Lorsch. 1967. *Organization and Environment*. Cambridge: Harvard University Press.

Leavitt, H. J. and T. L. Whisler. 1958. Management in the 1980's. *Harvard Business Review* 36:41-48.

Lee, D. 1973. Requiem for large scale planning models. *Journal of the American Institute of Planners* 39(2):136-78.

Leege, D. C. and W. L. Francis. 1974, *Political Research*. New York: Basic Books.

Levy, F. S., A. J. Meltsner, and A. Wildavsky. 1974. *Urban Outcomes*. Berkeley, Calif.: University of California Press.

Lindblom, C. 1968. *The Policymaking Process*. Englewood Cliffs, N. J.: Prentice-Hall.

Lindblom, C. and D. Cohen. 1979. *Usable Knowledge: Social Science and Social Problem Solving*. New Haven: Yale University Press.

Lineberry, R. L. .and I. Sharkansky. 1978. *Urban Politics and Public Policy*. New York: Harper & Row.

Lorsch, J. W. and J. J. Morse. 1974. *Organizations and Their Members: A Contingency Approach*. New York: Harper & Row.

Lowi, T. J. 1964. American business, public policy, case-studies and political theory. *World Politics* 16 (July), 16:676-715.

—— 1971. Distribution, regulation, redistribution: The functions of government. In R. B. Ripley, ed., *Public Policies and Their Politics*, pp. 27-40. New York: Norton.

—— 1972a. Four systems of policy, politics and choice. *Public Administration Review* 32(4):298-309.

—— 1972b. Government and politics: Blurring of sector lines. In *Information Technology: Some Critical Implications*, pp. 131-81. New York: The Conference Board.

—— 1978. Public policy and bureaucracy in the United States and France. In D. Ashford, ed., *Comparing Public Policies*, pp. 177-196. Beverly Hills, Calif.: Sage.

Lucas, H. C. 1975. *Why Information Systems Fail.* New York: Columbia University Press.

Majone, G. 1978. The uses of policy analysis. New York: Russell Sage. Unpublished paper.

Managing data for decision. 1971. *Public Management* 53(10):3–26.

Mann, F. C. and L. R. Hoffmen. 1960. *Automation and the Worker.* New York: Holt, Rinehart and Winston.

Mann, F. C. and L. K. Williams. 1960. Observations on the dynamics of a change to electronic data-processing equipment. *Administrative Science Quarterly* 5(2):217–56.

Marchand, D. and E. G. Bogan. 1979. *A History and Background Assessment of the National Crime Information Center and Computerized Criminal History Program.* Columbia, S.C., Bureau of Governmental Research and Service, University of South Carolina.

Markus, M. L. 1979. *Understanding Information System Use in Organizations: A Theoretical Perspective.* Ph.D. Dissertation. Cleveland, Ohio: Case Western Reserve University.

Marris, P. and M. Rein. 1973. *Dilemmas of Social Reform.* 2d ed. Chicago: Aldine.

Marx, K. 1906. *Capital.* Vol. 1. S. Moore and E. Aveling, trans. New York: Modern Library.

Masotti, L. H. and D. R. Bowen. 1965. Communities and budgets. *Urban Affairs Quarterly* 1(2):39–58.

Matthews, J., W. H. Dutton, and K. L. Kraemer. 1976. County computers. *Urban Data Service Reports* 8(2):1–10.

McDermott, J. 1977. Technology: The opiate of the intellectuals. In A. H. Teich, ed., *Technology and Man's Future*, 2d ed., pp. 180–206. New York: St. Martin's.

McPherson, C. B. 1977. *The Life and Times of Liberal Democracy.* New York: Oxford University Press.

Mendlin, A. 1968. Confidentiality and local information systems. *Public Administration Review* 28(6):509–18.

Mesthene, E. G. 1977. The role of technology in society. In. A. H. Teich, ed., *Technology and Man's Future*, 2d ed., pp. 156–79. New York: St. Martin's.

MITRE Corporation. 1971. *A Technology Assessment Methodology.* Vols. 2, 3, 4, 5, 6. Washington, D.C.: The MITRE Corporation.

Morse, P. M. and L. W. Bacon, eds. 1967. *Operations Research for Public Systems.* Cambridge, Mass.: MIT Press.

Moshowitz, A. 1976. *The Conquest of Will: Information Processing in Human Affairs.* Reading, Mass.: Addison-Wesley.

Mumford, L. 1970. *The Myth of the Machine.* New York: Harcourt, Brace, Jovanovich.

Nanus, B. 1972. The municipal framework. In H. Sackman and B. W. Boehm, eds., *Planning Community Information Utilities*, pp. 375–400. Montvale, N.J.: AFIPS Press.

Nelson, R. R. and S. G. Winter. 1975. Growth theory from an evolutionary perspective. *American Economic Review* 65(2):338–44.

Noble, D. 1977. *America by Design*. New York: Knopf.

Nolan, R. L. 1973. Managing the computer resource. *Communications of the ACM* 16(7):399–405.

Northrop, A. and W. H. Dutton. 1978. Municipal reform and group influence. *American Journal of Political Science* 22(3):691–711.

Oettinger, A. G. 1971. Compunications in the national decisionmaking process. In M. Greenberger, ed., *Computers, Communications, and the Public Interest*, pp. 74–114. Baltimore, Md.: Johns Hopkins University Press.

Ostrom, E. 1975. Interorganizational arrangements in urban police service. Paper presented at International Institute of Management Conference, Berlin, June.

O'Toole, J. 1974. *Work and the Quality of Life*. Cambridge, Mass.: MIT Press.

Pack, H. and J. R. Pack. 1977. The resurrection of the urban development model. *Policy Analysis* 3(3):407–27.

Parenti, M. 1979. *Democracy for the Few*. New York: St. Martin's.

Perrow, C. 1972. *Complex Organizations*. Glenview, Ill.: Scott, Foresman.

Perry, J. L. and J. N. Danziger. 1980. The adoptability of innovations. *Administration and Society* 11(4):461–92.

Perry, J. L. and K. L. Kraemer. 1979. *Technological Innovation in American Local Governments*. New York: Pergamon Press.

Pettigrew, A. 1973. *The Politics of Organizational Decisionmaking*. London: Tavistock.

—— 1975. Towards a political theory of organizational intervention. *Human Relations* 28(3):191–208.

Pettigrew, A. and E. Mumford. 1975. *Implementing Strategic Decisions*. New York: Longmans.

Piven, F. F. and R. Cloward. 1976. *Regulating the Poor*. New York: Random House.

Price, D. K. 1965. *The Scientific Estate*. Cambridge: Harvard University Press.

Primack, J. and R. von Hippel. 1974. *Advice and Dissent: Scientists in the Political Arena*. New York: Basic Books.

Quinn, R. 1976. The impacts of a computerized information system on integration and coordination of human services. *Public Administration Review* 36(2):166–74.

Redford, E. S. 1969. *Democracy in the Administrative State*. New York: Oxford University Press.

Rich, R. 1978. Instrumental versus conceptual uses of social science knowledge. In C. Weiss, ed., *Using Social Research in Public Policy Making*, pp. 147–65. Lexington, Mass.: Lexington Books.

—— 1979. Systems of analysis, technology assessment, and bureaucratic power. *American Behavioral Scientist* 22(3):393–416.

Rogers, D. 1968. *110 Livingston Street: Politics and Bureaucracy in the New York Public School System*. New York: Random House.

Row, F. A. and W. B. Boise. 1974. Organizational innovation. *Public Administration Review* 34(6):284–93.

Rule, J. 1974. *Public Surveillance and Private Lives*. New York: Schocken.

Sackman, H. and B. W. Boehm, eds. 1972. *Planning Community Information Utilities*. Montvale, N.J.: AFIPS Press.

Savas, E. S. 1978. The institutional structure of local government services. *Public Administration Review* 38(5):412–19.

Sayre, W. S. and H. Kaufman. 1965. *Governing New York City: Politics in the Metropolis*. New York: Russel Sage.

Scannel, T. 1979. CAC files suit against City of Cleveland. *Computerworld* 13(24), p. 2.

Schattschneider, E. E. 1960. *The Semi-Sovereign People*. New York: Holt, Rinehart and Winston.

Schick, A. 1966. The road to PPB: The stages of budget reform. *Public Administration Review* 26(6):243–58.

Schumpeter, J. 1947. *Capitalism, Socialism, and Democracy*. New York: Harper & Row.

Selznick, P. 1949. *TVA and Grass Roots: A Study in the Sociology of Formal Organization*. New York: Harper & Row.

Simon, H. A. 1957. *Models of Man*. New York: Wiley.

—— 1971. Designing organizations for an information rich world. In M. Greenberger, ed., *Computers, Communications, and the Public Interest*, pp. 106–25. Baltimore, Md.: Johns Hopkins University Press.

—— 1973. Applying information technology to organizational design. *Public Administration Review* 33(3):268–78.

—— 1975. *The Shape of Automation*. New York: Harper & Row.

—— 1977. *The New Science of Management Decision*. Englewood Cliffs, N.J.: Prentice-Hall.

Sonenblum, S., J. J. Kirlin, and J. C. Reis. 1975. Providing municipal services: The effects of alternate structures. Los Angeles, Calif.: University of California, Institute of Governmental Studies, September.

Stallings, C. W. 1972. A confidentiality and public access policy for local governments. Chapel Hill, N.C.: University of North Carolina, Department of City and Regional Planning.

Sterling, T. O. 1979. Consumer difficulties with computerized billing systems. *Communications of the ACM*, 22(5):283–89.

Stewart, R. 1971. *How Computers Affect Management*. Cambridge, Mass.: MIT Press.

Straussman, J. 1978. *The Limits of Technocratic Politics*. New Brunswick, N.J.: Transaction.

Suchman, E. A. 1967. *Evaluation Research*. New York: Sage.

Taylor, F. W. 1911. *Principals of Scientific Management*. New York: Harper.

Thompson, V. 1965. Bureaucracy and innovation. *Administrative Science Quarterly* 10:1–20.

Touraine, A. 1972. *The Post-Industrial Society, Tomorrow's Social History*. L. Mayhew, trans. New York: Random House.

URBIS Group. 1977. A survey of local government EDP practices. *Government Finance* 6(3):42–51.

URISA (Urban and Regional Information Systems Assocation). 1963. First

Annual Conference on Urban Planning Information Systems and Programs. Unpublished papers. Los Angeles: University of Southern California.

—— 1964. *Urban Information and Policy Decisions.* Selected papers from the Second Annual Conference on Urban Planning Information Systems and Programs.

—— 1965. *Proceedings of the Third Annual Conference on Urban Planning Information Systems and Programs.* Chicago, Ill.: American Society of Planning Officials.

—— 1966. *Proceedings of the Fourth Annual Conference on Urban Planning Systems and Programs.* Berkeley, Calif.: Department of City and Regional Planning and Development Research, University of California.

—— 1967. *Urban and Regional Information Systems for Social Programs.* Papers from the Fifth Annual Conference of the Urban and Regional Information Systems Association. Kent, Ohio: Center for Urban Regionalism, Kent State University.

—— 1968. *Urban and Regional Information Systems: Federal Activities and Specialized Systems.* Papers from the Sixth Annual Conference of the Urban and Regional Information Systems Association. Kent, Ohio: Center for Urban Regionalism, Kent State University.

—— 1969. *Urban and Regional Information Systems: Service Systems for the Cities.* Papers from the Seventh Annual Conference of the Urban and Regional Information Systems Association. Kent, Ohio: Center for Urban Regionalism, Kent State University.

—— 1970. *Urban and Regional Information Systems: Past, Present, and Future.* Papers from the Eighth Annual Conference of the Urban and Regional Information Systems Association. Kent, Ohio: Center for Urban Regionalism, Kent State University.

—— 1977. *Information Systems as Services to Citizens.* Papers from the Fourteenth Annual Conference of the Urban and Regional Information Systems Association. Chicago: URISA.

USAC (Urban Information Systems Inter-Agency Committee). 1976. Federal funding for municipal information systems. *Government Data Systems* 1(5):6.

U.S. Bureau of the Census. 1976. *City Government Finances in 1974–75.* Washington, D.C.: U.S. Government Printing Office.

Walker, C.R. 1957. *Toward the Automated Factory.* New Haven: Yale University Press.

Webb, E., D. Campbell, R. Schwartz, and L. Sechrest. 1966. *Unobtrusive Measures: Non-reactive Research in the Social Sciences.* Chicago: Rand McNally.

Webber, M. M. 1970. The politics of information. In N. K. Denzin, ed., *The Values of Social Science,* pp. 119–25 Chicago: Aldine.

Weick, K. E. 1969. *The Social Psychology of Organizing.* Reading, Mass.: Addison-Wesley.

Weiner, M. 1969. Service: The objective of municipal information systems. Storrs, Conn.: Institute of Public Science, University of Connecticut.

Weiss, C. 1980. Knowledge creep and decision accretion. *Knowledge* 1(3):381–404.

Weiss, C., ed. 1977. *Using Social Research in Public Policy Making*. Lexington, Mass.: Lexington Books.

Weizenbaum, J. 1976. *Computer Power and Human Reason*. San Francisco: Freeman.

Wessel, M. R. 1974. *Freedom's Edge: The Computer Threat to Society*. Reading, Mass.: Addison-Wesley.

Westin, A. and M. Baker. 1972. *Databanks in a Free Society*. New York: Quadrangle.

Whisler, T. L. 1967. The impact of information technology on organizational control. In C. A. Myers, ed., *The Impact of Computers on Management*, pp. 16–40. Cambridge, Mass.: MIT Press.

—— 1970. *The Impact of the Computer on Organizations*. New York: Holt, Rinehart and Winston.

Wildavsky, A., 1964. *The Politics of the Budgetary Process*. Boston: Little, Brown.

—— 1976. *Budgeting*. Boston: Little, Brown.

Wilson, J. Q. 1968a. *Varieties of Police Behavior*. Cambridge: Harvard University Press.

Wilson, J. Q., ed. 1968b. *City Politics and Public Policy*. Cambridge: Harvard University Press.

Winch, R. L. and D. T. Campbell. 1969. Proof? no. Evidence? yes. The significance of tests of significance. *American Sociologist* 4:140–43.

Winner, L. 1977. *Autonomous Technology*. Cambridge, Mass.: MIT Press.

Woodward, J. 1970. *Industrial Organization*. New York: Oxford University Press.

Yates, D. 1977. *The Ungovernable City*. Cambridge, Mass.: MIT Press.

Yin, R. K., P. M. Bateman, E. Marks, and S. K. Quick. 1979. *Changing Urban Bureaucracies: How New Practices Get Routinized*. Lexington, Mass.: Lexington Books.

Yin, R. K., K. A. Heald, M. E. Vogel, P. D. Fleischauer, and B. C. Vladeck. 1976. *A Review of Case Studies of Technological Innovations in State and Local Services*. Santa Monica, Calif.: Rand.

INDEX

Allison, Graham, xiii, 140, 163
Automated information in the policy
process, 136–69; conceptual role of,
142; control of access to, 164–69; and
decision alternatives, 152–56;
instrumental role of, 142; and policy
argument, 156–57; and policy
evaluation, 158–59; and policy
implementation, 157–58; and problem
definition, 150–51; and problem-
finding, 149–50; symbolic role of, 142,
159–60
Automated information systems, 20, 51,
137–40; and the policy-making process,
see Automated information in the
policy process
"Autonomous technology," 139

Bell, Daniel, 137
Biases in local government operation:
efficiency, 210–11; reform, 217–19, 220;
regulatory, 214–17; traditional service,
209–10
Brewer, Gary, 137
Brockton, Mass., 66–68
Bureaucratic control, 196, 201–08, 218
"Bureaucratic politics," 140, 163–69

Centralization of computing, 113–15,
125–26
Colton, Kent, 120
Computer-based information: patterns of
use by role-type, 180; and power shifts,
173–93
Computer elite, 85–86, 91–92, 98–99, 103,
106–10, 161–62, 225
Computer hardware: costs of, 25–26, 30;
decentralization of, 43; organizational
location of, 42–43
Computer package, 4–5, 8–11, 22–23, 26–
29, 44–48, 54, 55, 58; central processing
unit (CPU), 27, 33, 36, 46–48; change
in, 28–29, 44–48, 244; complexity in, 22–

24, 28–29, 227; decisional control over,
2, 9–12, 18, 20, 49–50, 54–55, 81–110,
132–33, 227–31; definition of, 5;
elements of, 26–27, 48, 49; and
equipment, 23–28, 35–39, 48–49; and
people, 22–23, 39–40; "reform" in, 244;
source; *see* Source of computing
services; suppliers, 83–85; and
technique, 41; users, *see* Users of
computing; *see also* Computer
technology
Computer resources, 12–18, 36–37, 48,
115–19, 92, 162; competition for, 119–
20, 123; distribution of, 115–18, 124–
27, 237; external funding for, 9, 53, 58,
59, 228; federal funding for, *see* federal
support; grants-in-aid for, 90; politics
of, *see* Resource politics; regulation of,
123
Computer software: costs of, 25;
development, 25, 27
Computer technology: central processing
unit (CPU), 27, 33, 36, 46–48;
complexity of, 22–24, 28–29, 35; costs
of, 24–25, 30, 37–39, 44–45, 121, 127–
29; development of, 23–28, 44–46, 112–
19, 125; and environment, 8–12, 46, 54,
59; equipment, 23–28, 33, 35–39, 48,
113–14; evolution of, 112–30; history of
use of, *see* History of computing;
generations of, 24, 25, 46–48, 243;
mainframes, 24, 36, 47, 48; proportion
of governments using, *see* Local
government; software development, 25;
speed of adoption, 55, 57, 58; unit
record equipment, 23; *see also*
Computer package
Computer uses: "known," 205–8;
"selected," 206–8
Computer utilization index, 57
Computing: financial commitment to, 45,
57–59; impacts, *see* Impacts of
computing; levels of use in local

277